AMNESIA

PERSPECTA 48

THE YALE ARCHITECTURAL JOURNAL

Edited by Aaron Dresben, Edward Hsu,
Andrea Leung, Teo Quintana

Some summers ago, we headed off to tread the pilgrim path. Though unspoken, the terms of the trip were clear: to find from amongst the trophies of popes and emperors the foundations of an advanced aesthetic. Like so many before us, we kept the obligatory sketchbooks, not failing to trace the subtleties of form, careful to consider the durability of the orders amongst the dusts of empire. Yet, leafing through the summer's sketches, we wondered if we were more in possession of an illustrated punch list than an object of serious inquiry.

If a century ago, gazing into the mirror of the past, Le Corbusier reformulated the lessons of the eternal city for his era, no such sleight of hand seems possible now. This should come as no surprise—history is not what it used to be. Our age belongs more to the tweet than the treatise. The habit of mind associated with the digital tends to flatten history. In this moment of rapidly accumulating facts, Allan Sekula neatly captures the zeitgeist when he notes that the archive serves as a sort of "clearinghouse of meaning." The more we gather, the less we grasp.

To confront this situation, we propose that amnesia, often seen as a destructive force, might also be understood as a productive one—that the gaps it creates might also provide spaces for invention. This journal explores the paradoxical nature of amnesia: how can forgetting be both harmful and generative? What sort of critical genealogies can be repurposed, suppressed, or manufactured to reenergize current practice? How might we construct counter-narratives, rebel histories, and alternative canons that are relevant to our present moment?

Perspecta 48 considers the uses and abuses of history to ignite a debate about the role of memory in architecture.

The Editors

Abelardo Morell, *Upright Image of the Coliseum inside Room #23 at the Hotel Gladiatori, Rome*, 2007.

The Two Faces
of Nostalgia

Karsten Harries

Thomas Kinkade, *Lamplight Lane*, 1993.

1

The built environment testifies to the power of nostalgia. Just about every neighborhood furnishes ready examples for which it matters little whether the builder looked back to a bygone America, England, or Mexico. We like to dress our buildings in finery borrowed from the past, evoking a more firmly rooted dwelling. This is hardly a new development. Consider the decorated sheds of the nineteenth century with their borrowed ornaments. Gesturing toward a past that cannot be resurrected, such buildings invite the label "kitsch."

Symptomatic of this tendency are the architectural visions of recently deceased artist Thomas Kinkade, self-styled "Painter of Light" and perhaps, at least in terms of sales, America's most popular religious artist. For some years his nostalgic interpretations of suburban dwellings, at home on Hallmark cards, have been translated into housing developments. As Dan Byrne, CEO of the Thomas Kinkade Company, puts it: "The Thomas Kinkade brand stands for the values associated with home and hearth, peace, joy, faith, family and friends. Partnering with HST in the creation of homes inspired by the artwork of Thomas Kinkade delivers on what collectors tell us inspires them most about Thom's work—that they wish they could step into the world created in the painting. The Thomas Kinkade Company is pleased to align itself with such a visionary home builder."[1] What was only a picture laden with nostalgia, a sort of dream, becomes reality. Indeed what is wrong with buildings that self-consciously edify, that are drawn from pretty pictures of a transfigured past, that invite us to forget the ugliness of the world we have created, in which we must make our way? Why not welcome such remembering, which is inevitably also a forgetting?

The changing fortunes of the word *edify* are instructive in this connection: once it meant simply to raise an edifice, a building. When religious and moral thinkers appropriated the word, they also raised spiritual structures in which human beings might discover their spiritual homes. This was Søren Kierkegaard's intent in *Edifying Discourses*. The term thus came to mean "to improve morally or spiritually" by offering guidance and strengthening faith. Why then did it eventually acquire an increasingly negative connotation, as suggested by synonyms such as *preach* and *indoctrinate*? Today "edifying art" suggests "kitsch." It conjures what has lost genuine life as if it were still alive but precisely because of this, succeeds only in preventing us from facing reality. This is how Arthur Schopenhauer viewed the popular return to Gothic architecture in the nineteenth century—in bad taste and born of what had become a mere simulacrum of faith: "In the interest of good taste, I am bound to wish that great wealth be devoted to what is objectively, i.e. actually, good and right, to what in itself is beautiful, not to that whose value rests merely on the association of ideas. Now when I see how this unbelieving age so diligently finishes the Gothic churches left uncompleted by the believing Middle Ages, it seems to me as if it were desired to embalm a Christianity that has expired."[2] Kinkade's architectural fantasies invite a similar response, providing us with a definition of kitsch supported only by an association of ideas drawn from the past yet no longer rooted in the experience of the sacred that once gave architecture its meaning. This is how Frank Lloyd Wright understood sentimentality in architecture: the "picture had now triumphed over architecture, and symbolism took the place of original inspiration."[3]

Yet what alternative can we point to in the absence of such experience or inspiration? Is bad faith perhaps better than no faith, and edifying kitsch preferable to Modernist irony or abjection? It is part of the human condition that, never quite at home in our world, we dream of a genuine homecoming,

1   "New Housing Community in Columbia, MO Features Thomas Kinkade Homes," Businesswire.com, August 14, 2006, accessed September 24, 2013, http://www.businesswire.com/news/home/20060814005221/en/Housing-Community-Columbia-MO-Features-Thomas-Kinkade.

2   Arthur Schopenhauer, *The World as Will and Representation*, vol. 2, trans. E. F. J. Payne (New York: Dover, 1966), 418.

3   Frank Lloyd Wright, *Genius and the Mobocracy* (New York: Horizon Press, 1971), xii.

Martin Heidegger's Hut, Todtnauberg.
Photo: Barbara Figal.

4   Martin Heidegger, "Building Dwelling Thinking," in *Poetry, Language, Thought*, trans. Albert Hofstadter (New York: Harper and Row, 2001), 160–61.

of paradise lost and regained, and look to the past for traces of a better world to project its promise into the future. Martin Heidegger invited architects to look back to an eighteenth-century Black Forest farmhouse, which he saw as a more authentic dwelling, quite aware that it would be foolish to build such a house today.[4]

Can such idealizing memories, in fact, cast a light into our world, giving us the strength to put up with its deficiencies while moving us closer to a genuine dwelling? In a world that we find difficult to call home, where too many demonstrate cold hearts, should we not welcome a bit of kitschy sentimentality, even when the energy, the will, and the means to transform reality are often lacking? The romantic nostalgia of Friedrich Schiller, Hölderlin, and Nietzsche for an imagined Greece that never quite was, or of Karl Friedrich Schinkel for an idealized version of the Middle Ages, fills many of us today with a longing for an age still innocent enough to allow such sentiment to shape its architecture.

In a world overshadowed by environmental and terrorist threats, memories of the Holocaust, two world wars, and various atomic disasters, who does not look back with tenderness at what writer Hermann Broch called the *Backhendlzeit*, the age of the Vienna fried chicken. But this urban environment, which gloried in its decorated sheds—was condemned as the capital of decadence by Modernists, who possessed a faith in reason that we no longer share. Buildings decked out in borrowed decoration—which our fathers and grandfathers, still filled with Modernist fervor and conviction, criticized wholeheartedly as inauthentic, sentimental, or false—may well suggest to us, despite and perhaps because of their backward-looking theatricality, our lost innocence. Bad faith can also be innocent. Think of the extraordinary popularity of the castles built by Ludwig II of Bavaria to idealize himself in the image of Louis XIV, in spite of the fact that his dream of an operatic kingship had no place in Bismarck's Germany. Why not try to forget the unpleasant present? To be sure, reality had the final word: the king paid with his life for the attempt to turn reality into a fairy tale.

But if our time is, as Broch thought, the age of the value vacuum, why call bad faith bad? Isn't bad faith better than no faith at all? Today many have become nostalgic for nostalgia itself—and what is wrong with nostalgia?

The Ringstrasse and Parliament, Vienna. Photochrom Print, c. 1890.

HARRIES

2

Nostalgia is a word, like *aesthetics*, whose birth we can locate with precision. Both terms originated in the Enlightenment and testify to dissatisfaction with the culture of reason created by the movement—that is to say, with our modern world. Have we lost sight of experiences vital to human flourishing? Both identify phenomena that in their seeming irrationality call the rule of reason into question.

Alexander Gottlieb Baumgarten became the founder of aesthetics by trying to make room for experiences of the beautiful within a fundamentally Cartesian framework. Aesthetics came to be understood, along with logic, metaphysics, and ethics, as one of the branches of philosophy. He coined the term to name the philosophical discipline he established in his dissertation of 1735, written when he was just twenty.[5]

Nostalgia antedates *aesthetics* by half a century. The term was invented by Johannes Hofer, an Alsatian medical student studying in Basel, in his 1688 dissertation by joining *nostos*, meaning a journey back home, and *algia*, meaning pain. This neologism describes what in the vernacular was called *Heimweh* ("homesickness"), which Hofer had come to understand as a potentially deadly disease that had not been properly recognized by the medical profession. In extreme cases the only cure was allowing the patient to return home.[6] Nostalgia, then, is a sickness born of an inability or unwillingness to be content with memories or dreams of a home left behind. The nostalgic feels an acute need to actually return home, preventing him from coping effectively with his current environment. As such, memories of home become an obstacle to making a new home in the wider world.

Hofer's subjects were Swiss, and the Swiss were especially associated with this strange ailment. This was a particular concern for the French government since the Swiss were sought-after mercenaries, and attacks of nostalgia induced, as Jean-Jacques Rousseau reports, by the *Ranz-des-vaches*, that Tune so cherished by the Swiss that they [not the Swiss] have forbidden it from being played in their Troops on pain of death, since it would cause those who heard it to dissolve in tears, desert, or die, so much would it arouse in them the ardent desire to see their country again."[7] Just what was it that drew them back home with such force—the air, the milk, the food? A convincing answer eluded the enlightened doctors.

5   Alexander Gottlieb Baumgarten, *Reflections on Poetry (Meditationes philosophicae de nonnullis ad poema pertinentibus)*, trans. Karl Aschenbrenner and William B. Holther (Berkeley and Los Angeles: University of California Press, 1954).

6   See Helmut Illbruck, *Nostalgia: Origins and Ends of an Unenlightened Disease* (Evanston, Illinois: Northwestern University Press, 2012), 5.

7   Jean-Jacques Rousseau, "Dictionary of Music," cited in Illbruck, *Nostalgia*, 88.

Ludwig Wittgenstein House, Vienna, c. 1930. Period postcard.

Neuschwanstein Castle, Upper Bavaria.
Photochrom Print, c. 1890.

In the late eighteenth and nineteenth centuries, nostalgia gradually ceased to be considered primarily a medical problem and figured increasingly into poetry and philosophy. It came to be recognized as a dissatisfaction with present reality that transforms a remembered or imagined past into a figure of some lost paradise. This presented the Enlightenment with a challenge: Was there something missing in the culture of reason or were nostalgics simply cultural laggards who had not yet recognized the countless ways in which the progress of reason had improved their lot? Rousseau thus points out that the Swiss who had come to appreciate the gifts of the Enlightenment no longer experienced attacks of nostalgia with the same intensity. Immanuel Kant—no doubt thinking of Rousseau and understanding the Enlightenment as humanity's coming of age—tended to dismiss nostalgia as a product of the troubled imagination of someone who refused to grow up.[8] When a nostalgic does manage to return home, Kant notes, reality is likely to shatter its imaginative construction and leave the sufferer disappointed. But while blaming the changes that have taken place, she is finally cured. What really has changed, however, is not the place but the individual. It is thus not so much a particular place, Kant suggests, that the nostalgic longs for, but rather a lost youth. But isn't it childish to want to be a child again?

If nostalgia is understood to be an "unenlightened disease," as Helmut Illbruck calls it in the title of his marvelous study, why should someone privileged to live in the age of Enlightenment—humanity's coming of age, as Kant understood it—long to return to a much less free, more circumscribed mode of existence? And yet, as Kant himself had to recognize, nostalgia is not quite so easily dismissed as a childish product of a troubled imagination. Casting a shadow on the Enlightenment and its achievements, Kant observed that nostalgia is more likely to afflict those who grew up in regions such as Switzerland (he also mentions Westphalia and Pomerania) that, while "poor in money," were socially more firmly knitted together. The nostalgic has not yet made *Patria ubi bene* her motto. Nostalgia implies a legitimate critique of an increasingly money-centered modernity that has paid for an increase in freedom with a loss of genuine community and dislocation. Nostalgia thus possesses a forward-looking, revolutionary potential. The longing for home can figure a legitimate longing, not so much for a particular place or childhood, as

8   Immanuel Kant, *Anthropologie in pragmatischer Hinsicht*, A85/B86.

Bruno Taut, Gardenstadt Falkenberg estate, Berlin, 1913–16.

Karl Friedrich Schinkel, *Cathedral Towering Over a Town*,
Oil on canvas, c. 1830.

HARRIES

for a sense of community lost with society's emphasis on individual freedom. As such, the progress of freedom calls into question the values reflected by the Kinkade brand: "home and hearth, peace, joy, faith, family and friends." Such values are not easily dismissed, even if the words and buildings that respond to them may be.

3

Kant's discussion of nostalgia evokes ambivalence: It is criticized for refusing to confront contemporary reality, with the nostalgic finding refuge in a past that is long gone. Yet for Kant the nostalgic recalled a way of life that contrasts favorably in certain ways with the money-centered environment in which he found himself. Schopenhauer recognized these two faces of nostalgia in a very different way: having lost faith in the Enlightenment, unlike Kant, and finding reality unsatisfactory, he understood dreams of homecoming all too well. The nostalgic is right not to feel at home in the world, to want to escape from it, but wrong in the desire to actually return to that home whose memory haunts him. Homelessness is the human condition. If Schopenhauer is right, any homecoming will inevitably disappoint. The nostalgic would do better to become absorbed in the beautiful illusions of art, which make reality bearable, at least for a time.

Is Schopenhauer right to insist that the human condition renders all dreams of genuine homecoming futile? Isn't it really the way a particular historical situation has distorted reality that is to blame, as Kant hints in his reference to the Swiss longing to return to a less self-centered way of life? As Frederic Jameson observes: "It is scarcely surprising that out of the alienating structures of nineteenth and twentieth century capitalism we should look back with a (not necessarily unrevolutionary) nostalgia at such moments in which life, and form, are still relatively whole, and which seem at the same time to afford a glimpse into the nature of some future non-alienated existence as well."[9] In the tradition of Johann Winckelmann, Friedrich Schiller, and Georg Wilhelm Friedrich Hegel, Karl Marx thought that art would never again be as beautiful as it was in ancient Greece and that humanity would never again unfold itself quite so beautifully. But to admit that what fills us today with nostalgic joy cannot be retrieved does not mean that it may not point towards a better future. Marx appeals to the joy we experience when we observe children: "A man cannot become a child again, or he becomes childish. But does he not find joy in the child's naiveté, and must he not try to reproduce its truth at a higher stage?"[10] Schopenhauer would have challenged such a claim. Not only will the nostalgic's return home inevitably disappoint, but so will any attempt to find meaning in the repetition of some lost naiveté "at a higher stage," as Nietzsche once hoped for a modern repetition of Greek tragedy. Nietzsche later condemned himself for his romanticism, understood as "the impossible attempt to resurrect what has died and lies irrecoverably behind us."[11] Weren't the Enlightenment's high estimation of Greek art and Romanticism's later embrace of the Gothic aesthetic responses to what the cult of reason destroyed yet longed for, based on constructions of a mythical paradise that never was and never will be?

Thus the general point of Marx's comment on our appreciation of Greek art: what moves us in great art, both as memory and promise, is the idea of a fuller humanity. Nostalgia plays a part in this appreciation and is not divorced from hope. All great art transcends the limited circumstances that gave birth to it, reaching beyond any historical period. Art expresses the power of human

9   Fredric Jameson, "Introduction," in Henri Arvon, *Marxist Esthetics*, trans. Helen Lane (Ithaca: Cornell University Press, 1973), xvii.

10   Karl Marx, *Grundrisse. Foundations of the Critique of Political Economy*, trans. Martin Nicolaus (New York: Vintage, 1973), 111.

11   Friedrich Nietzsche, *Dawn* III, par. 159.

self-transcendence and the freedom that allows us to dream up figures of what Kant called the highest good, of plenitude.

The inability to forget and let go of the past—whether in the form of nostalgia clinging to a past transfigured into paradise or to memories that have become a vision of hell—can blind us to what the present and future have to offer. It is with good reason that the principles of the Enlightenment portrayed "nostalgia" first of all as something to overcome, like a disease or some other aberration incompatible with humanity's true coming of age. Better to forget! As poet Hölderlin put it: *"Kolonie liebt, und tapfer Vergessen der Geist* [The spirit loves colony and brave forgetting]."[12] Here he touches on not only the importance but also the difficulty of forgetting, allowing it to be called "brave." We find it difficult to let go of the past; after all, it has made us who we are and provided us with orientation. Nostalgia and a desire to forget are thus mingled. A presupposition of the founding of a colony, of a new way of dwelling and building, is that the idea of home leaves those venturing into the new dissatisfied. They want something new and different, and yet the colony remains bound to that mythical home that continues to enthrall them. All responsible building is a creative repetition of the past that is open to new possibilities. And so, again and again, colonies have sought to preserve the image of home in a new environment, enacting a contest between nostalgia and the need to forget.

Nostalgia shows us two faces—one that looks to the past and the other to the future. One seeks to return home; the other is content to leave home a dream that projects its promise into the future. The former is destructive, the latter constructive. Every attempt to return home must shipwreck on the reef of reality. Dreams of home, on the other hand, can cast a light over the present that reveals hope for a better future. And what is life without such hope?

12 From a late version of the final stanza of "Brod und Wein," cited in Martin Heidegger, *Hölderlins Hymne "Der Ister," Gesamtausgabe,* vol. 53 (Frankfurt am Main: Vittorio Klostermann, 1984), 157.

UNIVERSITY OF VIRGINIA, AT CHARLOTTESVILLE.

The University of Virginia, Charlottesville, 1831.

HARRIES

In January 2015, Mies van der Rohe's New National Gallery closed and restoration work began.

In any restoration or reconstruction project there must be a clear philosophical framework within which technical and formal solutions can be developed. The complex issues raised during repair and restoration involve the consideration of often contradictory technical and philosophical concerns: we must consider the original intentions of the architect, inherent defects in the design, the issue of weathering and damage, modifications in program and use, and the status of any changes and alterations made to the original design. These issues must be clearly articulated and measured against one another.

Having been through this process many times, we endorse the saying, "better to repair than restore; better to restore than reconstruct." In this range of interventions, which swings from repair to restoration and finally to reconstruction, this project sits comfortably towards the repair end of the spectrum. The building has suffered no trauma; no fire has destroyed it. Its fabric is intact and rescuable.

In comparison to other projects that we have worked on, the intellectual and emotional issues are quite reasonable. We do not have to struggle with the enormous loss of material that confronted us with the Neues Museum; nor do we have to deal with the complex and contaminated history that confronts us with the Haus der Kunst in Munich; nor do we have to sift between the history of layers and modifications as with the Forum Museumsinsel. In real terms, our work does not require us to make any radical intrusion or alteration, but to both address the relatively modest yet still complicated issues that arise from the fabric of the building and also reinstate the integrity of its structure.

We have been asked many times why, if it is our intention to be invisible, do we want to do it?

We can say of course that it is an honor; that it is a responsibility; or even that we don't trust anyone else! We can also profess our deep appreciation for the building, which is a critical component in such a task. But in the case of the New National Gallery, there is something else that has motivated us: that is the possibility to consider and discuss in a coherent and intelligent environment the physical stuff of architecture.

In what we might call "normal practice," the architect is often fighting for physical and material ideas that are difficult to describe and protect. The architect does this usually isolated and with little evidence, only with promises. The architect must fight against the more obvious forces of money, time, and deliverability. It is no accident that contemporary architecture tends towards form over substance, skin over bones. The ability to carefully consider these essential elements of architecture with others who share a belief in their importance has been a regenerating experience.

Repairing Mies's great utopian work puts us into a stark relationship with the elements of an architecture that asserts the importance of each physical decision. This is an engagement of reduced building substance and spatial composition in which the mullion, the structure, the sheet of glass are all engaged in the idea of the building. There is nothing covered; everything is what it is, an unforgiving assembly of parts in service of a singular idea.

Even at the early stages of this process, a few revealing observations have emerged about the functionality of the building. It is well understood and an accepted part of its story that the building does not work so well, that Mies was not sufficiently concerned with function.

Most of the criticism of the building, though, is aimed at the main hall. Conceived as a changing exhibition space it certainly did not make things easy for itself. However if we go downstairs, it is interesting that after nearly fifty years the building has hardly changed. By this time we would expect an institution, which as a group is not usually very respectful, to have made countless interventions in the front of house and especially back of house areas. One would anticipate a huge amount of work to strip away all of these provisional modifications introduced in the intervening years. It is striking how few changes have been made in this instance. The explanation for this is likely twofold. Firstly, and against the common idea, this was a very well worked out plan. Secondly, and most importantly, the planning has a clear authority and near classical simplicity that maintains a slightly loose relation to program.

I do not think Mies subscribed to the idea of form following function as it suggests an unrealistic precision about use. With Mies it seems that function follows good form, intelligent and clear planning, and a certain lack of specificity.

A final observation returns to the criticism of the exhibition spaces. Firstly, we can be bold enough to say that the downstairs galleries have no problems. They work perfectly well. Simple exhibition spaces, perhaps a bit low, but clearly organized with simple circulation and orientation, and light provided by the courtyard window—a very intelligent solution to the issue of daylight and artificial light. Returning to the exhibition hall, the room is clearly difficult and not an ideal space for changing exhibitions. We must understand its gesture: a room at the scale of the city. A room that mediates between the sensible internal workings of the lower museum and the complex context in which it sits. This is the ultimate expression of Mies's ideas of a non-specific space, defined not by function but by purpose; a space that has been adopted by the citizens of the city and by the curators and artists who have learned to work with it.

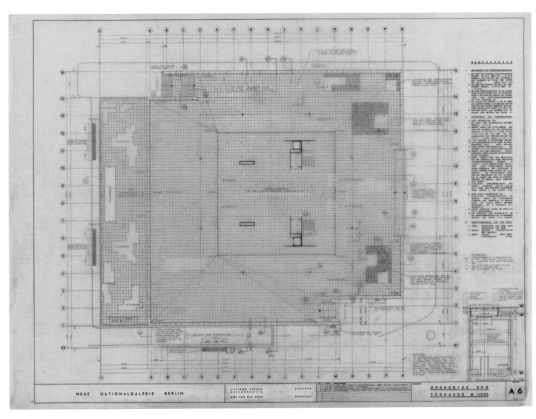

Ludwig Mies van der Rohe, New National Gallery, Berlin, 1967. Floor plan of the terrace.

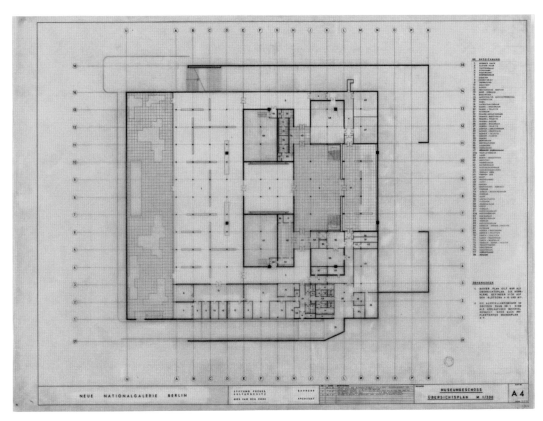

Ludwig Mies van der Rohe, New National Gallery, Berlin, 1967. Plan of museum floor.

Previous spread: New National Gallery, View from Potsdamer Straße, Berlin, 1968. Photo: Reinhard Friedrich.

Making Presence

Saskia Sassen

If we think of amnesia as rendering invisible what was once visible, then we can argue that "making presence" is one mode of trespassing into amnesia—its spaces and symbols, its shadows and silences. *Making* presence is an operation that can engage empty space, material or mental.[1]

There is much that can be rendered invisible in complex systems, intentionally or unintentionally.[2] In this regard, there is much in these structures that can enter into the space of amnesia and be forgotten. The instruments, intentions, and accidental outcomes leading to or generating this invisibility vary enormously across different epochs and their particular systems. Further, what may remain invisible in one type of system, even though present and consequential, can be highly present but much less significant in another.

In this brief think piece I explore such interactions between visible formalizations and invisible facticities. I use the concept of "visible formalizations" to capture conditions that acquire a kind of presence because they are part of a formal system. For instance, an area zoned for manufacturing makes us "see" the buildings within it as marked by manufacturing, even though they may actually be storage buildings or completely empty and unused. I use the concept of "facticity" to capture conditions that have attributes of the empirical or material but are not necessarily recognized as such.[3] Along those lines, an early 1900s Soho or TriBeCa warehouse building today is completely detached from its origins: it is seen as a luxury residential building in spite of its original function as a turn-of-the-century warehouse.

"Presence" is a complex condition that goes beyond the material and visible. It can be ephemeral even when it is deeply material because materiality by itself, and the visibility of the material, are not enough to *make* presence. Presence is not a mere function or attribute of materiality: it is produced by a building's shape, aura, witnesses, and passersby, as suggested by the previous examples. Another kind of example is Frank Gehry's Bilbao Guggenheim, whose presence extends well beyond the actual building. It is an icon whose invocation is enough to conjure up not just the building, but also the transformation of a decaying city into a destination for experts and tourists alike. In contrast, a deeply material condition can become invisible to the passerby because it has become routinized or because its edges have become lost in the larger complex of buildings. This is a form of invisibility that harkens back to amnesia—the impossibility of hanging on to the clear image. Against this backdrop "making presence" is an antithesis to amnesia.

Addressing these issues as a social theorist has meant working with several systems of representation and constructing spaces of intersection.[4] There are analytic moments when two different systems of representation intersect. These are easily experienced as spaces of silence, absence, and amnesia. One challenge is to detect what happens in those spaces, which we barely notice and therefore experience as empty and silent. In my own work, the question becomes what operations (of analysis, power, or meaning) take place when we experience the intersection of two systems of representation as a silence, or an absence. In short, we do not see anything happening in these spaces because we do not have the conceptual bridge that would allow us to see the operations present (analytic operations, issues of power and meaning, etc.).

To address these kinds of questions, I have developed notions of the active "*making* of presence," of rescuing from the silence of absence. I am especially interested in understanding how groups, activities, and events at risk of invisibility due to societal prejudices can become present to themselves and to others both like and unlike themselves. What I seek to capture is a very specific feature that would allow the making of presence where there has been silence and absence.[5] In my experience this takes work, often very hard work. One question that comes up is what kind of work would it take to make the lost or forgotten in architecture and cities present once again. A city like New York, with many different immigrant and minority groups, could become a space where they can make themselves present to one another. What they can make collectively in a large city is different from what they could do in a large corporate farm in California, for example, where their powerlessness is elementary because it is harder to escape control and make their own, even if partial, histories, as is possible in a New York neighborhood. Nonetheless, even if they do experience this difference, this gain of complexity, they may still remain invisible to the larger city's residents.

The deep issue here is how slippery our grasp is on real, concrete facts. One cannot help but think that some of what we lose track of and explain as amnesia may have little to do with amnesia. Rather the source might be the absence of bridges between systems of representation that we think of or experience as unconnected.

1. See "Does the City Have Speech?" *Public Culture* 25, no. 2 (2013): 209–21, http://www.saskiasassen.com/PDFs/publications/does-the-city-have-speech.pdf.

2. This also holds for what we designate as "the" economy. See Saskia Sassen, "What All Is Getting Expelled … and Once Expelled Is Invisible," *Open Democracy*, June 26, 2014, http://www.opendemocracy.net/can-europe-make-it/saskia-sassen/what-all-is-getting-expelledand-once-expelled-is-invisible; and Sassen, "The Language of Expulsion," *Truthout*, July 30, 2014, http://www.truth-out.org/opinion/item/25235-the-language-of-expulsion.

3. "Visible Formalizations and Formally Invisible Facticities," *Indiana Journal of Global Legal Studies* 20, no. 1 (2013).

4. See *Territory, Authority, Rights: From Medieval to Global Assemblages* (Princeton, New Jersey: Princeton University Press, 2008), chap. 8.

5. See "Imminent Domain: Saskia Sassen and Hans Haacke on the Spaces of Occupation," *Artforum*, January 2012.

Opposite: Hilary Koob-Sassen, *Vista of World Organs*, 2004.

Michael Wesely, *9 August 2001 – 2 May 2003 The Museum of Modern Art, New York, 2001–03.*

What does *amnesia* mean in the urban context, marked as it is by continuously shifting visual orders and soundscapes? I think of a city as a vast amplification of presences and absences repeated and duplicated across neighborhoods, train stations, parks, parking lots, and so on. Notwithstanding the enormity of immobile physical structures, what marks the urban is the continuous sliding and shifting—of meaning, perspective, and materiality. Every person, street, and window is a different vector into it all. Even the materiality of buildings can be changed significantly without destroying them; they can simply become the object of a new perspective, a new gaze. Historical ruins can survive centuries of transformation with their shapes intact, but they may lose presence or acquire a radically different one, shifting from grandiosity to pathos, as in Rome, for example.

How can presence be secured in a city, or amnesia resisted? In my experience, this can be quite counterintuitive. For instance, there is a type of urban condition that dwells between the reality of massive structures and that of semi-abandoned places, often waiting to be developed. For some passersby these places are unmarked and invisible, yet they could function as operational spaces for others who are able to recall past histories lost to destructions of what was once in the now empty patches of land. We can conceive of these spaces as ironic versions of the *terrae nullius* of a previous era, when the unknown or unused was represented as an empty place at the edge of an empire or in a desert land.

I think such *terrae nullius* are central to the experience of the urban environment. They can function as spaces where long-term dwellers of a city can reconnect with past presences now destroyed. It is precisely the empty space left behind that enables a long-gone building to become present. At the other extreme, these voids can make legible transitions from "uselessness" to new developments. Examples include the massive development of the long semi-abandoned Docklands in London, which eventually became a new financial center, and the severely underused Atlantic Yards area of Brooklyn, just acquired by Chinese investors who plan to transform the vast semi-industrial area into fourteen enormous, high-rise luxury apartment buildings. These places have gone from *terrae nullius* to luxury complexes. Large cities have continuous unsettlements of specific spatiotemporal configurations, some positive and others not.

A different version of unmarked urban space is the in-between of infrastructure—for instance, the intersections of multiple transport and communication routes, recycling plants, and water-purification systems—spaces that are distant from the milieu of everyday life. They are easily forgotten, remaining unseen or unnoticed despite often having enormous dimensions. This is a sort of urban amnesia. Some cities are beginning to see the value of these underutilized surfaces and are trying to make the most out of this "suddenly" available space—exiting the zone of amnesia and entering into that of making presence.

One way to approach these tensions, contradictions, and juxtapositions is to ask: How can we develop an open-source urbanism that will take in these seemingly non-urban spaces and *terrae nullius*? I have developed the notion of "open-source urbanism" to underline the extreme differentiation of these diverse spaces within cities and the specific forms of knowledge they contain about the city. Open-sourcing a neighborhood means bringing the specific knowledge of its residents and institutions into the broader knowledge space of the city. In this context, we could say that open-source urbanism would contribute to the repositioning of amnesia as a condition that has many refracting surfaces, depending on where in the city one experiences it.[6]

Architectural interventions that make use of problematic or unusual spaces are key here. Architects must be able to navigate several forms of knowledge to create architecture for, to make present, spaces where the naked eye and the engineer's imagination see no shape or possibility for form, only pure infrastructure or utility. In this manner, architecture can make presence to replace the formal silence and nonexistence of genuinely undistinguished terrain vague, such as an ambiguous, underutilized, or useless vacant plot in a city. That is to say not only a grand *terrain vague*, such as an abandoned steel factory that becomes magnificent through the scale of its decay, but also a small old structure in a nondescript section of a city.

This opens up a salient dilemma about the current urban condition beyond fairly transparent notions of high-tech architecture, virtual spaces, simulacra, and theme parks, all mere fragments of an incomplete puzzle. What concerns me in terms of terrain vague or *terra nullius* is a type of urban condition that dwells between the reality of massive structures and that of semi-abandoned places: the urban condition of a plot where a building has been demolished but a new one has not yet appeared. This condition is central to the urban experience, and it makes legible transitions and unsettlements of specific spatio-temporal configurations. Architecture and urban design can also function as critical artistic practices that allow us to capture something more elusive than what is represented by strategies like the "theme-parking" of city centers or the *installing* of meaning into an empty place by building a shopping mall, for instance.

The effect of the types of intervention I am after in this regard is a recovery of presence. For me, this experience is at the core of urbanity and is to be understood as a more transcultural mechanism than our Western European notion of the urban life of the piazza. It is rather the urbanity of the "global street," a space marked by indeterminacy and crowds.[7]

The multiplication of material elements in a city provides an experience of intensity rather than the endless repetition of an office park or a suburb. Indeed, the active *making* of multiplication unsettles the meaning of endless repetition. Although there is plenty of repetition in any city, it is alive despite its seemingly inert materiality. In these conditions and actions, we may see an escape from amnesia, even if we may never gain full recollection. The effect is that of making presence, whether in intense built environments or in terrains vagues.

6. See "Open-Sourcing the Neighborhood," Forbes.com, October 11, 2013, http://www.forbes.com/sites/techonomy/2013/11/10/open-sourcing-the-neighborhood.

7. See "The Global Street: Making the Political," *Globalizations* 8, no. 5 (2011): 573–79, http://www.tandfonline.com/doi/full/10.1080/14747731.2011.622458.

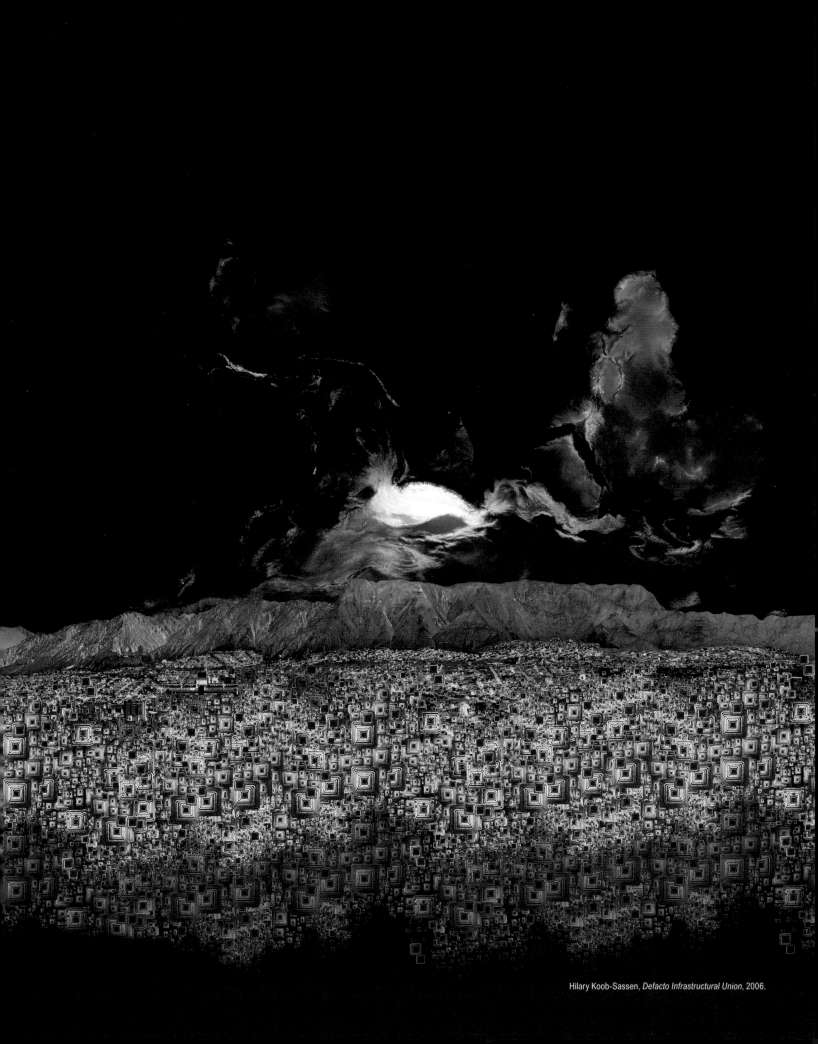

Hilary Koob-Sassen, *Defacto Infrastructural Union*, 2006.

Dredging Up the Unknown:
Interpretive Notes on Edward Forbes's
Ægean Expedition

Edward Eigen

Now let us turn to our richest geological museums, and what a paltry display we behold! That our collections are imperfect is admitted by every one. The remark of that admirable palaeontologist, Edward Forbes, should never be forgotten, namely, that very many fossil species are known and named from single and often broken specimens, or from a few specimens collected on some one spot.

Charles Darwin, *Origin of Species* (1859)

An easily overlooked, distantly recollected architectural detail relating to "resurrectionist times,"[1] which culminated in (but did not end with) the Anatomy Act of 1832, casts a shuttered and shuddering light on the fragile and vulnerable bodies that are wrested from obscurity by the forensic desire—guided by scientific method, though sometimes abetted by felonious intent—to know where and how things (come to an) end. Before describing the "sliding pannel [sic]" in the lecture room at No. 10 Surgeon's Square, Edinburgh, where Dr. Robert Knox conducted his learned and eloquent anatomical lectures in the presence of rapt auditors and arrested demonstration subjects, let us put forth the more general claim of this brief essay lest we lose sight of its oceanic ambition: to chart the metes and bounds of graspable knowledge. Simply stated, things—even or especially precious and singular ones—have a natural-seeming tendency to become misplaced, even when remanded for safekeeping or more or less

randomly designated for study. Things of no apparent meaning or value—one potential phase in an object or person's life history—are more typically neglected until their place in the elastic if not amorphous order of things is belatedly perceived. What follows is a historical case study on the depth of investigation at which the sense of things meaningfully begins to (dis)appear. *Keywords*: Dredging, the Blind Homer, Brittle Stars (Ophiuroidea), Ægean Sea, the Xanthian Marbles, Bodysnatchers.

In his unfinished memoir of Edward Forbes, George Wilson, the Regius Professor of Technology at the University of Edinburgh, recounts the mundane and peculiar circumstances of the Manxman's arrival at the "Athens of the North" in autumn, 1831.[2] As regards the naturalist's earlier formative years, Wilson notes the difficulty of separating the topography, natural history, and cultural heritage of the Isle of Man. To Forbes the island's "natural charms were of more interest than its architectural ruins or archaeological remains; but in truth the time-honored monuments of a country, which have been witnessed from early childhood side by side with its great natural features, are unconsciously identified with the latter, as if they were part of them."[3] Wilson offers a Manx fortress and the rock upon which it stands as an example of this coeval psycho-intellectual stimulation. These, he observes, "have been where we see them ever since we remember, together

---

1   See George MacGregor, *The History of Burke and Hare and of the Resurrectionist Times: A Fragment from the Criminal History of Scotland* (Glasgow: Thomas D. Morison, 1884).

2   MacGregor, *History of Burke and Hare*, 20.
3   Ibid.

constituting what seems a natural whole, and as such giving a character to the landscape."[4] Observation and recollection thus conspire in the production of a mnemonic topography of feeling and association. But Forbes's speculative reason was not girded by the insular patriotism born of his "small fatherland," one that "identifies itself with the visible objects within the horizon of their cradle or dwelling-place."[5] His theater of study would be the "vast deep sea region," that finest and forbidding, but as yet unvisited, "field" of "submarine study."[6]

Leaving Douglas on October 31, 1831, Forbes sailed by steamer from Ramsay Bay to Glasgow. After reaching Edinburgh on November 3, 1831, he immediately matriculated in the university.[7] In his notebook, by which Wilson retraces his steps, Forbes indicates the "£3. 5s. 0d." fee for Knox's lectures at the Extra-Academical Medical School. Wilson does not fail to notice the tyro's "error in summation" while accounting for his overall tuition, which he considered "eminently characteristic of Forbes's arithmetic."[8] Whether this sort of miscalculation contributed to what, in the aftermath, was considered his conspicuously faulty conception of a region of "life-zero," an abyss of permanent darkness, its "confines yet undetermined," is not here specifically a matter of speculation.[9] It should be mentioned, however, that in May 1832 Forbes's accounts record that he went on a dredging expedition, and thereafter, as Wilson writes, entered "formally on the study of Natural History."[10] A related entry indicates that he acquired a dredge for "1s. 7d." It was this rudimentary but effective instrument, which operated at a tethered distance, and not the finely edged knives purchased by Forbes in conjunction with the outlay of £2 for the leg of a subject, which "implied the direct handling of the dead body in [Dr. Knox's] dissecting room," that led and governed Forbes's search for life in the most remote aqueous recesses of the globe.[11]

Wilson's discussion of Edinburgh's resurrection men and the even less scrupulous West Port murderers whose wares, it was alleged in court, were punctually delivered to No. 10 Surgeon's Square, is more picaresque than it is probative. His moral accountancy of William Hare and William Burke's fatal depredations is nonetheless splendidly sardonic. While they spread terror and indignation throughout the country, "in reality their crimes had saved the graves of the dead from desecration."[12] Knox, for his part, knew how to encrypt the evidence of what he evidently regarded as his inculpable and, in any case, scientifically sanctioned involvement in the body trade. According to Wilson, "the janitors of the anatomical room detected a law officer through the most cunning disguises, and had always extreme difficulty in understanding his errand when he produced a warrant to search for a body missed from its grave." If at length the law officer was admitted, "it was not till the *corpus delicti* had vanished through a hole in the wall, or had otherwise disappeared, and with looks of innocence or indignation every one disclaimed all knowledge of the matter."[13]

---

4   Ibid.

5   Ibid.

6   Edward Forbes and Robert Godwin-Austen, *The Natural History of the European Seas* (London: John Van Voorst, 1859), 27. Godwin-Austen completed the unfinished book following Forbes's death in 1854.

7   George Wilson and Sir Archibald Geikie, *Memoir of Edward Forbes* (London: MacMillan and Edmonston Company, 1861), 87.

8   Wilson and Geikie, *Memoir of Edward Forbes*, 138.

9   See C. Wyville Thomson and John Murray, *Report of the Scientific Results of the Voyage of H.M.S. Challenger during the Years 1873–76*, vol. 1, "Narrative, First Part" (London: Longmans & Co., 1885), xi.

10 Forbes enrolled in botany classes under Robert Graham and in natural history under Robert Jameson. In 1854, he succeeded Jameson as professor of natural history.

11 Wilson and Geikie, *Memoir of Edward Forbes*, 140.

12 Wilson and Geikie, *Memoir of Edward Forbes*, 92.

13 That one of these janitors, David Patterson, whose responsibilities included "carrying away and burying the offals of the dissecting-rooms," was himself an accessory after the fact emerged at the murder trial of Burke and his accomplice, Helen M'Dougal. Adduced as a witness for the prosecution *qua socius criminis*, a procedure typically resorted to when there was a *penuria testium*, Hare was afforded immunity from prosecution. See "Joint statement of Dr. Knox's principal assistants," in *Trial of William Burke and Helen M'Dougal before the High Court of Justiciary, at Edinburgh, on Wednesday, December 24, 1828, for the Murder of Margery Campbell, or Docherty*, John Macnee (Edinburgh: Robert Buchanan, 1829), 30. Patterson sought to implicate his employer, Knox, in the anonymous pamphlet addressed to Sir William Rae, "The Echo of Surgeon's Square, Letter to the Lord Advocate, Disclosing the Accomplices, Secrets and Other Facts relative to the Late Murders; with a Correct Account of the Manner in which the Anatomical Schools are Supplied with Subjects" (Edinburgh, 1829).

It was rumored that on such occasions the detective was well remunerated for taking part in the charade. Wilson mentions the discovery, during demolition work, of the architectural trace of this vivid but morbid passage from the annals of the empirical sciences. The lecture room in Surgeon's Square was provided with "a sliding pannel through which *subjects* were hoisted into a dark garret whenever the approach of a sheriff's officer was signaled from the gate."[14] Perhaps not incidentally, *pannel* is the Scottish legal term used for a defendant. It was in this room that Forbes delivered his first scientific lectures.[15]

Yet for the purposes of this essay, the room is most significant as the place where Forbes met fellow student John Goodsir. On that day, Wilson recounts, the usual crowd of Knoxites who "haunted" the space were absent at the hospital or elsewhere, and the "living" were represented only by Goodsir, who was busy in a corner dissecting a head.[16] The talented Fife anatomist was to become a steady companion and collaborator in Forbes's expeditionary science, their lasting amity commemorated by the similar miniature granite obelisks marking their side-by-side graves in Edinburgh's Dean Cemetery.[17] These adamantine monuments—their historical models subjected more than most any other immovable-seeming architectural artifacts to displacement or spoliation—serve as our point of departure for (the study of) unknown and potentially unknowable regions, including a stop at the lost and forgotten burial place of the Blind Homer.

The appointment of twenty-four-year-old Forbes to the committee for researches with the dredge, established at the August 1839 Birmingham meeting of the British Association for the Advancement of Science, confirmed rather than initiated the Manxman's contributions to study of the sea.[18] At the meeting Forbes presented the zoological researches he had made with Goodsir in the Orkney and Shetland Islands.[19] At the time, Forbes and Goodsir shared the garret floor of a house at No. 21 Lothian Street, adjacent to the university. Their rooms were an unhomely combination of menagerie, mortuary, laboratory, and, when space permitted, a "barracks" for the emerging ranks of scientific society.[20] Following the Birmingham meeting Forbes returned to the Isle of Man, where he remained for two months, "naturalizing, as was his wont."[21] His first research station was a scallop bank in twenty fathoms of water, which lay about five miles off the coast of Ballaugh.[22] Two weeks later, in a letter to the London publisher John Van Voorst, he wrote, "For some time back, under the most favourable circumstances, [I have] been collecting materials for the natural history of the molluscous and radiate animals."[23]

A theoretical conspectus of his seven years of accumulated observations of the scallop bank appeared in his paper "On the Associations of Mollusca on the British Coasts, considered with reference to Pleistocene geology." Here Forbes related his understanding of the bank as a mutable formation shaped by migration, succession, and occasional recurrence of faunas, each phenomenon leaving distinct traces. He also presented his schematic division of the British Coasts into four faunally distinct zones of depth.[24] The delicate and

---

14 Wilson and Geikie, *Memoir of Edward Forbes*, 93.

15 Wilson and Geikie, *Memoir of Edward Forbes*, 93.

16 Wilson and Geikie, *Memoir of Edward Forbes*, 144.

17 Henry Lonsdale, "Biographical Memoir," in *The Anatomical Memoirs of John Goodsir*, ed. William Turner (Edinburgh: Adam and Charles Black, 1868), I: 194.

18 "Synopsis of Sums appropriated to Scientific Objects by the General Committee at the Birmingham Meeting," in *Report of the Ninth Meeting of the British Association for the Advancement of Science; Held at Birmingham in August 1839* (London: John Murray, 1840), xxvi.

19 Edward Forbes and John Goodsir, "Notice of Zoological Researches in Orkney and Shetland during the month of June 1839," *Report of the Ninth Meeting of the British Association for the Advancement of Science; Held at Birmingham in August 1839*, 79–82.

20 Henry Lonsdale, "Biographical Memoir," I: 97–98.

21 Wilson and Geikie, *Memoir of Edward Forbes*, 249.

22 Edward Forbes, "On a Shell-bank in the Irish Sea, considered Zoologically and Geologically," *Annals of Natural History* 4 (1840): 217.

23 Forbes to John Van Voorst (Douglas, Isle of Man, September 16, 1839), cited in Wilson and Geikie, *Memoir of Edward Forbes*, 250.

24 Edward Forbes, "On the Associations of Mollusca on the British Coasts, considered with reference to Pleistocene geology," *Edinburgh Academic Annual* 1 (1840): 177–83.

Edward Forbes, *The Natural History of the European Seas* (London: John Van Voorst, 1859), viii.

vibrant nonmollusk creatures that lived on the edges of the scallop bank appeared in Forbes's *History of British Starfishes, and other animals of the class Echinodermata* (1841), published by Van Voorst and warmly dedicated to Louis Agassiz.[25]

When Agassiz came to Edinburgh following the 1840 Glasgow meeting of the British Association, he paid a visit to the "attic" on Lothian Street,

where he was "in ecstasies with the living urchins, star-fishes, and ophiurae" kept by Forbes in his aquarium.[26] Yet this class of animals presented both real and perceived difficulties of observation and description that might be seen to prefigure what Forbes saw (or failed to) in his survey of the Ægean. The name *Ophiuridae* (brittle stars) derives from the Greek word *ophis*, for "snake," from whence come specific epithets such as *caput medusa*, for the serpent-tressed Gorgon. The *Ophiuridae* came to pieces seemingly at the mere presentiment of being

25 In his "On the Asteriadae of the Irish Sea," *Memoirs of the Wernerian Natural History Society* 8 (1838): 114–28, Forbes cites Louis Agassiz's "Prodrome d'une monographie des Radiaires ou Echinodermes," *Mémoires de la Société des Sciences Naturelles de Neuchâtel* 1 (1835): 168–99, as a model of clarity.

26 Wilson and Geikie, *Memoir of Edward Forbes*, 264.

handled or seen. Forbes was initiated early into the ordeal of observation: that which escapes from view. When dredging the Irish Sea in October 1834, he took several specimens of Comatula, apparently the rare *Comatula rosacea*. He placed them without examination in a tin case along with some shells and mollusks, "intending to examine them minutely when I had landed."[27] When he returned home, however, all he found within were shards of life.

Engaging in a speculative form of reasoning, Forbes interpreted the scallop bank's geological meaning by supposing it "converted into a fossil bed similar to the shell-marls of the Pleistocene or newer Pliocene era."[28] Writing (natural) history in the future anterior, he anticipated which classes of animals would remain in the proleptic fossil record. "We should be able to form a pretty accurate idea of the testaceous mollusca inhabiting it, but not of the naked mollusca, as the latter would wholly disappear." As for the Chitons, "they would scarcely be met with in consequence of their fragility and disorganization after death, though abundant on the bed in a living state."[29] However constancy was observed in the appearance or disappearance of the Echinodermata. "We should find the remains of sea urchins only; and as they generally fall in pieces like the Chitons, we should be obliged to determine the species from fragments."[30] A note Forbes received from the Cork surgeon and naturalist John Vaughan Thompson, who was the first to describe the Pentracrinoid stage of the Comatulidæ (feather stars), described the process with photogramlike instantaneity. "The power of this animal to break itself up," Thompson writes of the brittle star, "is exemplified in an interesting manner by a specimen in Mr. Ball's collection." Robert Ball, director of the Natural History Museum at the University of Dublin, where a number of the specimens described

in *A History of British Starfishes* were housed, designed the dredge that was widely used by British naturalists, in Forbes's case to indiscriminate effect. Ball placed the brittle star on a sheet of paper "and glued down each part as it broke it off, thus exhibiting the appearance presented by the fossil species."[31]

As the name suggests, the *Ophiuridae* educed a special form of petrification. Forbes writes, "I have seen a large dredge come up completely filled with them; a most curious sight, for when the dredge was emptied, these little creatures, writhing with the strangest contortions, crept about in all directions, often flinging their arms in broken pieces around them, and their snake-like and threatening attitudes were by no means relished by the boatmen, who anxiously asked permission to shovel them overboard, superstitiously remarking that 'the things weren't right.'"[32] Brought to light by the naturalist, the gaze-defying brittle stars were destined to be pitched by the superstitious boatmen into a watery grave in sunless depths.

Forbes was similarly disconcerted by his attempt to study *Luidia fragilissima* (Asteroida). In a gesture of seeming self-reflection, he dedicated the genus to Edward Lhuyd, "one of the earliest observers of our native Star-fishes." Robert Plot's successor as keeper of the Ashmolean Museum, Lhuyd "united a comprehensive and philosophical mind with an observing eye." In naming the genus after him, Forbes was compensating for the "strange" fact that "his name is omitted in many of our cyclopedias, which devote whole pages to men of less repute."[33] As for the sea star, while it was among the most remarkable and largest of British species, and generally distributed, it had long "altogether escaped observation, or rather description." The implied hiatus between observation and description is a telling one. Forbes narrates his failing attempt to capture it: "Never having seen one before, and quite unconscious of its suicidal powers, I

27 Edward Forbes, "Reports of Dredging," *Magazine of Natural History* 8 (1835): 69.

28 Forbes, "On a Shell-bank in the Irish Sea," 222.

29 Forbes, "On a Shell-bank in the Irish Sea," 223.

30 Ibid.

31 Edward Forbes, *A History of British Starfishes and Other Animals of the Class Echinodermata* (Edinburgh: John Van Voorst, 1841), 52.

32 Forbes, *A History of British Starfishes*, 63.

33 Forbes, *A History of British Starfishes*, 136.

OPHIURIDÆ.   *OPHIURÆ.*

COMMON BRITTLE-STAR.

Ophiocoma rosula.   Link.

Edward Forbes, *A History of British Starfishes, and Other Animals of the Class Echinodermata* (London: John Van Voorst, 1841), 60.

spread it out on a rowing bench, the better to admire its form and colours. On attempting to remove it for preservation, to my horror and disappointment I found only an assemblage of rejected members. My conservative endeavours were all neutralized by its destructive exertions, and it is now badly represented in my cabinet by an armless disk and a diskless arm."[34] What was a star without its rays?

In his revision of Forbes's *British Echinodermata*, the Rev. Alfred Merle Norman draws attention to the figure of *Asterius savignyi* (*Luidia fragilissima*) that appears in the *Description de l'Égypte* as a "marvelous example of the perfection to which the engraving of objects of natural history can be carried." (Regrettably Jules-César Savigny provides no information regarding how the specimen was collected.) Not content with the possible perfection of the engraver's art, Norman goes on to suggest that "nature has been, as it were, photographed—and

that, too, before photography was discovered—by the artist on his plate."[35] It was nature, not art, that conspired against Forbes as he tried to observe and describe the disintegrating sea star. "In despair I grasped at the largest, and brought up the extremity of an arm with its terminating eye [pigment spot], the spinous eyelid of which opened and closed with something exceedingly like a wink of derision."[36]

Forbes's failure to wholly grasp these self-dismembering beings, first encountered by him in a state of unconsciousness to their seeming derisive resistance to being apprehended, assumes a changed aspect in light of his exploration of the Ægean. His progress marked by a hundred or more dredging stations, what he found—or rather speculated upon as a result of his empty dredge—was a telling and resounding absence of life. In April 1841, Forbes was appointed naturalist aboard the HM Surveying Ship *Beacon*. Under the command of Captain Thomas Graves, the vessel was engaged in hydrographical work along the coasts of Crete. As if replicating the disquieting arrangement of his rooms on Lothian street, the captain's cabin, which Forbes was liberally invited to share, was turned "into a kind of museum, laboratory, and storeroom, where the various animals brought up from the deep were dissected, drawn, or stowed away in bottles."[37] In a letter to Dr. John Percy, Forbes indicated that he was "devoting my time more to observation than to mere collecting, and I am especially occupying myself drawing all the unpreservable animals (which in these seas have been sadly neglected) that fall in my way."[38] The fear, again revived, was of that which falls from view, or fails to enter into it.

34 Forbes, *A History of British Starfishes*, 138.

35 Rev. Alfred Merle Norman, "On the genera and species of British Echinodermata," *Annals and Magazine of Natural History*, series 3, vol. 15 (1865): 118.

36 Forbes, *A History of British Starfishes*, 139; Victor Audouin, "Explication sommaire des plantes d'échinodermes de l'Égypte et de la Syrie, publiés par Jules-César Savigny," *Description de l'Égypte*, vol. 1 "Histoire Naturelle," pt. 4 (Paris: Imprimerie Impériale, 1809), 207–208.

37 Wilson and Geikie, *Memoir of Edward Forbes*, 275–76.

38 Wilson and Geikie, *Memoir of Edward Forbes*, 277. Percy befriended Forbes when he was a medical student under Charles Bell in Edinburgh.

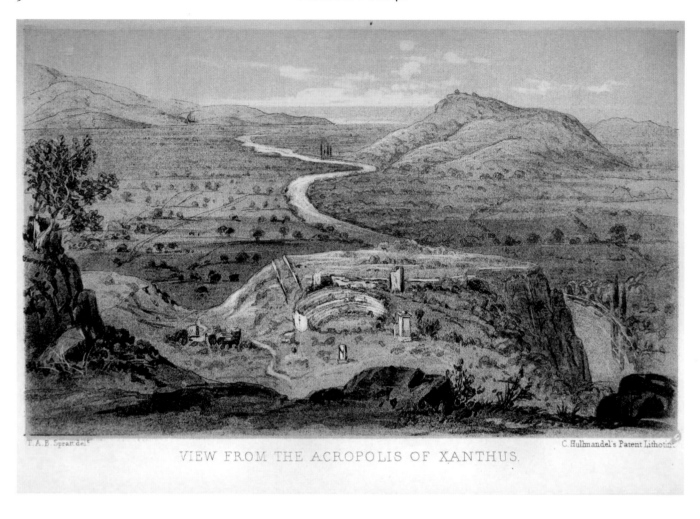

VIEW FROM THE ACROPOLIS OF XANTHUS.

Thomas Abel Brimage Spratt and Edward Forbes, *Travels in Lycia, Milyas, and the Cibyratis* (London: John Van Voorst, 1847), 29.

Along with its survey operations, the *Beacon* was charged with securing the antiquities of Xanthus (Antalya Province, Turkey), the capital of ancient Lycia. With the archaeologist Charles Fellows on board "to point out the monuments to be removed,"[39] the operation induced in Forbes visions of a geological unconformity. During January and February 1842 the crew of the *Beacon* was employed to excavate among the ruins, assisted by the HM Survey Ship *Medea*, which was detailed to the operation when the *Beacon*'s hull proved unsuited to receiving the rare cargo. "Its proud monuments had been despoiled of their ornaments," Forbes writes, "and its long-buried treasures, brought to light. On the platform before our habitation lay between seventy and eighty huge cases, containing relics of its former grandeur, destined to adorn the national Museum of a distant land—one which, when Xanthus flourished, was yet more wild and barbarous than the land of the Xanthians is now."[40] The anomalous redistribution of past and present, parceled into just so many numbered crates, was not the only lesson offered by the Xanthian interlude. Rather the quandary as posed by Fellows was the extent to which the treasures brought to light represented others that remained buried. In October 1841, the trustees of the British Museum, having received information that a *firman* (decree) had been obtained from the

39 Charles Fellows, *The Xanthian Marbles: Their Acquisition, and Transmission to England* (London: John Murray, 1843), 9.

40 Thomas Abel Brimage Spratt and Edward Forbes, *Travels in Lycia, Milyas, and the Cibyratis* (London: John Van Voorst, 1847), I: 45–46.

Sublime Porte, urgently requested from Fellows "full instructions as to what objects were to be removed, and to make maps, plans, and descriptions as to where each fragment was to be sought by the Captain of such of Her Majesty's ships as might be appointed to the service."[41] Fellows was apprehensive about what *might* be seen or missed by an as yet unnamed captain: "I feel certain that the removal of one stone would bring to light others, probably better preserved and more valuable, and that the *visible* formed but a fraction of what might be obtained, but could not be enumerated in written order, which might probably be only literally obeyed."[42]

On August 5, 1841, with the *Beacon* anchored at Paros, Forbes departed aboard the tender ship *Isabella* on a six-week triangulation expedition led by Lieutenant Abel Brimage Spratt, assistant hydrographer of the Mediterranean Survey. Bound for Cerigo (Kythera) and the southern end of the Morea (Peloponnese peninsula), Forbes, who as a student produced a translation of the *Iliad*, was irresistibly drawn to Nio (Ios), the legendary burial place of Homer. Two years earlier, in 1839, the Halle classicist Ludwig Ross had visited Nio to "retrace" the aporetic narrative of self-styled Dutch nobleman Heinrich Leopold Pasch van Krienen.[43] In 1771 the archaeological adventurer took leave of the Russian navy, to which he had lent his services during its engagement with the Ottoman fleet, in the Ægean to conduct excavations near the creek at Plakotos, in the northern part of the Cycladic island of Ios. The marble inscription on the third tomb Pasch van Krienen uncovered convinced him that it was "truly that of the great prince of poetry."[44] Consistent with

the text that appears in the pseudo-Herodotean *Life of Homer* (ca. 50–150 CE), the elegy read:

> Here the earth has covered that sacred head,
> adorner of warriors and heroes, the godly
> Homer.[45]

Casting his lot in an unequal struggle against what he regarded as the "blithe skepticism" of *Altertumswissenschaft* (knowledge of human nature in antiquity) articulated and practiced unsparingly by Friedrich August Wolf in his *Prolegomena ad Homerum*, Ross sought to defend the (counterfeit) count's discoveries against the imputations of fraud made by Wolf's own teacher and later critic, Göttingen humanist Christian Gottlob Heyne. In his tract, *The Pretended Tomb of Homer* (1794),[46] Heyne was not insensitive to the umbrageous allure of the already legendary tale that the skeleton of the blind poet, found seated upright, fell to dust at the moment of being distinctly seen. But Pasch van Krienen's renderings of the inscriptions were the source of considerable doubt and uncertainty. Ross feebly replied that Pasch van Krienen was not sufficiently skilled as an epigrapher and antiquarian to have forged the inscriptions.[47]

Having found no evidence during his investigation of Ios, Ross did not end his search for the fate of Homer's tomb. In a letter from July 21, 1858, addressed to *The Athenæum*, he prevailed on traveler and antiquarian Lieutenant-Colonel William Martin Leake, British Museum Egyptologist Samuel Birch, and Sir Charles Fellows, whose excavation of the Xanthian Marbles (January–February 1842)

41 Lord Ponsonby to Fellows (March 7, 1840), cited in Fellows, *Xanthian Marbles*, 3.

42 Fellows, *Xanthian Marbles*, 4.

43 On Pasch van Krienen's true identity see Jan Paul Crielaard, "A 'Dutch' Discoverer of Homer's Tomb," in *Homeric Questions: Essays in Philology, Ancient History, and Archaeology, Including the Papers of a Conference Organized by the Netherlands Institute at Athens (15 May 1993)*, ed. Jan Paul Crielaard (Amsterdam: J. C. Gieben, 1995), 313–316.

44 Conte Pasch di Krienen, *Breve Descrizione dell'Arcipelago e Particolarmente delle Diciotto Isole Sottomesse l'Anno 1771 al Domino Russo* (Livorno, Italy: Tommaso Masi e Comp., 1773), 45.

45 Martin L. West, ed. and trans., *Homeric Hymns, Homeric Apocrypha, Lives of Homer*, Loeb Classical Library (Cambridge, Massachusetts: Harvard University Press, 2003), 411.

46 Ludwig Ross, *Reisen auf den griechischen Inseln des ägäischen Meeres* (Stuttgart: J.G. Gotta'scher Verlag, 1840), I: 6. Christian Gottlob Heyne, *Das vermeinte Grabmal Homers* (Leipzig: Weidmannischen Buchhandlung, 1794). Ross's vindication of Pasch van Krienen was harshly critiqued by Friedrich Gottlieb Welcker in "Grab und Schule Homers in Ios und die Betrügereien des Grafen Pasch van Kreinen," *Zeitschrift für die Alterthumswissenschaft* 2 (April 1844).

47 Ross, *Reisen auf den griechischen Inseln*, I: 168.

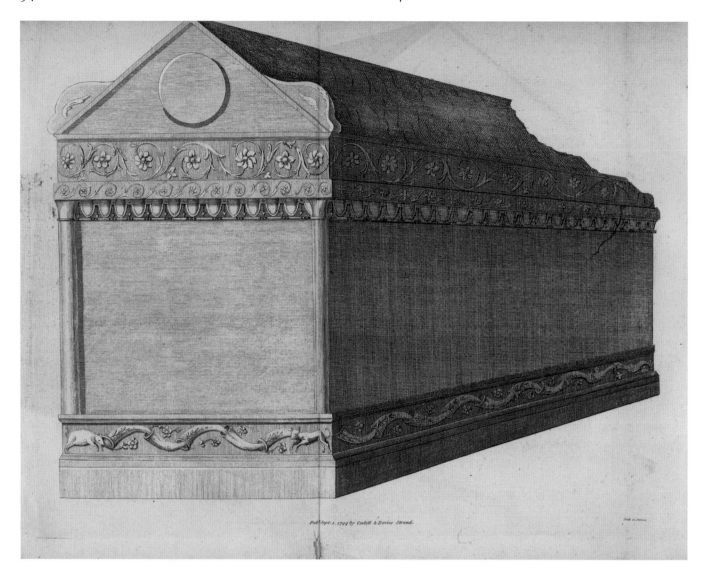

Johann Dominik Fiorillo after M. Le Chevalier, frontispiece from *The Pretended Tomb of Homer*
by Christian Gottlob Heyne (London, T. Cadell, Jun. and W. Davies, 1795).

was keenly observed by Forbes during his prolonged sojourn in Lycia, to pursue some compelling if not neglected clues.[48] Most intriguingly, during his visit to London in spring, 1822, Göttingen classicist Karl Otfried Müller copied an inscription found in the cellars of the British Museum that matched one in Pasch van Krienen's *Breve descrizione dell'Arcipelago*. Müller's mentor, Wolfian classicist August Böckh, published the discovery in the *Corpus Inscriptionum Graecarum*, though under the rubric *inscriptiones locorum incertorum* ("inscriptions of uncertain origin"). While Fellows's expatriated Lycian ruins were assured an "honorable enshrinement" alongside the Elgin Marbles,[49] the dismembered remains of

---

48 "Foreign Correspondence," *Athenæum* 1605 (July 31, 1858): 140. First published as Ludwig Ross, "Die Grabschrift Homer's vielleicht im britischen Museum?" *Archäologische Zeitung* 9 (1857): 220–21. The trail leads back to the report made by Swedish Orientalist and manuscript collector Jacob Jonas Björnståhl, from Leghorn in June 1772, where Pasch van Krienen was attempting to sell his "crated up" collection to Frederick the Second of Prussia. The negotiations having failed, "he and his antiquities have been completely lost sight of." Jacob Jonas Björnståhl, *Briefe auf seinen ausländischen Reisen an den Königlichen Bibliothekar C.C. Gjörwell in Stockholm* (Stralsund, Germany: Christian Lorenz Struck, 1778), II: 169–71.

49 William Watkiss Lloyd, *Xanthian Marbles: The Nereid Monument; an Historical and Mythological Essay* (London: William Pickering, 1845), 91; see also Samuel Birch, "Observations on the Xanthian Marbles Recently Deposited in the British Museum," *Archaeologia* 30 (1844): 176–204.

Homer's tomb were "deposited, buried, and forgotten *in subterraneis Musei Britannici.*"[50] Ross preserved the hope that it might "again be brought to light, and once more dug from its hiding place."[51] That is if in fact it still or ever existed. Wolf proposed a realistic and unsettling solution for the Homeric question: "It is certain that, alike in the *Iliad* and in the *Odyssey*, the web was begun, and the threads were carried to a certain point, by the poet who had first taken up the theme. [...] Perhaps it will never be possible to show, even with probability, the precise points at which new filaments or dependencies of the texture begin."[52]

Forbes's research in the Ægean, where the study of marine animals was said to have begun under the tutelage of Aristotle, posed related questions as to what was grasped by or lost to an instrument tethered to a line descending into once inconceivably remote depths. For Forbes the results of dredging presented themselves according to a double-sided point of view. In order to "ascertain the exact relations of animals and plants to each other" so as to have a "good basis for the illustration of certain points in geology and philosophical zoology," it was necessary to carry out "more precise, and, at the same time, more *generalized* observation of the Mediterranean than has hitherto been gone into."[53] In seeking to reconcile the precise and generalized, a final comment on Homer's Homeric diversion on the island of Ios might be suitable, particularly considering that Forbes's indiscriminate "idea of a life-zero"

was as beguiling to his followers as Odysseus's evasive self-introduction, "I am Nobody" (οὖτις) was to the Cyclops Polyphemus. The pseudo-Herodotean author relates that an ailing Homer was resting along the shore of Ios when some fisher-boys arrived and posed the following riddle: "What we have done is leave behind what he caught, and what we didn't catch we're carrying." Met with silence, the boys explain that they had no success in catching fish, but to pass to the time they deloused themselves, and all the lice they caught they left behind, but all the ones they missed they carried with them. One legend, which the pseudo-Herodotus author critically dismisses, suggests that Homer became depressed and died when he was unable to work out the riddle.[54]

The riddle—the word and the thing—prefigures the findings (or leavings) of the dredge in the most profoundly mundane sense. *Riddle* derives from an Indo-European root shared by the Latin *cribrum* ("sieve") and the Greek *krinein* ("to decide" or "to discriminate"), which was akin to *kritikos* ("critic"). Describing the process of discrimination, Robert Ball writes, the contents of the dredge are best examined by means of sieves, of which three should be used, one over the other, first a riddle, next a wheat sieve, and third an oat sieve. These may be fastened together, the contents of the dredge being emptied into the riddle, and water being poured upon them. The mud and other detritus will be washed off, and the contents separated so as to be easily examined; by this plan a hundredfold more will be discovered than can be found by searching in mud or sand in the usual manner. Numbers of crabs, starfish, sea urchins, worms, corals, zoophytes, algae, et cetera are procured by the dredge.[55]

Forbes presented his Ægean dredging results and conclusions at the August 1843 meeting of the British Association, held at Cork, where William Thompson presided over "Section D: Natural

50 Müller to Böckh (London, May 27, 1822), in *Briefwechsel zwischen August Boeckh und Karl Otfried Mueller* (Leipzig, Germany: Druck und Verlag, 1883), 79–83; August Böckh and Johannes Franz, eds., *Corpus Inscriptionum Graecarum*, vol. 4, pars 39: "Inscriptiones locorum incertorum" (Berlin: Ex Officina Academica and G. Reimer, 1856), 36, no. 6953: "In subterraneis musei Britannici in tabula marmorea litteris magnis; habeo ex schedis Odofr. Mülleri"; Ludwig Ross, *Graf Pasch van Krienen. Abdruck seiner italienischen Beschreibung des Griechischen Archipelagus* (Halle, Germany: Schwetschkescher Verlag, 1860), 42.

51 "Foreign Correspondence," 140.

52 Wolf's preface to the 1794 edition of the *Iliad*, xxviii, cited and translated in R. C. Jebb, *Homer: An Introduction to the Iliad and the Odyssey* (Glasgow: James Maclehouse and Sons, 1887), 109.

53 Wilson and Geikie, *Memoir of Edward Forbes*, 277. See also Richard Hoskyn, "Narrative of a Survey of part of the South Coast of Asia Minor, and of a Tour into the Interior of Lycia in 1840–1," *Journal of the Royal Geographical Society of London* 12 (1842): 143–61.

54 *Lives of Homer*, 411.

55 Robert Ball, "The Dublin University Museum, January 1846," *Dublin University Magazine* 27 (January 1846): 15.

FIG. 45.—'Ball's Dredge.'

Robert Ball's Dredge. C. Wyville Thomson,
The Depths of the Sea (London: Macmillan and Co., 1873), 240.

History." Thompson had joined Forbes as a naturalist aboard the *Beacon* but quit the expedition in June 1841, when there was no prospect of visiting Crete; and he "was sick of the sea."[56] Nonetheless, Forbes kept Thompson apprised of his work in the Ægean: "I have found star-fishes alive at 200 fathoms; *Tellinae* and *Rissoae* at 150 (!); a bed of chalk full of *Foraminifera*, and the shells of Pteropoda

forming at the bottom of these seas! Moreover, the most characteristic shells of this hitherto unknown region are species only known to conchologists as fossil: *I* only have seen them alive and kicking. You can appreciate the value both to geology and zoology of the discovery of this new sea-country. We have dredged deeper than ever was done before (as recorded), but it could never have been effected except by Ball's little dredge, which has proved invaluable. Tell Ball so."[57]

After his disappointment while collecting brittle stars—"little creatures, writhing with the strangest contortions"—Forbes could be forgiven his exuberance at seeing species known only in fossil form "alive and kicking." While he happily expressed his gratitude to Ball for having contrived the dredge by which they were collected, the moment of observation was his alone: "*I* only have seen them." It is what eluded the dredge and his expectant eye, in spite of a concern for recording all that was recovered from the previously unsampled depths, that committed Forbes to improbable conclusions in his report at Cork. Having sifted the British Coasts into four zones of depth, he identified eight in the Ægean, the final one having a range more than twice that of all the other regions combined. "Throughout this great, and I may say hitherto unknown province, for the notices we have had of it have been but few and fragmentary, we find an uniform and well-characterized fauna distinguished from those of all the preceding regions by the presence of species peculiar to itself. Within itself the number of species and of individuals diminishes as we descend, pointing to a zero in the distribution of animal life as yet unvisited. It can only be subdivided according to the disappearance of species which do not seem to be replaced by others."[58]

"If he erred," Archibald Geikie wrote of Forbes, "it was from an over-anxiety to reach the meaning

56 Wilson and Geikie, *Memoir of Edward Forbes*, 280. Thompson did manage to produce notes on migratory birds from the survey vessel. William Thompson, "Notice of migratory Birds which alighted on, or were seen from, HMS *Beacon*, Capt. Graves, on the passage from Malta to the Morea at the end of April 1841," *Annals and Magazine of Natural History* 8 (1842): 125–29.

57 Forbes to Thompson [September 1841], cited in Wilson and Geikie, *Memoir of Edward Forbes*, 294–95.

58 Edward Forbes, "Report on the Mollusca and Radiata of the Ægean Sea, and on their distribution considered as bearing on Geology," (ref. 61), 167.

of isolated observations, which sometimes, perhaps, led him to theorize on too narrow a basis, and to over-estimate the value of negative evidence."[59] But it was also the case that the disciples of great men tend to assert dogmatically what their master suggested hypothetically, and it was so with the followers of Forbes. Thus they "view the life-zero not as a probability, but as a certainty, building their belief more on the *a priori* absurdity of creatures being able to live in the absence of light and air, and under the great pressure which must prevail in the depths of the sea, than on any direct evidence."[60] One ruthlessly lucid contemporary philosopher of the unknown has thoroughly tested the origin and import of the proposition: "Absence of evidence isn't evidence of absence."[61] A more fitting model for considering Forbes's conceptual misadventure might be the thought experiment devised by Edinburgh-born mathematical physicist James Clerk Maxwell that arguably bears some structural resemblance to the "sliding pannel" in Knox's lecture room. In his desire to "pick a hole" in the "2nd law of $\Theta\Delta cs$," to adopt his private notation for the universal tendency of energy to be "dizzypated," Maxwell imagined the intervention of a "doorkeeper, very intelligent and exceedingly quick," who could sort slow- (colder) from fast-moving (hotter) molecules passing between adjoining chambers.[62] To understand a matter it is often necessary, and certainly advisable, to place it side by side, like the fortress and the rock on which it stands, to sort out the similarities and differences.

The specific status, no less than the significance, of this demonic "guiding agent" has been a matter of speculation ever since. But for Maxwell the statistically supported probabilistic implication was clear: "Moral: The 2nd law of Thermodynamics has the same degree of truth as the statement that if you throw a tumblerful of water into the sea you cannot get the same tumblerful of water out again."[63] The sea is an agent and a harbor of indifference, yet it is marked and transected by zones and regions and levels of differentiation. Knowing how things (come to an) end might well depend on operating the door or sliding the panel that releases the observing subject, rather than the subject of observation, from its self-entrapping empirical vigilance. Failing that, there is something to be said for forgetting ourselves for a while, before once again indulging the lament expressed by Fellows that "the *visible* formed but a fraction of what might be obtained" (from our grasping desire for self-possession).

A potentially misplaced faith in what is to come animates its own species of fear and dread. George MacGregor, the Glaswegian historian of Burke and Hare, observes that "the 'something beyond' the mortal sphere caused a peculiar regard for the dead." This was a reverence, however, that the people of Scotland did "not always pay to the living." In any case, their "belief in a resurrection was rather material, and it was thought impossible by many that when the last trump should sound the dead could rise if the bodies were cut up in dissection."[64] Forbes's own dredging disclosed the presumed depths where no life remained, where the very possibility of life's existence diminished with the gradual but fatal extinction of light. He was bound to go wrong, illuminatingly so.

59 Wilson and Geikie, *Memoir of Edward Forbes*, 549.

60 *Report on the Scientific Results of the Voyage of HMS Challenger*, xl.

61 Errol Morris, "The Certainty of Donald Rumsfeld (Part 4)," *New York Times*, March 28, 2014.

62 See Edward Eigen, "The Housing of Entropy," *Perspecta* 35 (2004): 62–73.

63 James Clerk Maxwell to John William Strutt (December 6, 1870), in P. M. Harman, *The Scientific Letters and Papers of James Clerk Maxwell: Volume II: 1862–1873* (Cambridge: Cambridge University Press, 1995), 583.

64 MacGregor, *The History of Burke and Hare*, 14.

Eric Kahn & Russell Thomsen, *Pin Drawing*, 2015, IDEA.

Is it because the Holocaust will always go beyond the limits of representation? Is it because the Holocaust seems to stand outside narratable and representable history, so that the monuments commemorating it are reduced to the status of mere signs, like numbers or helpless syllables, unable to carry a meaning and to be anything more than pure and naked reference? Hence, can the Holocaust monument never properly be said to be a commemorative representation of the Holocaust because no Holocaust monument could ever add meaning to pure and naked reference?

—F. R. Ankersmit, *Historical Representation*, 2001

Until recently, a great deal of the controversy, debate, and anxiety over the question of what to do with Auschwitz has centered on the camp at Auschwitz I. Most of the remaining buildings, railway tracks, and grounds, along with the notorious mocking gateway, stand there. The iconic displays of confiscated suitcases, shoes, spectacles, prosthetics, and the shorn hair belonging to the victims are located in a retrofitted museum there, and ongoing discussions about how to curate the visitors' experience have focused on it. The Polish government made a pragmatic decision in the early 1950s to house the museum and exhibitions in the masonry buildings at Auschwitz I (there simply weren't sufficient funds to deal with the larger, more fragile camp at Auschwitz II-Birkenau). An Austro-Hungarian army barracks from the First World War before its transformation by the Nazis into a *Konzentrationslager*, the durable buildings were more easily restored and provided de facto the iconic presence required to effectively represent the state's version of the atrocities committed there.[1]

Several kilometers away, the much larger extermination camp at Auschwitz II-Birkenau—the synecdoche for the Holocaust—is disappearing. Nature and time are slowly erasing the physical presence of the camp and its grounds. The memory of the Holocaust, embodied in the words of both survivors and perpetrators, and the palpable experience of the place itself are slowly moving from firsthand forms of knowledge to more mediated historical representations.

The Birkenau site is already in an advanced state of ruin. Within the vast figure of almost 400 acres delimited by barbed-wire fencing and iconic guard towers spaced at regular intervals, a seemingly endless field of brick chimneys surrounds the few remaining buildings, emphatic vertical lines marking locations where row after row of wooden prisoner barracks once stood. Erasure began as early as 1944, when Jewish prisoners led a failed rebellion, dynamiting Crematorium IV using smuggled explosives. Shortly thereafter, as the Russian army approached, the Nazi SS hastily blew up the

1   Timothy W. Ryback, "Evidence of Evil," *New Yorker*, November 15, 1993. During the war, Auschwitz was already a household name in Poland: this was the camp to which Polish intellectuals, priests, members of the Resistance movement, and indeed ordinary Poles arrested in street roundups were sent. As many as 75,000 ethnic Poles were murdered in Auschwitz; their families knew where they were since they could send them postcards, and even food parcels. Auschwitz (or Oświęcim in Polish) became synonymous with the horrors of the Nazi occupation. Little wonder that after the war, the communist government preserved the place as a reminder of the evils of fascism, and a visit there was an obligatory part of the school curriculum.

2   Michael Kimmelman, "Auschwitz Shifts from Memorializing to Teaching," *New York Times*, February 18, 2011. "Each generation has gotten the stories it wants from the site. Under communism, Auschwitz served as a national memorial to Polish political prisoners, who were the camp's first victims. Birkenau, where hundreds of thousands of Jews from Poland, France, Germany, Hungary, the former Soviet Union and elsewhere were murdered, lapsed into neglect, because it didn't fit the narrative."

3   Jonathan Webber, *The Future of Auschwitz*, "Frank Green Lecture Series" (Oxford: Oxford Centre for Postgraduate Hebrew Studies, 1992), 3. "The need for Jewish cultural privacy to nurse the grief, to attempt to recover from the overwhelming ignominy, implies that Auschwitz should not be intruded on, that it should not be cluttered with other messages, with moral and cultural irrelevancies deriving from elsewhere—a Christian convent, for example."

4   For an extensive discussion of postwar Holocaust narratives, see James E. Young, *The Texture of Memory: Holocaust Memorials and Meaning* (New Haven, Connecticut: Yale University Press, 1993).

remaining crematoria in an attempt to erase Birkenau's architecture of genocide and any concomitant evidence of atrocities. In the months following the liberation of the camp, an acute shortage of building materials resulted in many of the barracks being dismantled and removed. Whatever remained was left largely untouched over successive decades, lapsing into neglect.

Today, prosaic events continue to assault the fragility of Auschwitz. In 2009, the theft of the infamous ironwork entry sign, *Arbeit Macht Frei,* from Auschwitz I marked the loss of an original artifact. In 2010, massive floods inundated Birkenau and again prompted international calls for a plan to deal with the future of the site and its environs before it simply passed away from neglect. The subtractions, erasures, modifications, edits, and subsequent additions to the camp complex as a tourist site have created additional historical and evidentiary problems. Tours are offered daily, bringing multitudes of visitors to the towns of Oświęcim and Brzezinka; an average of more than one million people annually visit the combined sites of Auschwitz I and Birkenau. The physical impact of this many visitors strains the already fragile, accessible portions of Birkenau. It is ironic that the fragile historical evidence embodied in the camps is such a popular draw that the site requires infrastructural additions that endanger those very artifacts. Moreover, the Auschwitz-Birkenau Museum, gift shop, bus station, parking lots, and restaurants, as well as a planned (as of 2010) visitor center, have challenged the quest to maintain authenticity, resulting in a compromised and problematic site.

As a memorial site and as a symbol, Auschwitz has played a schizophrenic role in regard to its nationalist significance. On one hand it has been a powerful symbol for the Polish-centric resistance to Nazi ideology, especially during the decades of communist rule following the end of the war (as a satellite state of the Soviet Union during the Cold War and as a symbol of the Holocaust, Auschwitz was subsumed by a larger, state-sponsored narrative warning against the evils of fascism).[2] On the other hand, it has always had an altogether different significance for the global Jewish community.[3] As a result, postwar Auschwitz narratives have been contentious, polarized, and widely debated.[4]

The future of the concentration camp at Auschwitz I and the extermination camp at Birkenau remains uncertain and contested. The Auschwitz-Birkenau Memorial and Museum currently maintain the camps and grounds in counsel with the International Auschwitz Council (IAC) and UNESCO. While the Auschwitz-Birkenau Foundation has made a clear and impassioned commitment to restoration in the near future, the more distant future of the camp, especially at Birkenau, is

Eric Kahn & Russell Thomsen,
Ruins at Birkenau, 2015, IDEA.

less certain.[5] Cultural historian Robert Jan van Pelt has described the inherent difficulty in restoring the ruins there, observing that inevitably the site will grow less authentic with the passage of time. "You're seeing basically a reconstruction of an original site. It's a place that constantly needs to be rebuilt in order to remain a ruin for us."[6]

Needless to say, the issues are contentious and animated by deep emotions, opinions, and politics. While some call for maintaining, even restoring, the buildings and grounds at Birkenau as a perpetual (albeit static) sign of remembrance, others advocate leaving them to ruin and allowing them to disappear back into the surrounding forest.[7] Both sides are passionate and argue their positions in earnest, remaining diametrically opposed. Thus without any clear direction, a question emerges: How can the disappearing evidence of the Holocaust at Auschwitz remain vital without being framed solely as a curated museum, a cemetery, or a progressively inauthentic, static memorial?

The goal of our proposal "Thinking the Future of Auschwitz" is twofold: first, to engage the broad cultural questions of memory, evidence, and preservation within the context of a physical site with a traumatic past; and second, to advance and expand the potential role of architecture within a critical interdisciplinary dialogue already in progress. The project suggests that we are approaching a clear tipping point, a paradigmatic shift in the relationship between the Holocaust as an event and its subsequent myriad forms

5 BBC News Europe, "Auschwitz Memorial: Germany Gives $80m for Preservation," December 15, 2010, http://www.bbc.co.uk/news/world-europe-12004610. The Auschwitz-Birkenau Fund, established in 2009, has a number of contributors, including Germany, Austria, Netherlands, Switzerland, and the Czech Republic. (The strategic conception of the present/future of the camps is based on a default preservationist model that does not acknowledge the asymmetry between the physical and metaphysical natures of Auschwitz I and Auschwitz II [Birkenau]).

6 Andrew Curry, "Can Auschwitz Be Saved?" *Smithsonian*, February 2010.

7 Statements by former Polish foreign minister and Auschwitz survivor Wladyslaw Bartoszewski and cultural historian Robert Jan van Pelt, in "Cash Crisis Threat to Auschwitz," January 26, 2009, http://news.bbc.co.uk/2/hi/europe/7827534.stm.

Eric Kahn & Russell Thomsen, *Area Plan*, 2015, IDEA.

8   Arthur A. Cohen, *The Tremendum:
    A Theological Interpretation of the Holocaust*
    (New York: Crossroad, 1981), 27–58.

9   Robert Jan van Pelt and Carroll William Westfall,
    Architectural Principles in the Age of Historicism
    (New Haven: Connecticut: Yale University
    Press, 1993), 341. "Cohen derived the term
    tremendum from Rudolf Otto's classic
    The Holy (1923). Otto described God as the
    utter mystery, the enormous mystery, the terror
    mystery, the *mysterium tremendum*. This
    original and awesome holiness, from which all
    the other attributes of God emanate, is
    countered by the human *tremendum*. This
    tremendum Cohen defined as "the enormity of
    an infinitized man" who fears death so
    completely and denies it so "to placate death by
    the magic of endless murder." Cohen identified
    the Nazi destruction of the Jews as the
    tremendum of our own times, "for it is the
    monument of a meaningless inversion of life
    to an orgiastic celebration of death, to
    a psychosexual and pathological degeneracy
    unparalleled and unfathomable to any person
    bonded to life." Cohen believed that it
    had not been accidental that the victims of the
    tremendum had been the Jews: their 4,000-year-
    long history was, after all, "a celebration
    of the tenacity of life."

of memorialization. Thus an imminent and urgent dilemma: preserving the physical site as evidence for eternity is both impossible and progressively destructive, while passive indifference (leading to erasure) ultimately deprives future generations of one of the most powerful means to comprehend the gravity of what occurred at Auschwitz. It is within this dilemma that this project seeks to propose an alternative.

Auschwitz as a place has come to connote a single iconic entity; it has become a historical metonym for the Holocaust in general. In reality, it is a large complex made up of multiple camps and subcamps, and collapsing them together as a whole fails to distinguish between the different roles played by each constituent part, physically and metaphysically. Understanding the difference between the two primary camps, Auschwitz I and Birkenau, is to acknowledge their asymmetric roles in the Nazi apparatus of genocide and locate their destinies within separate and very different notions of time. American Jewish scholar Arthur A. Cohen adopted the terms *tremendum* (from Rudolf Otto) and *caesura* (from Martin Buber) to describe the abyss of history opened up by the Holocaust.[8] For Cohen, the human *tremendum* of our time was the Nazi destruction of the Jews, and the *caesura* was the catastrophic fissure in the foundation of Jewish existence.[9] By conceptually splitting Auschwitz I and Birkenau, we create a productive abyss, producing

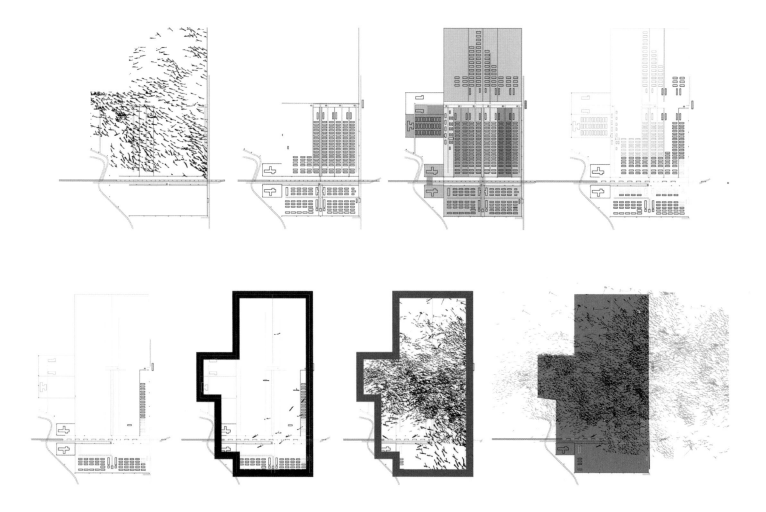

Eric Kahn & Russell Thomsen, *Timeline*, 2015, IDEA.

an interruption that echoes Cohen's description of tremendum as caesura: the "interruption of conventional time and intelligible causality."[10] The tremendum allows us to think of the catastrophe as a vast abyss without filling it; "as *Grund*, but also and simultaneously as *Abgrund*, abyss."[11] For various reasons, both historical and largely unintentional, the current reality is that Auschwitz I and Birkenau are for the most part already individuated, and the way forward must acknowledge their different trajectories as they contribute to the future of the whole.

"Thinking the Future of Auschwitz" imagines that two modes of control would articulate the splitting of the camps. Auschwitz I would continue to be maintained and programmed by the Auschwitz-Birkenau Museum; the buildings and grounds would be conserved as evidence and house a museum to exhibit the narrative of its history. It would endure as a didactic institution—a place of curated coherence, order, signs, signifiers, symbols, facts, use, and mnemonic reference points. It would hold steady as an arrested past manifest as memorial. But rather than simply abandoning Birkenau and allowing it to be subsumed by nature (and ultimately erased), the second act of the project sets it on an alternative course. In 2045, a *Tel Olam* would be constructed at Birkenau, after the last survivor and perpetrator would have passed from this world. Originally cited in Deuteronomy, *Tel Olam* is a biblical term for a place whose physical past should be blotted out forever and rendered inaccessible.[12] Translated as a perpetual heap, it would produce a traumatic figure steadfastly delimiting a perimeter. It would be realized as a procedural event; felled tree trunks, harvested from each of the countries from which victims were deported, would be stacked to form a perimeter wall approximately thirty feet high. The Tel would act as both a palpable, physical presence on the site and an object deeply saturated with meaning derived from its making. Encircling the grounds, the tree trunks would effectively separate the ruins of the camp from the surrounding world, barring entrance from the outside. Initially the stacks would be orderly and solid, but the logic of nature would contribute to their inevitable decay, and the physical remains would be transformed through a signless entropy. In contrast to the didactic memorial site at Auschwitz I, Birkenau would be set into perpetual drift as it moves out of the regime of culture (human time) and into that of nature (geological time), finally released from the mission of maintaining its traumatic landscape.

After viewing the Memorial Museum at Auschwitz I, visitors would move to Birkenau and walk the perimeter of the Tel Olam, creating an emergent ritual that would allow for an assertion and

10 Arthur A. Cohen and David Stern, *An Arthur A. Cohen Reader: Selected Fiction and Writings on Judaism, Theology, Literature, and Culture* (Detroit: Wayne State University Press, 1998), 246.

11 Pierre Joris, ed., *Paul Celan: Selections* (Berkeley: University of California Press, 2005), 5. "The perpetual ruin as both physical ground and figurative abyss is noted by Pierre Joris in relation to the poetry of Paul Celan: [in German] *Grund*, but also and simultaneously *Abgrund*, abyss."

12 F. R. Ankersmit, *Historical Representation* (Stanford, California: Stanford University Press, 2001), 178. "In a most perceptive essay, Jonathan Webber associated the Holocaust with a *Tel Olam*, a biblical term for a place whose physical past should be blotted out forever. That is to say, the Holocaust should remain to us forever an 'empty place,' a place that we can never hope to possess or actually occupy in the way that the historian hopes to appropriate or to come into possession of the past with the help of his metaphors. The discourse of memory is 'indexical,' it points to or indicates the past, it encircles the past—but without ever attempting to penetrate into it."

Eric Kahn & Russell Thomsen, *Emergent Ritual*, 2015, IDEA.

13 In describing the motivations for his design of the "Memorial to the Murdered Jews of Europe," architect Peter Eisenman addressed the issue of representation and the Holocaust: "I think it was something that defies representation; I think you cannot represent it. And what I've tried to do is say if you go to Auschwitz, if you go there, it's horrific: you're reminded of all these images, et cetera. But you can reassimilate your internal mechanisms to say, OK, that was then and here we are now. What I tried to do in Berlin was to do something that couldn't necessarily be as easily reassimilated." Peter Eisenman, "'Liberal Views Have Never Built Anything of Any Value': Interview by Robert Locke," *Archinect*, July 27, 2004, http://archinect.com/features/article/4618/ peter-eisenman-liberal-views-have-never-built-anything-of-any-value.

recording of the camp in absentia. The perimeter condition would acquire new significance contingent on the perpetual line that differentiates inside from outside. The various paths inscribed into the landscape by the wanderings of the multitudes of visitors would slowly accumulate over the years, marking a common journey without common answers. In shifting the perception of Birkenau from cultural to geological time, a new ontology for the camp would emerge. The camp's interior would communicate a presence of absence (a *blanking*), a withholding that would transform how it is apprehended as the manifestation of the ineffable, that which cannot be named.

Birkenau's echo of the "machinic" order (as a means for mass extermination) would cease to project its authoritative trauma and instead remain without narration and beyond comprehension. If understanding can be argued as one of the first steps toward assimilation and closure (and ultimately forgetting), the *blanking* of the extermination camp at Birkenau would confound conventional explanations.[13] Subject to a caesuric act of separation from the world, Birkenau would be ritually expelled and placed outside of humanity, rendering its landscape purposeless and thereby radically opening up a future for the whole of Auschwitz. After a long passage of time, when the perimeter wall will have decayed to the point where it has been breached and will soon become indistinguishable from the nature reclaiming it, we will ask again, "What is the future of Auschwitz?" But there will never be a definitive answer. Instead cyclical reconsideration will perpetuate memory as an incomplete but enduring future yet to be imagined.

In memory of Eric Kahn, 1956–2014.

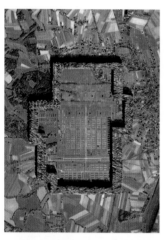
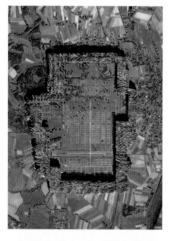

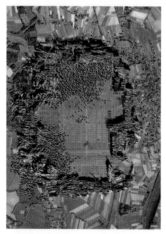

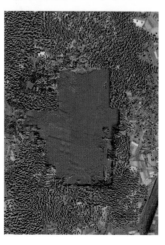

Eric Kahn & Russell Thomsen, *Perimeter Stacks*, 2015, IDEA.

Selected References

Abrams, Janet, and Peter Hall, eds. *Else/Where: Mapping—New Cartographies of Networks and Territories*. Minneapolis: University of Minnesota Design Institute, 2006.

Agamben, Giorgio. *Remnants of Auschwitz: The Witness and the Archive*. New York: Zone Books, 2003.

Améry, Jean. *At the Mind's Limits*. New York: Schocken Books, 1986.

Ankersmit, F. R., *Historical Representation*. Stanford, California: Stanford University Press, 2001.

Arendt, Hannah. *Eichmann in Jerusalem: A Report on the Banality of Evil*. New York: Viking Penguin Books, 1963.

Bellamy, Elizabeth J. *Affective Genealogies: Psychoanalysis, Postmodernism, and the "Jewish Question" after Auschwitz*. Lincoln: University of Nebraska Press, 1997.

Burleigh, Michael, and Wolfgang Wippermann. *The Racial State: Germany 1933–1945*. Cambridge, Massachusetts: Cambridge University Press, 1991.

Cohen, Arthur A. *The Tremendum*. New York: Crossroad, 1981.

Czech, Danuta. *Auschwitz Chronicle 1939–1945*. New York: Henry Holt & Co., 1990.

Eisenman, Peter, and Hanno Raugerberg. *Holocaust Memorial Berlin*. Zurich: Lars Müller Publishers, 2005.

Gilbert, Martin. *The Holocaust*. New York: Henry Holt, 1985.

Gutman, Yisrael, and Michael Berenbaum, eds. *Anatomy of the Auschwitz Death Camp*. Bloomington: Indiana University Press in association with the United States Holocaust Memorial Museum, 1994.

Hansen, Oskar. *Towards Open Form*, Edited by Jola Gola. Frankfurt: Revolver Publishing, 2005.

Hilberg, Raul. *Perpetrators Victims Bystanders*. New York: Harper Perennial, 1992.

Joris, Pierre. *Paul Celan: Selections*. Berkeley: University of California Press, 2005.

Katz, Steven T. *The Holocaust in Historical Context*. New York/Oxford: Oxford University Press, 1994.

Landau, Ronnie S. *The Nazi Holocaust*. London: I. B. Tauris & Co., 1992.

Lang, Berel. *The Future of the Holocaust Between History and Memory*. Ithaca, New York: Cornell University Press, 1999.

Lang, Berel. *Holocaust Representation: Art within the Limits of History and Ethics*. Baltimore, Maryland: Johns Hopkins University Press, 2000.

Langer, Lawrence L., ed. *Art from the Ashes: A Holocaust Anthology*. New York: Oxford University Press, 1995.

Langer, Lawrence L. *Holocaust Testimonies: The Ruins of Memory*. New Haven, Connecticut: Yale University Press, 1991.

Levi, Primo. *Survival in Auschwitz*, trans. Stuart Woolf. New York: Simon & Schuster, 1958.

Lifton, Robert J., and Eric Markusen. *The Genocidal Mentality*. New York: Basic Books, 1990.

Liss, Andrea. *Trespassing through Shadows: Memory, Photography, and the Holocaust*. Minneapolis: University of Minnesota, 1998.

Matz, Reinhard. *Die Unsichtbaren Lager*. Hamburg: Rowholt, 1993.

Moss, Herbert. *Holy Holocaust*. London: Janus, 1998.

Myers, David M., and David B. Ruderman, eds. *The Jewish Past Revisited: Reflections on Modern Jewish Historians*. New Haven, Connecticut: Yale University Press, 1998.

Rees, Lawrence. *Auschwitz: A New History*. New York: Public Affairs, 2005.

Rittner, Carol, and John K. Roth, eds. *Different Voices: Women and the Holocaust*. New York: Paragon House, 1993.

Roth, John K., and Michael Berenbaum, eds. *Holocaust: Religious and Philosophical Implications*. New York: Paragon House, 1989.

Schleunes, Karl A. *The Twisted Road to Auschwitz*. Urbana-Champaign: University of Illinois Press, 1990.

Smoleń, Kazimierz, ed. *KL Auschwitz Seen by the SS*. Warsaw: Interpress Publishers, 1991.

Swiebocka, Teresa, ed. *Auschwitz: A History in Photographs*, trans. Connie Wilsack. Oświęcim, Poland: Auschwitz-Birkenau State Museum; Bloomington: Indiana University Press, 1993.

van Pelt, Robert Jan, and Carroll William Westfall. *Architectural Principles in the Age of Historicism*. New Haven, Connecticut: Yale University Press, 1991.

Webber, Jonathan. *The Future of Auschwitz*. Oxford: Oxford Centre for Postgraduate Hebrew Studies, 1992.

Wiese, Christian, and Paul Betts. *Years of Persecution, Years of Extermination: Saul Friedlander and the Future of Holocaust Studies*. London: Continuum, 2010.

Wiesel, Elie. *Night*. New York: Bantam, 1982.

Young, James E. *At Memory's Edge*. New Haven, Connecticut: Yale University Press, 2000.

Young, James E. *The Texture of Memory: Holocaust Memorials and Meaning*. New Haven, Connecticut: Yale University Press, 1993.

Mario Carpo

BIG DATA AND

At the time of writing, in the summer of 2014, *Big Data* is a cultural trope more than a technical term. Yet the expression originally referred simply to our technical capacity to collect, store, and process increasing amounts of data at decreasing costs, and this original meaning still stands, regardless of hype, media improprieties, or semasiological confusion. Historians of information technology would be hard pressed to see this as a novelty: Moore's law, which describes a similar trend, has been known since 1965, and it holds true to this day. Yet, even more than the adoption of the term by specialists and in some professions, the "Big Data" phenomenon indicates that some crucial qualitative threshold may indeed have been crossed of recent—or at least, suggests a general belief that it may soon be. And there may be more to that than media hype. Today, for the first time in the history of humankind,

THE END OF HISTORY

data is abundant and cheap, and getting more so every day. If this trend continues, one may logically infer that at some point in the future an almost infinite amount of data could be recorded, transmitted, and retrieved at almost no cost. Evidently, a state of zero-cost recording and retrieval will always be impossible; yet this is where today's technology seems to be heading to, asymptotically. But if that is so, then we must also come to the inevitable conclusion that many technologies of data-compression currently in use will at some point become unnecessary, as the cost of compressing and decompressing the data (sometimes losing some in the process) will be greater than the cost of keeping the raw data in its pristine state for a very long time, or even forever. When we say data-compression technologies, we immediately think of JPEGs or MP3s. But let's think outside of the box for a second.

Data-Compression Technologies We Don't Need Anymore

Big Data, which many today see as a solution, was more often a problem throughout the history of humankind. For example, hand-processing big numbers with traditional arithmetic tools takes time and effort—and the bigger the numbers, the higher the risk of errors. Hence that glorious invention of baroque mathematics, logarithms, which use tables of conversion in print to turn big numbers into small numbers, and the other way around; and, crucially, convert the multiplication of two big numbers into the addition of two smaller ones. Laplace, Napoleon's favorite mathematician, famously said that logarithms, by "reducing to a few days the labor of many months, doubled the life of the astronomer." As well as, we may add, of many twentieth-century engineers: logarithms are at the basis of that other magical tool, the slide rule, whereby engineers of the twentieth-century could calculate almost everything in almost no time. But, even though I myself still studied logarithms in school for many months, I never learned to use my father's slide rule, because by the time I was fifteen I could buy a Texas Instruments pocket calculator for next to nothing. That worked much faster and more precisely than all the logarithmical tables and slide rules combined. Today, logarithms are a relic of an age gone by: a fascinating chapter in the history of early modern mathematics, which no astronomer or engineer would waste time on. Logarithms are a technology of data compression we don't need any more.

To take another example closer to the daily life of today's design professionals: scaled drawings in plans, elevations, and sections have been the basic tool of the designer's trade since the Renaissance, and the geometrical rules of parallel projections were famously published in 1799 by Gaspard Monge under the name of descriptive geometry (fig. 1). But seen from a historical perspective, and from today's vantage point, descriptive geometry is another cultural technology typical of a Small Data environment, as descriptive geometry uses parallel projections to compress big 3D objects into a set of small flat drawings, which can be easily recorded, stored, and transmitted on simple sheets of paper. In this instance, the compression of data is also a visible and physical one. No one could store the Seagram Building in reality—it is quite a big building—but many offices could store (and some did, in fact) the batch of drawings necessary to make it, and, if needed, to remake it. Today, however, using digital technologies, we can store not only a huge number of planar drawings, but also full 3D avatars of buildings, on a single memory chip—including all the data we need to simulate that building in virtual reality, or to build it in full. And technologies already exist that allow designers to operate directly in 3D, hence avoiding the mediation of planar drawings and of the geometrical projections underpinning them. In short, if buildings can be entirely notated as informational models in three dimensions from the start, the ways to represent them may change at all times based on need, and in many cases without falling back on plans, elevations, and sections. Descriptive geometry is another cultural technology for data compression already on the way out (and in fact, few schools of architecture still teach it).

The list of cultural technologies that have been with us from time immemorial, but which are being made obsolete by today's Big Data, is already a long one. To take an unusual suspect, the alphabet is a very old and effective technology for data compression: a voice recorder, in fact, that converts an infinite number of sounds into a limited number of signs, which can be easily notated, recorded, and transmitted across space and time. This strategy worked well for centuries, and it still allows us to read transcripts from the voices of famous people we never listened to and who never wrote a line, such as Homer, Socrates, or Jesus Christ. Yet today's technologies allow us to record, transmit, retrieve, and process speech as sound, without converting it into alphabetical signs (for the time being, the machine still does it, unbeknownst to us; but this may change, too). Thus today we can already speak to some machines without using keyboards, and receive answers from machines that vocalize words we no longer need to read. Keyboards used to be our interface of choice to convert the infinite variations of our voice (Big Data) into a short list of standardized signs (Small Data), but this informational bottleneck, typical of Small Data environments, is already being bypassed by today's speech-recognition technologies.

If the prospect of building without drawing frightens many architects, a civilization without writing may appear more than apocalyptic—almost a contradiction in terms. Yet, in purely informational terms, most technologies of notation (from numerals to Euclidean geometry; from musical scores to the Laban scripts for dancers) are tools we created in order to convert complex, data-rich phenomena into stripped-down and simplified transcriptions that are easier to keep, edit, and forward to others. These transcriptions are less and less necessary today as, thanks to Big Data, we can record, transmit, and manipulate digital avatars that are almost as rich in data as the originals they replace (and far richer in metadata). Of course, no digital replica will ever replace a natural phenomenon in full, as every copy implies some degree of abstraction, hence some data will always be left out or lost in the process. But in

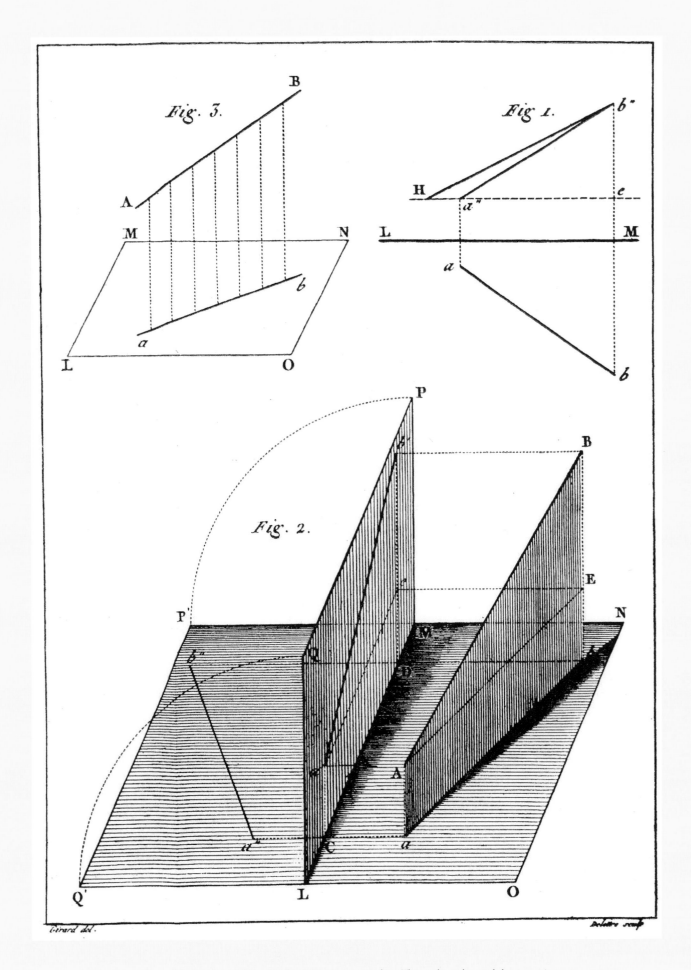

practice, once again, it is the tendency that matters, and this tendency has already started to affect today's science, technology, and culture.

Let's take another example—and one well-known one among architects, as it has been at the core of digitally intelligent design for the last twenty years: the calculus-based, digital spline. Calculus, another great invention of baroque mathematics, is the ultimate Small Data technology, as it compresses an infinite number of points into a single short notation, in the format $y = f(x)$. In practice, the script of a function contains all the points we may ever need to draw or produce that line (curve, or, adding one letter, surface) at all possible scales. But let's put ourselves, again, into a Big Data state of mind, and let's assume we can have access to unlimited, zero-cost data storage and processing power. In that case, we could easily do away with any mathematical notation, and simply record instead a very long, dumb log: the list of the positions in space (X,Y,Z coordinates) of many points of that line—as many as necessary, perhaps a huge number of them (fig. 2). That file will record the individual positions in space of a cluster or cloud of points that may not appear to follow any rule or pattern—any rule or pattern would in fact be of no use, so long as the position of each point is known, measured, and recorded, in two or three dimensions. This is exactly the kind of stuff humans don't like, but computers do well. A long time ago we invented dimensionless Euclidean points and continuous mathematical lines to simplify nature and translate its unruliness into short, simple, elegantly compressed notations: Small Data notations, made to measure for the human mind; notations we could write down, and work with. But today computers do not need any of that any more. Today's digital avant-garde has taken due notice: some digital designers have already discarded the Small Data, calculus-based spline (Bézier's spline), which was so important for the digital style of the 1990s, and have started to use Big Data and computation to engage the messy discreteness of nature as it is, in its pristine, raw state—without the mediation of elegant, streamlined mathematical notations (figs. 3, 4, & 5).

Search, Don't Sort: The End of Classical and Modern Science

This new trend in today's post-spline digital style may be discounted as a fad, a quirk, or an accident. It shouldn't be. All major, pervasive changes in our visual environment are signs of a concomitant change in our technical, economic,

and scientific paradigms. Indeed, if we look back at our data-starved past from the perspective of our data-opulent present, all the instances just mentioned (and more could be added) suggest that Western science as a whole, from its Greek inception, could be seen today as a data-compression technology developed over time to cope with a chronic shortage of data storage and processing power. Since the data we could record and retrieve in the past was limited, we learned to extrapolate and generalize patterns from what data we had, and we began to record and transmit condensed and simplified formal notations instead of the data itself. Theories tend to be shorter than the description of most events they apply to, and indeed syllogisms, then equations, then mathematical functions, were, and still are, very effective technologies for data compression. They compress a long list of events that happened in the past into very short scripts, generally in the format of a causal relationship, which we can utilize to describe all other events of the same kind, including future ones. In his last book, *Discorsi e Dimostrazioni Matematiche*, which had to be smuggled out of Tuscany and printed in a Protestant country to escape the Inquisition's censorship, Galileo reported and illustrated a number of experiments he had made to study how some beams break under load. But we need not repeat any of his experiments, nor any other, to determine how standard beams will break under most standard loads, because, generalizing from Galileo's experiments and many more that followed, we have obtained a handful of very general laws, which all engineers study in school: a few, clean lines of mathematical script, easy to commit to memory, which derive from all the beams that broke in the past, and describe how most beams will break in the future under similar conditions. This is how modern science worked—until now.

For let's imagine, again, that we can collect an almost infinite amount of data, keep it forever, and search it at will at no cost. We could then assume that every one of those experiments—or more generally the experiential breaking of every beam that ever broke—could be notated, measured, and recorded. In that case, for every future event we are trying to predict, we could expect to find and retrieve a precedent, and the account of that past event would allow us to describe the forthcoming one without any mathematical formula, function, or calculation. The spirit of Big Data, if there is one, is probably quite a simple one, and it reads like this: whatever happened before, if it has been recorded, and if it can be retrieved, will simply happen again, whenever the same conditions reoccur. This is not very different from what Galileo and Newton thought. But Galileo and Newton did not have Big Data; in fact, they often had very little data indeed. Today, instead of calculating predictions based on mathematical laws and formulas, using Big Data we can

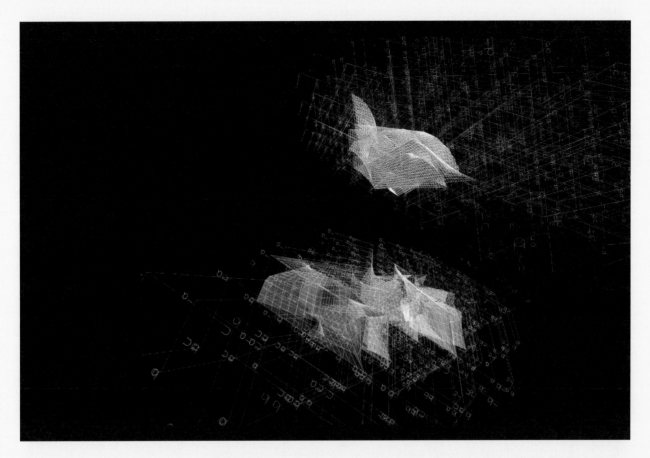

fig. 2   Karl Chu, X Kavya, *The Turing Dimension*, 2010.

fig. 3   Michael Hansmeyer and Benjamin Dillenburger, *Phenomena*, 2015.

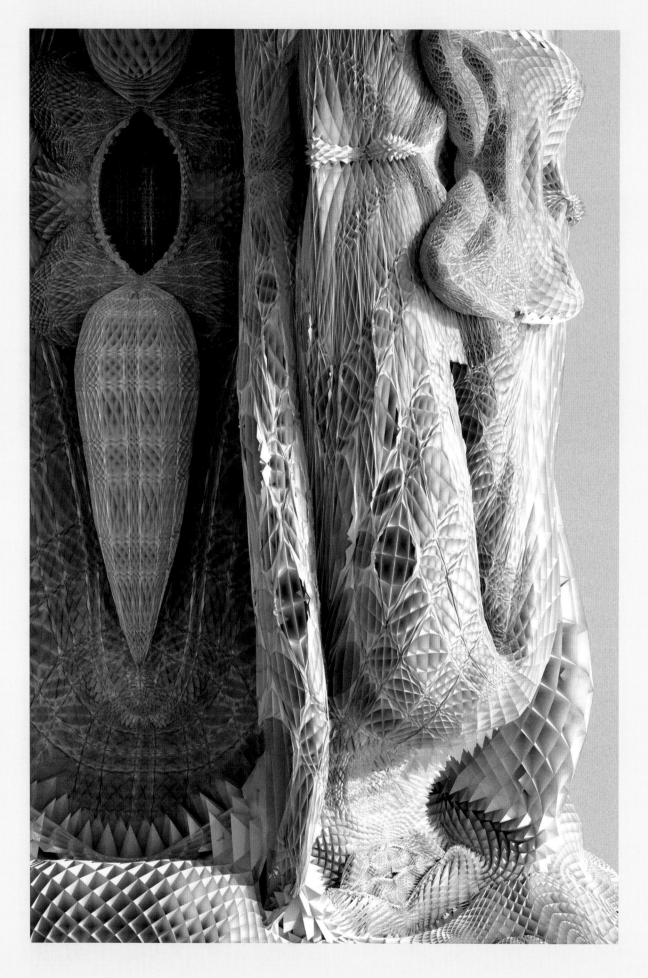

fig. 4   Michael Hansmeyer, *Hall of Columns*, 2010.

fig. 5 Roland Snooks, *Kazakhstan Symbol*, 2013.

simply search for a precedent for the case we are trying to predict, and retrieve it from the almost infinite, universal archive of all relevant precedents that ever took place. When that happens, Search will replace the method of modern science in its entirety.

This apparently weird idea is not science fiction. This is already happening, in some muted, embryonic way, in several branches of the natural sciences, and more openly, for example, in weather forecasting. Once again, this may not be either a rational or a palatable fact, but it is a tendency—it is in the air, whether we like to admit it or not. And sure enough, some historians of science have already started to investigate the matter—with perplexity and reservations, as we could expect. Indeed, from an even more general, philosophical point of view, mathematical abstractions such as the laws of mechanics or of gravitation, for example, or any other grand theory of causation, are not only practical tools of prediction but also, perhaps first and foremost, ways for the human mind to make sense of the world—and some could argue, as many did in the past, that the laws thus discovered are Laws of Nature, that disclose and unveil inner workings. Conversely, if abstraction and formalization (i.e., most of classical and modern science, in the Aristotelian and Galilean tradition) are seen as merely contingent data-compression technologies, one could argue that in the absence of the technical need to compress data in that particular way, the human mind can find many other ways to relate to, or interpret, nature. Epics, myth, religion, and magic, for example, offer vivid historical examples of alternative, non-scientific methods; and nobody can prove that the human mind is or ever was hardwired for modern experimental science. Many postmodern philosophers, for example, would strongly object to that notion.

This is probably not a coincidence, since the postmodern science of Big Data marks a major shift in the history of the scientific method. Using the Big Data approach to science (i.e., prediction by search and retrieval of precedent, instead of prediction by the transmission of general laws), modern determinism is not abandoned, but employed at a new, granular scale. Western science used to apply causality to bigger and bigger groups, or sets, or classes of events—and the bigger the group, the more powerful, the more elegant, the more universal the law that applied to it. Science, as we knew it, tended toward universal laws, which bear on as many different cases as possible. Today's new science of Big Data is just the opposite: using information retrieval and the search for precedent, Big Data causality can be applied to smaller and smaller sets, and it works best when the sets it refers to are the smallest. Indeed, the new science of Big Data only works in full when it does not apply to a class or group of events, but only to

one, specific, individual case—the one we are looking for. In that too Big Data represents a complete reversal of the classical (Aristotelian, scholastic, and modern) scientific tradition, which always held that individual events cannot be the object of science: most Western science only dealt with what Aristotle called forms (which today we more often call classes, universals, sets, or groups).

In social science and in economics, this novel Big Data granularity means that instead of referring to generic groups, social and economic metrics can and will increasingly relate to specific, individual cases. This points to a brave new world where fixed prices, for example, which were introduced during the industrial revolution, will cease to exist (and famously, this is already happening). Likewise, the cost of medical insurance, calculated as it is today on the basis of actuarial and statistical averages, could become irrelevant, because it will be possible to predict, at the granular level, that some individuals will never have medical expenses, hence they will never need any medical insurance, and some will have too many medical expenses, hence no one will ever sell medical insurance to them. This is a frightening world, because the object of this new science of granular prediction will no longer be a statistical abstraction—it will be each of us, individually. This may be problematic from a philosophical and religious point of view, as it challenges traditional ideas of determinism and free will; but in more practical terms, it is also simply incompatible with most principles of a liberal society and of a market economy in the traditional, modern sense of both terms.

In the field of natural sciences, however, the picture is quite different, and apparently less frightening. Following the old (i.e., the "modern") scientific method, natural sciences too used to proceed by generalization and abstraction, applying more and more general formulas to larger and larger swaths of the natural world. To the contrary, using the new method of granular retrieval of precedent, we are no longer limited to predicting vast and general patterns—we can try and predict smaller and smaller events, up the most singular ones. As recent works by Neri Oxman, Achim Menges, and others have proven, we can now design structural materials at minuscule, almost molecular scales, or quantify and take into account the infinite, minute, and accidental variations embedded in all natural materials (fig. 6, fig. 7). This runs counter to the method of modern science, which traditionally assimilated all materials, natural and artificial alike, to homogeneous chunks of continuous matter: for the last two centuries the main mathematical tool at our disposal to describe structural and material deformations was differential calculus, which is a mathematics of continuity, and abhors singularities; to allow for mathematical modeling (i.e., a quantitative prediction of their behavior), new

fig. 6 Neri Oxman and Stratasys in collaboration with Prof. W. Craig Carter (MIT), *Stratasys*, 2012.
3D printed with multi-material 3D-printing technology.

fig. 7   Institute for Computational Design (Prof. A. Menges)
and Institute of Building Structures and Structural Design (Prof. J. Knippers) at the Universität Stuttgart.
ICD/TKE Research Pavilion, 2014.

industrial materials were designed to be isotropic and continuous, and natural materials were doctored, processed, and tinkered with to achieve some degree of homogeneity. To the contrary, using the granularity of Big Data, we may now model the structural behavior of each individual part in a hypercomplex, irregular, and discontinuous 3D mesh, including the behavior of the one part we are interested in—that which will fail, one day. Used this way, the new science of granular prediction does not constrain but liberates, and almost animates, inorganic matter.

Search, Don't Tell: The End of Classical and Modern History

Since data scarcity has been a universal human condition across all ages, cultures, and civilizations, we can expect to find similar strategies of data compression embedded in most, if not all, cultural technologies we have been familiar with to this day. Historiography, or the writing of history, codified as an academic discipline and cultural practice in the course of the nineteenth century, is no exception. Like the modern scientist, the modern historiographer must infer a theory (in the case of history, more often an argument or a story) from a vast archive of findings. This data is not reported as such (even though today facts and sources are often listed or referred to in footnotes), but it is subsumed and transfigured, as it were, in a larger narrative—namely, a history—that derives from the original findings, but encompasses and describes them in more general terms. In this sense the historiographer, like a bard or ancestral storyteller, must condense and distill an accumulation of accidental experiences into one streamlined sequence or story, following a linear plot that is easier to remember and to recount, while most of the factual events that inspired it are destined to remain anecdotal—i.e., literally, unsaid. Halfway between the storyteller's plot and the scientist's theory, the historiographer's narration, or history, weaves endless anecdotes into one meaningful narrative. This narrative, once again, functions as a lossy data-compression technology: only the story thus construed will be recorded and transmitted and will bear and convey memories, wisdom, or meaning, whereas most of the individual events, experiences, or (in the Aristotelian sense of the term) accidents that inspired it will be discarded and forgotten.

Yet, as Walter Benjamin had already intuited, today's increasingly abundant dissemination of raw information goes against this ancestral strategy of story-building and story-telling. Let's imagine, once again pushing the argument to its limits, that a universal archive of historical data may be collected, recorded, transmitted, and searched at will, by all and forever. The term "historical" would become ipso facto obsolete, as all facts must have occurred at some point in time in order to have been recorded, hence all data in storage would be "historical," and none more so than any other. And since Google has already proven that no two searches are the same, every search in this universal archive would likely yield new results—based on user preference, context, endless more-or-less secret parameters, and the sheer complexity and whim of search algorithms. Consequently, at that point no "narrative," theory, story, or sequence would be stronger than any other; in fact no narrative, theory, sequence, or story would even be needed or warranted any more. Only the data would speak—forever, and whenever asked, never mind by whom, and every time anew.

Again, it is easy to dismiss this Big Data scenario (which, it will be noted, is structurally similar to the postscientific, prediction-by-retrieval paradigm I outlined earlier) as a sci-fi nightmare. Yet, once again, signs of this impending change can already be seen in today's technology and culture, and they are seeping through contemporary social practices. Take this example, which will sound familiar to many scholars of my generation: for all undergraduates studying architectural history in Italy (and elsewhere, for that matter) in the late 1970s or early '80s, the architectural history survey was basically a book, sometimes two, outlining a much simplified, teleological and ideological narrative of the rise of the modern movement in architecture (in Pevsner's and Giedion's historiographical tradition, that was the Hegelian and Marxian story of a linear rise to culmination, with no fall ever to ensue). Our textbooks (no names mentioned) contained a limited selection of small, and often very poor black-and-white pictures of the buildings under discussion, and these pictures, in most cases, were the only available evidence of buildings that few students, and indeed not many of our teachers, had ever seen. This is why we went to class, when we could: not so much to hear but to see. Giovanni Klaus Koenig's lectures were popular across the whole university of Florence (and beyond) not only because of Koenig's unparalleled talent as a jocular storyteller, but also because of the color slides he showed, which he had taken while traveling by car to Germany, Austria, and Switzerland (therefore no images of French or American buildings, for example, were ever shown). Most of the learning we could glean in such a technocultural environment was indeed, and could not have been other than, a narrative: a story, or a theory, which we got to know much better than any of those famous buildings upon which those stories were supposedly predicated. As for the buildings themselves, some we could visit when traveling, and some we would get a glimpse of, somehow, through a handful of color photographs in the relatively few books we could peruse at university libraries or buy in bookshops. A quarter of a century after Malraux's *Musée Imaginaire*, even the most famous buildings of the twentieth century were then still known exclusively through a very limited repertoire of authorial pictures, often due to some well-known photographers working in collaboration with the architects. Before I first traveled to Berlin as a student, I knew Ezra Stoller's photographs more than Mies van der Rohe's buildings.

Compare that situation—which was the norm throughout the age of printing and of modern mechanical technologies—to today's wealth of visual and verbal documentation, available at the click of a mouse, by tapping on a touch-screen, or—as I just did—by saying "Mies van der Rohe" to my smartphone. One generation ago, the same scant data was imparted to all. Today, information is so abundant and easily searchable that each user can find her or his own. But due to the largely unauthorial, raw or crowdsourced nature of most of this wealth of information, each person doing the same search will likely come up with slightly different results, and sometimes with conflicting or incompatible information. That is indeed the way Big Data works, for scientists no less than for students or for the general public: Big Data is useful and usable only on average, and in the aggregate. Failing that, each end-user will construct her or his own argument based on a random or arbitrary selection from an extraordinary array of data, and each selection will likely be different from all others. Each narrative or argument thus put together will therefore tend to idiosyncrasy and ephemerality. Anyone who has tried to teach a research seminar in the traditional way (i.e. expounding a sequential argument) in front of a group of doctoral students busily ferreting out odd happenstances, Photoshopped images, and wrong information from their tablets in real time will be familiar with this predicament. This does not mean that a thousand anonymous pictures on Instagram and a promenade through Google Earth are worth less than a single shot by Iwan Baan—in fact, in statistical terms, the opposite is true. But this does mean that many cultural habits we used to take for granted were in fact the accidental fallout of data-skimping, and are already incompatible with the data-rich environment we live in. Whether we like it or not, when an infinite amount of facts are equally available for anyone's perusal, search, and retrieval, we may no longer need theories, stories, histories, or narratives to condense or distill data, and to present them in a linear, clean, and memorable array. Again, one may argue that we will always need theories and stories for a number of other reasons, but—as mentioned earlier—that is difficult to prove.

So it would appear that many antimodern and post-modern ideological invocations or vaticinations, from Nietzsche's "eternal recurrence" and Lyotard's "fragmentation of master narratives" to Baudrillard's or Fukuyama's "end of history," to name a few, all came, in retrospect, a bit too early—but all may soon be singularly vindicated by technological change. What ideology could not accomplish in the twentieth century, technology is making inevitable in the twenty-first. If Search is the new science, *Big Data* is the new history. But not the history we once knew.

1 On the origin and different meanings of the expression, see Victor-Mayer Schönberger and Kenneth Cukier, *Big Data: A Revolution that Will Transform How We Live, Work, and Think* (Boston and New York: Houghton Mifflin Harcourt, 2013), 6 and footnotes.

2 Pierre-Simon de Laplace, *Exposition du système du monde* (Paris: Imprimerie du Cercle-Social, IV–VI [1796-98]), vol. II, 5, IV, p. 266. ("[Kepler...] eut dans ses dernières années, l'avantage de voir naître et de profiter de la découverte des logarythmes, artifice admirable, dû à Neper, baron écossais; et qui, réduisant à quelques heures, le travail de plusieurs mois, double, si l'on peut ansi dire, la vie des astronomes, et leur épargne les erreurs et les dégoûts inséparables des longs calculs ; invention d'autant plus satisfaisante pour l'esprit humain, qu'il l'a tirée en entier, de son propre fonds. Dans les arts, l'homme emploie les matériaux et les forces de la nature, pour accroître sa puissance; mais ici, tout est son ouvrage.")

3 I discussed this in "Breaking the Curve: Big Data and Digital Design," *Artforum* 52, no. 6 (2014): 168–73.

4 Galileo Galilei, *Discorsi e Dimostrazioni Matematiche intorno à due nuove scienze, attinenti alla mecanica e i movimenti locali* (Leiden: Elzevir, 1638), 116–33.

5 In July 2008, a groundbreaking article by Chris Anderson first argued for a scientific revolution brought about by Big Data ("The End of Theory," *Wired* 7 [2008], 108–9). Although that issue of *Wired* was titled "The End of Science," the other essays in the "Feature" section of the magazine did little to corroborate Anderson's vivid arguments. The main point in Anderson's article was that ubiquitous data collection and randomized data mining would enable researchers to discover unsuspected correlations between series of events, and to predict future events without any understanding of their causes (hence without any need for scientific theories). A debate followed, and Anderson retracted some of his conclusions (Schönberger and Cukier, 2013, 70-72 and footnotes). From an epistemological point of view, however, what was meant by "correlation" in that debate did not differ from the modern notion of causality, other than in the practicalities of the collection of much bigger sets of data, and in today's much faster technologies for data processing. Both classical causation and today's computational "correlation" posit quantitative, cause-to-effect relationships between phenomena; and at the beginning of the scientific enquiry, both the old (manual) way and today's computational way need some hypotheses to select sets of data among which even unexpected correlations may emerge. Evidently, today's computational processes make the testing of any such hypotheses much faster and more effective, but the methodological and qualitative changes that would follow from such faster feedback loops between hypotheses and verification were not part of that discussion. A somewhat similar but more promising debate is now taking place in some branches of applied technologies, such as structural engineering. See Mario Carpo, "The New Science of Form Searching," forthcoming in "Material Synthesis: Fusing the Physical and the Computational," ed. Achim Menges, special issue, *AD: Architectural Design* 85 (2015): 5.

6 See D. Napoletani, M. Panza, and D. C. Struppa, "Agnostic Science: Towards a Philosophy of Data Analysis," *Foundations of Science* 16 (2011): 1, 1–20.

7 As a search always starts with, and aims at, one individual event, the science of search is essentially a science of singularities; but the result of each search is always a cloud of many events, which must be compounded, averaged, and aggregated, using statistical tools. Thus, there are no limits to the level of "precision" of a search (a lower level of precision, or less intension, will generate more hits, or a larger extension in the definition of the set).

8 On this aspect of Aristotelian science, see Carlo Diano, *Forma e evento. Principi per una interpretazione del mondo greco* (Venice: Neri Pozza, 1952). The rejection of modern science as a science of universals is central to the postmodern philosophy of Gilles Deleuze and Félix Guattari. In *Milles Plateaux*, in particular, Deleuze and Guattari opposed the "royal science" of modern science, based on discretization ("striated space") to the "smooth space" of "nomad sciences," based on "nonmetric, acentered, rhizomatic multiplicities that occupy space without counting it and can be explored only by legwork," which "seize and determine singularities in the matter, instead of constituting a general form... they effect individuations through events or haecceities, not through the object as a compound of matter and form." Deleuze and Guattari saw the model of nomad sciences in the artisan lore of medieval master builders, i.e. in the past, before the rise of modern science; and they had no foreboding of the then nascent technologies that would inspire digital makers one generation later. See Gilles Deleuze and Félix Guattari, *A Thousand Plateaus: Capitalism and Schizophrenia*, trans. B. Massumi (London and New York: Continuum, 2004), 406-9 and 450-51. (First published in French as *Milles Plateaux* [Paris: Les Editions du Minuit, 1980]).

9 See Mario Carpo, "Micromanaging Messiness: Pricing, and the Costs of a Digital Nonstandard Society," in "Money," *Perspecta* 47 (2014): 219-26.

10 See Neri Oxman, "Programming Matter," in "Material Computation: Higher Integration in Morphogenetic Design," ed. Achim Menges, special issue, *AD: Architectural Design* 82 (2012): 2, 88-95, on variable property materials; Achim Menges, "Material Resourcefulnes: Activating Material Information in Computational Design," ibid., 2, 34-43, on nonstandard structural components in natural wood.

11 This vindicates the premonitions of Ilya Prigogine, another postmodern thinker whose ideas were a powerful source of inspiration for the first generation of digital innovators in the 1990s. See in particular Ilya Prigogine and Isabelle Stengers, *Order Out of Chaos: Man's New Dialogue with Nature* (New York: Bantham Books, 1984). (First published in French as *La Nouvelle Alliance: métamorphose de la science* [Paris: Gallimard, 1979]).

12 Walter Benjamin, "The Storyteller: Reflections on the Works of Nikolai Leskov," in *Illuminations: Essays and Reflections*, trans. Harry Zohn, ed. Hannah Arendt (New York: Schocken Books, 1968), 83-109. (First published as "Der Erzhäler: Betrachtungen zum Werk Nikolai Lesskows," in *Orient und Okzident* [City: Publisher, 1936]). However, Benjamin considers the ancestral storyteller and the oral chronicler as the conveyors of raw data, and sees only the modern novel and historiography as abstract, simplified linear narratives that are construed independently from the events on which they are based and from which they derive. After the works of Marshall McLuhan and particularly of Walter Ong on the cultures of orality, it is easier today to see the bard's/storyteller's recitals as tools of abstraction and memory devices.

13 See note 7.

14 Nietzsche's first mention of "eternal recurrence" is in aphorism 341 of *The Gay Science* (*Die fröliche Wissenschaft*, 1882-87). Lyotard spoke of the "décomposition des grand Récits," or "métarécits": Jean-François Lyotard, *La condition postmoderne* (Paris: Les Éditions de Minuit, 1979), 31. The "end of history" may have been first proclaimed by Jean Baudrillard, *Simulacres et Simulations* (Paris: Galilée, 1981), 62-76 (see in particular p. 70: "l'histoire est notre référentiel perdu, c'est-à-dire notre mythe"). Francis Fukuyama, *The End of History and the Last Man* (New York: Free Press, 1992). See also Fukuyama, "The End of History?" *The National Interest* 16 (Summer 1989): 3-18.

Painting and Uprising: Julie Mehretu's Third Space

T.J. Demos

Julie Mehretu's *Mogamma (A Painting in Four Parts)*, 2012, takes as its subject the mammoth government building located on Tahrir Square in Cairo. First shown in 2012 at dOCUMENTA (13), the four large paintings—or rather single painting in four parts—comprise linear architectural drawings scored by gestural markings in ink and acrylic, presenting scenes of conflict and multiplicity. The four fifteen-by-twelve-foot canvases that make up *Mogamma* stage complex interactions between the structural and the social, the tactile and the mechanical, calling up disjunctively assembled geographical spaces and defining multiple temporalities to resonate with the revolutionary present.

Although Cairo is the nominal focus, the painting's palimpsests of architectural renderings reference numerous city squares that have seen social and political uprisings, from the fraught era of modernity into our own discordant times, including Red Square in Moscow; Plaza de la Revolución in Havana; Assahabah Square in Darnah, Libya; Manara Circle in Ramallah; and Firdos Square in Baghdad. The artist's exploration of the relay between architectonic structure and bodily gesture that is perceptible in *Mogamma* surely builds on her past work—think of her *Stadia I* and *Stadia II* of 2004, for example, with their linear armatures, always rendered with meticulous draftsmanship, counterposed against loose black markings and multihued vectors, that join together the signs of national pageantry, the global sports industry, and mass-spectacle culture. Recognizable as well is the painterly engagement with networks, social composition, and the interrelated schemata of geopolitical sites that reverberate with global conflict, transnational media flows, and rebellious social energies. The fractured and entropic system of *Mural*, 2009, for instance, visualizes a contemporary financescape of macroeconomic complexity—what Mehretu calls "an exploration of the space-time of globalization." Or take *Dispersion*, 2002, with its swirling curved lines, cyclonic composition, and fiery chromatic explosions that suggest so many planetary metabolic clashes, part social, part climatic. *Excerpt (Riot)*, 2003, unleashes whirling storms and angry vortexes in grayish black, Prussian blue, and blood red, translating the violent elements of revolt into a powerful visual analogue. The *Mogamma* paintings and related recent work, including *Aether (Venice)*, 2011, and *Invisible Line (Collective)*, 2010–11, develop these tensions between geopolitical spaces and social movements, advancing them in particular in relation to the Egyptian revolution and, more widely, the Arab Spring. As such, they constitute startling contributions to Mehretu's already impressive practice of exploring complex geoaesthetics via the complex multi-nodal and interlinked surfaces of her canvases.

During those days of rage in January and February 2011, millions of Egyptians occupied Tahrir Square, driven to fury by years of government corruption and military repression, the stifling of free expression and democratic practice, and grinding poverty and economic inequality. Triggered by uprisings in Tunisia—the events of which are also alluded to in *Mogamma*'s architectural renderings of Tunis's Independence Square and Sidi Bouzid's Place des Martyrs—the Egyptian demonstrations eventually brought down the seemingly invincible regime of Hosni Mubarak, and in retrospect they can collectively be seen as a model of democratic self-determination in the Middle East and North Africa (even if the revolution remains unfinished). The Egyptian demonstrations also resonated with the quickly internationalizing Occupy movement, and indeed the signs of Zuccotti Park also make an appearance in the *Mogamma* paintings. Rather than acting as a silent witness to these events, the Mogamma building on Tahrir Square itself acted as an inspiring agent in the uprisings, and this complexity of architectural function also registers in Mehretu's approach. Long associated with the autocratic regimes of Egypt's successive post-independence military administrations, beginning with Nasser's in the early 1950s and ending with Mubarak's, the Mogamma was constructed in the early 1950s with money given by the Soviet Union to Egypt under King Farouk. An example of 1940s architectural modernism, designed by Egyptian architect Kamal Ismail, the fourteen-story building, housing some 18,000 civil servants, has long been the common

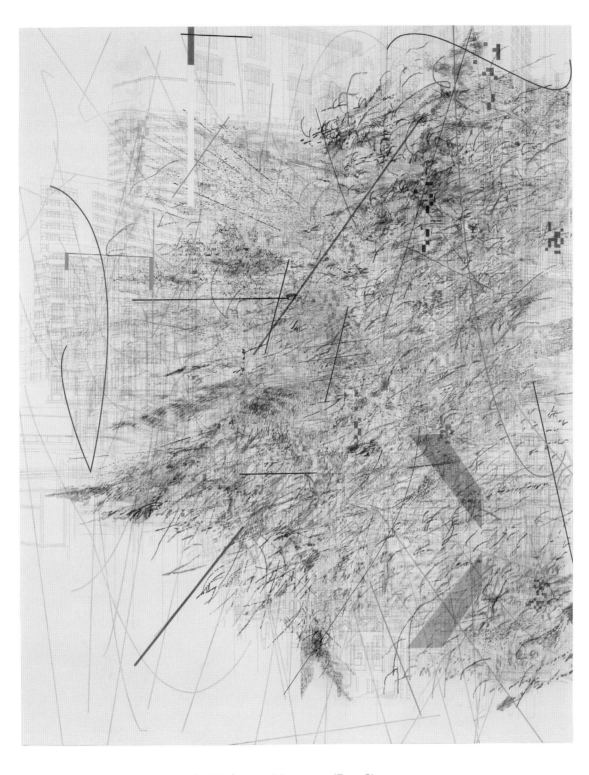

Julie Mehretu, *Mogamma (Part I)*, 2012.

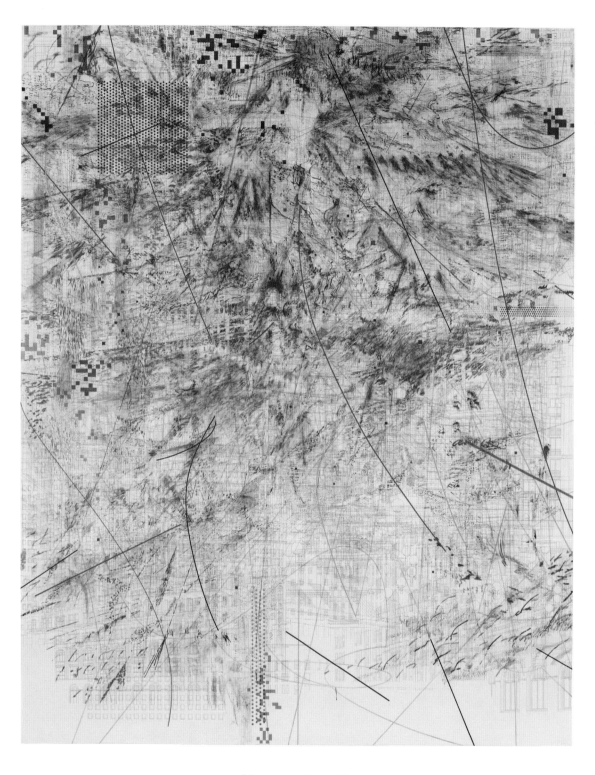

Mogamma (Part II).

destination for those seeking a driver's license, residency visa, or passport. Vilified for its snaking queues and Kafkaesque labyrinth of corridors and offices, the Mogamma has, not surprisingly, inspired much ire as a symbol of massive and inefficient government bureaucracy and itself has become the object of numerous recent protests, which have blocked the building's entrances and effectively shut down governmental operations there.[1]

Yet the appearance of the Mogamma building in Mehretu's paintings is not a simple representation of, or metonymy for, the detested governmental regime; instead, the building, and more broadly the square on which it sits, unfolds in Mehretu's work to a complex past of multiple determinations, forms of agency, and shifting socio-political usages. The painting builds up a complex accounting of the space of Tahrir Square and its diverse architectural environment through the inclusion of drawings of various buildings found there, including the Museum of Egyptian Antiquities, designed in the early twentieth century by French architect Marcel Dourgnon; the Nile Hilton, built in the 1960s in the international style; and the neo-Mamluk-styled princely palaces that populate the city, built in the late-nineteenth century. As noted by architectural historians, this area of Cairo has been associated with various geopolitical formations over the course of its history, beginning in July 1798, when Napoleon landed in Egypt with his occupation army.[2] Indeed, the city's colonial-era buildings, which can be seen as popular sites for symbolic competition between Britain, France, the US, and the Soviet Union, have also jostled for recognition with such anti-colonial monuments as the statue commemorating Omar Makram, who led the struggle to oust the French in 1800, and later architectural expressions of Arab and Egyptian nationalism. Named "Tahrir"—meaning "liberation"—in September 1945, the square references Egypt's success at negotiating an end to the British presence and the liberation of the country from the last traces of colonial occupation. The site thus defines a complex array of historical periods, geopolitical forces, and social struggles, and its architecture resists coding in any single or simple manner. It is appropriate then that in Mehretu's paintings, Tahrir opens onto a field of multiple perspectives, appearances, and imagined social uses, all of which escape any single determination.

Mehretu energizes this architectural-spatial multiplicity by presenting drawings of overlapping buildings, their forms based on computer-generated projections showing various one-point and bird's-eye perspectives, which are overlaid with abstract gestures and markings. Facades of linear constructions—complete with indicated fenestration, canopies, arches, cornices, and cupolas—emerge and intermix on the surfaces of the four *Mogamma* canvases. Various architectural elements—entablatures, spandrels, and sills—are plotted on elevations and perspectival renderings, which sometimes appear upside down, especially near the upper quadrants of the paintings. As a result, no single geographical armature or architectural space-time continuum unites the compositions; instead, the conjoining and intermingling schemata remain discontinuous, fragmentary, stranded, and monstrously hybridized. As a kind of geopolitical echo chamber of repetition and transmutation, the structurings call up various historical episodes, geographical contexts, and scenes of past revolutions and uprisings, but the relationship they propose between the elements remains unstable and uncertain.

The paintings, consequently, render their viewing points similarly compound—even structurally impossible—always incomplete when viewed from any single location. Lacking of modernist presentness, the whole of each painting is simply too perceptually expansive to register at once, or even after sustained periods of attention. As such, Mehretu's is a modeling of painting that challenges the limits of apprehension—spatially and historically—and thus defies the master

1 For an account of how the Mogamma building figured in the Egyptian uprising, see Mohammed Abouelleil Rashed, "The Egyptian Revolution: A Participant's Account from Tahrir Square," *Anthropology Today* 27, no. 2 (April 2011); 22–27.

2 See Nasser Rabbat, "Circling the Square: On Architecture and Revolution in Cairo," *Artforum* 49, no. 8 (April 2011); 182–191. This essay was particularly important to Mehretu in the planning of *Mogamma*.

(or colonial) gaze. One walks around and looks from various angles and distances, with a mobility of perception that allows one to encounter the temporal prolongation and perceptual process the works engender. There is no way to look at the canvases so as to draw together the various visualizations in or between them. In fact, the all-over compositions—with structures and markings seeming to both continue beyond the individual canvases' edges and dissolve into an endless interiority—indicate an environmental infinitude. In this regard, the architectural spatialization across time correlates with a representational entropy. The viewer is situated within the intervals between the four paintings, cast into a dizzying perceptual experience of disarray and spatio-historical multiplicity. She is at once inside the virtual expanse of the four vertically oriented canvases (which, when together, wrap around into a surrounding, panoramic horizontality) and outside in a site of uncertainty. (This effect was particularly powerful when encountered in the enclosing diamond-shaped installation created by architect David Adjaye for the spring 2013 exhibition of the work at White Cube Gallery in London). Immersion in such a geopolitical psycho-geography becomes a durational event: the paintings not only represent multiple perspectives, they engender mobile and shifting viewing points from which spatial expansiveness can ramify historical allusions and geopolitical connections.

The structural stability and symbolic power of the Mogamma building is consequently undone from within; if the building's symbolic gravity and massive scale suggest a mode of architectural determinism, Mehretu's painterly intervention draws alternate potentialities out of the edifice, thereby extending the approach of her past work with even greater intricacy at the level of drawing and referencing. To the extent that the plan functions as a blueprint for the building's intended use and implicit understanding of its political functions, Mehretu deconstructs it. As she does so, however, the plan gives way to numerous possible alternate realizations, as it holds within itself the force of indeterminacy, which is particularly evident in the large white expanse at the bottom of the first of the canvases and in the sudden unfinished endings to the drawings also found in that area. As the paintings make evident, there is no essentialism that can render architecture's meaning certain. Rather, the Mogamma is subjected to multiple views, conceptualizations, uses, and potential re-purposings. With Mehretu's canvases, we encounter an unbuilding, a de-architecturization, of built space; a revolution, in other words, in painterly form. If, in these works, architecture provides the foundation for the abstract gestural marks, then that basis, dedicated to precise structural renderings and perspectival mappings, is already largely unstable, multiple, unfixed.

Mehretu's painterly daubs and smudges advance this de-determination even while at times suggesting various patternings. Mathematically shaped groupings, amorphous swarms, and linear trajectories appear to correspond to manifold collective assemblages and social movements. At times, one sees flocking formations of graphic characters, including blurred groupings that intimate a collective merging in rapid movement. Others appear as if suddenly scattering into explosive dispersals and energized distributions. Appropriately, "mogamma" means "collective" in Arabic, and the paintings—which have themselves been collectively produced, with Mehretu overseeing a team of assistants as they laid the architectural-drawing groundwork—pushes this terminological association toward the insurrectionary rather than suggesting a unified social totality. This socialization is not only *represented in* the panels—visualized through so many figurations and collectivizations of marks—it is *performed by* the panels insofar as they make numerous invitations to the viewer to enter their virtual arenas and become part of their social, material intensity. Not only does the work's sheer size indicate an architectural scale that encloses viewers in its vertical and horizontal span (especially when arranged in its surrounding installation), it also includes various moments in which the viewer is visually summoned to enter the virtual space. A stairway near the center of the first of the *Mogamma* panels, for example, leads from the viewer's sightline into the aesthetic melee of networked layers. And, in the second panel, as if carving out a safe seclusion

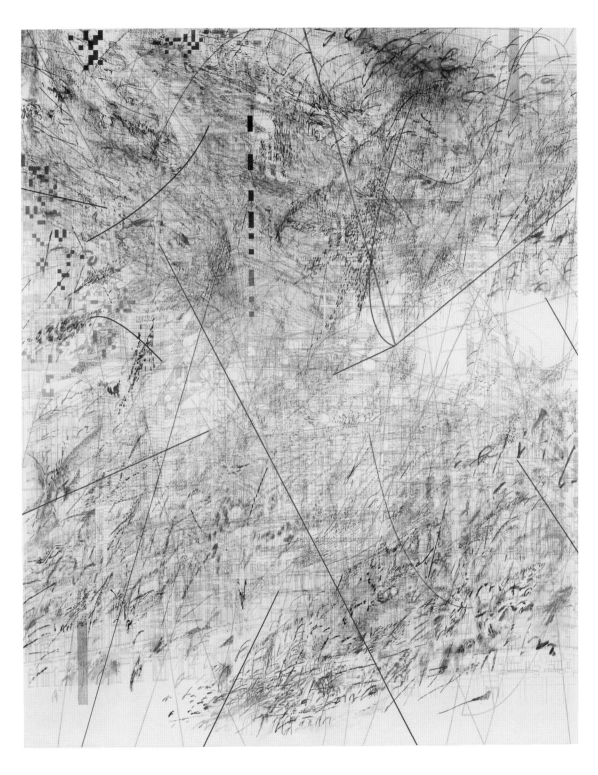

Mogamma (Part III).

Mogamma (Part IV).

of calm amidst the spatial disjunctions and chaotic massifications in the social field, a dome-like architectural canopy offers visual refuge.

Adding to this complexity of spaces, social groupings, and time zones are numerous large, colored shapes—red and green trapezoids, a light greenish circle, thin orange rectangles—that attract visual attention by virtue of their large-scale and chromatic punctuation but whose meaning and conceptual contribution to the paintings remains uncertain. Are these forms the stranded language of modernist abstraction—El Lissitzky and Malevich come to mind—that strangely migrated into our present, detached from utopian politics and avant-garde purpose only to gaze as mute outsiders onto the revolutionary energies they themselves failed to inspire over the course of the twentieth century? Or are they repurposed as integral to this emergent revolutionary dynamic? In addition, sweeping vectors in burgundy, purple, and yellow arc across the canvases, forming bowed pathways of seemingly topographical connection, or indicating directions of social movements distilled to molecular energy. Finally, grid-like assemblages of small circular shapes and sequences of squares reminiscent of architectural drawings and digital code appear on the different canvases of *Mogamma*, as if mapping forests of columns or designating solid architectural spaces seen from above. These abstract jottings seem at times both to underlie the architectural renderings, especially when present in faded hues, and to float atop when more saturated in black.

The question remains how these abstract shapes and gestural markings relate to the architectural drawings with which they share pictorial space. One temptation is to see the paintings as cartographic or representational. Yet this would miss their affective force, the way they unleash an event—an uprising in aesthetic terms—that materializes duration and openness, one that is generative, transformative, and non-representational.[3] In this sense, the paintings' system of architectural drawings, marks, and vectors doesn't map out a single space, geopolitical context, revolutionary history, or continuous surface, and it doesn't propose an image of a coherent spatiotemporal location. Rather, it constructs what Mehretu herself calls a "third space," a term that provocatively designates the visual relations between architecture and gesture, representation and abstraction, a relationality that remains determinedly and productively uncertain.[4] Consider, in this vein, the way the elegant and rhythmical round shapes that pattern the second of *Mogamma*'s canvases visually echo the street lamps in Meskel Square in Addis Ababa (where Mehretu was born and retains family ties).[5] Inexplicably, but as a result enticingly, Mehretu's lamps appear transparent to the background architecture while remaining opaque to the graphic figures that course in front of the buildings and behind the lamps' circular forms. Paradoxical, these passages propose sites of intermediacy between time zones and spatial extensions, and as such are exemplary areas where the paintings' elements defy resolution and define moments of incommensurable relationality between, for instance, Meskel Square and Tahrir Square, and between Egyptian and Ethiopian revolutionary times. Mehretu's work, in this regard, stresses the non-correlation between layers, spaces, references, and marks, proposing something of a painterly parataxis. While the vector lines might at first appear to literalize the spatial trajectories between locations plotted on the architectural diagrams, and while the dottings might initially seem to describe the movements of figures or people, as if mapping a chaotic protest, Mehretu's is no neo-futurist attempt to portray the vitalism of urban space. Instead, these are visualizations that open up a third space of conceptual and visual potentiality, where systems defy a coherent plan or unified cartography.

3   See Deleuze and Guattari's description of the revolutionary "event": "An event can be turned around, repressed, co-opted, betrayed, but there still is something there that cannot be outdated. Only renegades would say: it's outdated. But even if the event is ancient, it can never be outdated: it is an opening to the possible. It goes as much inside individuals as in the depths of society." Gilles Deleuze and Félix Guattari, "May '68 Did Not Take Place," in *Two Regimes of Madness: Texts and Interviews 1975–1995*, ed. David Lapoujade, trans. Amy Hodges and Mike Taormina (New York: Semiotext(e), 2006), 233.

4   Conversation with the author, New York, March 13, 2013.

5   This detail of the square is present in the photographs included in the extensive documentary archive Mehretu used to produce the paintings.

Certainly, these are energetic surfaces, but they transcend a correlative logic or onomatopoetic aesthetics. Rather, the various elements—multitudes, architectures, revolutionary histories, and lines of flight—take on indeterminate relations to one another, where there is no shared or unified temporality—and no predictability or final determination. Their resolution remains a future potential but present impossibility.

Of course the notion of "third space" has long been important to postcolonial theory. First articulated in the late 1980s by figures such as Homi Bhabha, the term has been reprised recently as a way to understand the contemporary world of globalization, with its info-networks, multicultural ethnoscapes, and financial and cultural flows. As a site of transcultural translation, multilingual becoming, and socio-political liminality, it names a place of "incommensurability" where "coexistent kinds of activity" come together, clash, conflict, and thus redefine social, cultural, and political concepts that exceed conventional modes of understanding.[6] In the representational register, the third space characterizes the openness of the sign, where the "thickness of culture" is "as enigmatic as the obliquity of the signifier through which it is enunciated."[7] Mehretu's third space advances this definition further by materializing its workings in a transdisciplinary engagement situated between monumental history painting, abstraction, and architectural drawing. Adding to this transdisciplinarity is an aesthetic engine of temporal differentiation and spatial multiplicity; as such, it's perhaps best not to isolate and reify painting or drawing as mediums in a neo-Greenbergian modernist taxonomy—as different, say, from photography or film. One could argue instead that Mehretu develops not only a "dialectic of matrix and grapheme" that is internal to drawing and painting, as Catherine de Zegher has provocatively argued,[8] but also a "trialectics of spatiality," to invoke Edward Soja's definition of "thirdspace," one that implicates and cross-references structure, mark, and time, and operates via a physical, mental, and social transversality.[9] Accordingly, Mehretu's work catalyzes a hybridized aesthetic (anti-) system that remains radically open. In some ways, this aesthetic is continuous with that of the moving image, as well as with the necessarily time-based experience of space in architecture. As such, Mehretu's palimpsestual modeling of a diagrammed space-time image—an exploded system of spatialized montage packed with a durational phenomenology—both differs from and resonates with filmic montage, which sequences images over distinct frames, defining a mode of what Deleuze famously termed the "time-image." Likeminded contemporary media artists such as Hito Steyerl and the Otolith Group have similarly folded multiple geographies into their distinct montage-based film-essay practices, where a postcolonial-engaged geopolitics is allegorized by a new modeling of geo-aesthetics. Such practices provide a useful, if unexpected, contextualization of Mehretu's work, which develops a further, albeit singular approach to third-space geoaesthetics.[10]

That said, "third space" cannot but also reference the geopolitical designation of the "third world," as well as the militant anti-colonial and revolutionary aesthetics embodied in such movements as "third cinema."[11] In the past, "thirdness" defined an alternative to Cold War alignments

6 See Jonathan Rutherford, "The Third Space: Interview with Homi Bhabha," in *Identity: Community, Culture, Difference*, ed. Jonathan Rutherford (London: Lawrence & Wishart, 1990), 207–221. Also see Homi Bhabha, *The Location of Culture* (London: Routledge, 1994).

7 Homi Bhabha, "Preface: In the Cave of Making: Thoughts on Third Space," in *Communicating in the Third Space*, ed. Karin Ikas and Gerhard Wagner (London: Routledge, 2009), xiii.

8 Catherine de Zegher, "Julie Mehretu's Eruptive Lines of Flight as Ethos of Revolution," in *Julie Mehretu: Drawings* (New York: Rizzoli, 2007), 27.

9 See Edward Soja's discussion of "thirdspace" as a "trialectics of spatiality," one that defines a "recombinational" force and a "radically open" site, in "Thirdspace: Toward a New Consciousness of Space and Spatiality," in *Communicating in the Third Space*, 50, 53, and 57.

10 See my book *The Migrant Image: The Art and Politics of Documentary During Global Crisis* (Durham: Duke University Press, 2013) for discussions of the work of The Otolith Group and Hito Steyerl, as well as the analysis of Deleuze's theory of the time-image in relation to contemporary art.

11 On "third cinema," see Fernando Solanas and Octavio Getino, "Towards a Third Cinema," in *Movies and Methods: An Anthology*, ed. Bill Nichols (Berkeley: University of California Press, 1976), 44–64; and the special issue of *Third Text* 25, no. 1 (January 2011), on "The Militant Image: A Ciné Geography," guest edited by Kodwo Eshun and Ros Gray.

with the capitalist West or the communist East, taking on a direct relation to the underdeveloped world of the global South, just as it now connotes an alternative to the stale oppositions of art versus activism and gallery versus street. In today's context, the concept of the "third" also suggests a location of transcultural relationality between uneven geographies, and offers a critical resource whereby postcolonial claims for justice can contest the hegemony of resurgent Empire. It is within this genealogy, with its aesthetic and geopolitical alliances, that we should situate Mehretu, whose modeling of painting seems to declare its solidarity with the revolutionary uprising against the architecture of neo-colonialism, to which she contributes her own rebellious energy. In so doing, she adds specific political references to those poststructuralist renderings of indeterminacy, flows, and networks with which her work has often been associated.[12] In this regard, Mehretu's family background, linked to Ethiopia, remains significant in accounting for the artist's identification with an African and "third worldist" sensibility and political affinity—and indeed, Mehretu has been included in surveys of African art;[13] although emphasizing such an identitarian positioning is far from necessary in justifying a social-political alliance with the emancipatory aims of the revolutionary movement in Egypt.

In relation to her recent paintings, Mehretu has spoken of them as inciting feelings of "fear," "hopefulness," and "exhilaration."[14] It's remarkable—though not altogether unsurprising—that these emotions and revolutionary affects are precisely the ones named by some participants in the uprisings in Tahrir Square.[15] Yet situated in the artistic domain, they also express a certain trepidation around the question of the very viability of painting—and by extension of art itself—in an era of revolutionary social transformation. Does art have a place amidst such momentous events, and if so, what would that be? Mehretu's third space addresses this quandary without offering any simple solutions. She proposes a place between worlds, first and third, that echoes and points toward multiple geopolitical sites of transnationality and transformation, identity and alliance, structure and event. And her third space opens onto a transdisciplinary site, a location of translation and conflict between aesthetic experiences, mediums, and spatiotemporal logics, between modes of representation and as-yet-unfulfilled revolutions. But her practice also operates in the irreconcilable, even impossible, space between painting and uprising. For how could an art practice based on a post-Warholian model of quasi-industrial production, situated in an art-market context, reconcile itself with the radical social egalitarianism, the horizontalist organization, and the anti-neoliberal strivings of the revolution as displaced within painting's aesthetic zone? Which makes it all the more remarkable that Mehretu courageously takes on this very subject. Providing no easy answers, she refuses to abandon the aesthetic space of sensation and critical contemplation in the face of social emergencies and political imperatives, instead placing painting and uprising in unlikely proximity. At the same time, she rejects the occlusion of such a network of relationalities, as well as the idea that painting could, somehow, return to its hermetic enclosure without reference to the pressing social and political world beyond its frame.

Previously published in Julie Mehretu, Julie Mehretu: Liminal Squared *(New York: Marian Goodman Gallery, 2013).*

---

12   See De Zegher, "Julie Mehretu's Eruptive Lines of Flight as Ethos of Revolution"; Rebecca R. Hart, "Mapping, Erasing, Drifting," in *Julie Mehertu: City Sitings* (Detroit: Detroit Institute of Arts, 2009); and Peter Eleey, "Julie Mehretu's 'Perfect' Pictures," *Afterall* (Autumn/Winter 2006).

13   See, for instance, her inclusion in Okwui Enwezor and Chika Okeke-Agulu, eds., *Contemporary African Art Since 1980* (Bologna: Daniani, 2009).

14   Conversation with the author, New York, March 13, 2013.

15   Rashed, "The Egyptian Revolution."

Sam Jacob

PUT THE
NEEDLE
ON THE
RECORD

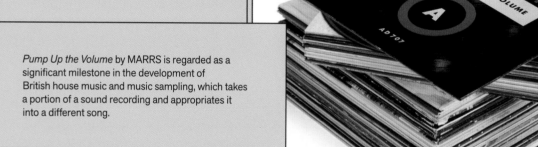

Pump Up the Volume by MARRS is regarded as a significant milestone in the development of British house music and music sampling, which takes a portion of a sound recording and appropriates it into a different song.

"Put the needle on the record / When the drum beat goes like this" runs a sample in the 1987 hit *Pump Up the Volume* by MARRS. One of the first British house records, it was a tour de force of sampling, then a new technique of making music out of music that had already been made. You no longer needed real people playing real instruments. All you needed was a record collection. Before the rise of sampling, records were exactly what their name suggests: recordings of the physical act of playing music. The vibrations caused by bashing a drumhead and twanging guitar strings were recorded into the spiraling grooves of peaks and troughs across the surface of the record. When you put the needle on it, the physical form translated back into noise. Vinyl disks, in other words, are a kind of materialized memory of events that can be reperformed again and again.

Pump Up the Volume was a song about records, about how playing with vinyl could be a new way to make music, and about the creative possibilities

of resurrecting events embedded in the physical substance of a disk. By choreographing bits of various recorded events from across time and space, something completely new and different could be made, something that does not resemble any one of those individual moments. Sampling is a technique that delves into and cuts up physical sounds, rearranging and composing them into something that never actually happened. We can think of sampling as a false memory turned creative act.

Records have since become fetish objects, symbols of a bygone era revived nostalgically by a generation whose native form of recording is digital. Part of the attraction is the direct connection to the recorded event, an immediate imprint of vibrations created by your favorite artists on a piece of plastic you can hold in your hand. Think for a moment about this relationship of object to memory: everything we make is a record of its own making, both result and record of its manufacturing process. Its material, shape, and assembly are

altogether the de facto record of the forces brought to bear on its original substance, of the labor involved. As anthropologists might tell us—in the way they can extrapolate information about an entire civilization from a fragment of bone or a stone, about the knowledge, reach, and nature of the society that organized that particular interaction of material and labor—objects are records of the worlds that make them. With the right kind of needle, we could play back the memories inscribed within every man-made object. In this way, every museum would house a cacophony of ghost civilizations and every home would be filled with the dissonance of countless voices.

This revelation came to me not in the rarified atmosphere of an ivory tower or in the fug of a late-night talk but in the course of bureaucratic architecture office administration. ISO 9001 is a quality-management certification necessary for many RFQs. It rates the way your office workflow is managed to ensure the quality of information you produce. Clients like it because it gives them an easy way to check a box that apparently ensures professionalism. We hired an ISO 9001 accreditor to help us put the necessary systems in place, and his take on record keeping performed what seemed like a conceptual double salvo that cracked the sky with its Confucian simplicity: "You don't keep records do you?" he asked. "No," I replied, guiltily. "But you do generate records," he added. What he was saying was that every act is a record of itself. An invoice, for example, is both an invoice and a record of that invoice; a drawing is both a drawing and a record of its own existence, and so on.

Although wrapped in the management speak of quality assurance, this is an idea that goes deep to the heart of human culture. Map and territory are revealed as one and the same. And if this is true of the professional conduct of an architecture office, it might also hold true for the built product of the office. Everything, according to this ISO creed, is a record—both the thing and the memory of the thing. Think of memory itself: it is the biological form of record management that stores our personal experiences within our own physiology. Our brain organizes and reorganizes itself in response to those experiences. Its shape and structure change as it processes each new experience, causing our synapses to fire in ways that alter the brain's neural circuits. Biochemical reactions alter the substance of the brain, forming pieces of memory scattered throughout our gray matter. Experience is both something that is remembered and the way it is committed to memory. As the structure of the brain changes, so does memory. Memory in our brain is, in other words, a physical, formal, and organizational thing—a biological recording akin to architecture.

If we can think of memory as a physical entity—that is, as architecture—we can also think of architecture as memory. An architect's work is usually concerned with the future, with propositions for the world as it could be. But architecture, as we experience it, always becomes the past in the present. In other words, buildings are historical documents as well as structures. As they come into the world, they write a record of themselves into the world, a record of the physical act of building, brick upon brick; of the intentions of the designer; and of all of the legal, economic, social, and political forces that have brought it into the world. Architecture's physical and spatial substance is a form of memory that exists not as interior psychology but as the world we inhabit, the present that surrounds us. Both architecture and the city are collective social and historical forms of materialized memory. There are, of course, forms of architecture that explicitly trade in memory. Memorials and monuments actively construct memory and history in the present. Trajan's Column, for example, was erected in the Roman Forum to narrate victory over the Goths. Its spiral bas-relief (much like the grooves of the wax cylinder) broadcasts the story (the victors, as always, writing history) from the center of the Roman world. Its object form is both the document and the means of transmission.

Memory can also be performed at the scale of the city. Trafalgar Square, built at the heart of imperial London, commemorates the victory of the British fleet over the French. Thus, its triumphal narrative is set into the very fabric of the city. The square is positioned at the top of Whitehall, a principal thoroughfare lined with government offices, where from atop a monumental column guarded by giant lions, Admiral Nelson looks out toward Buckingham Palace and over his fleet, represented by models of ships placed on lampposts along the Mall. Memory is encoded into the city through spectacle as well as the sequencing of everyday urban activities. The densely layered narratives of power remain unnoticed from day to day but are resurrected at every state occasion, where ceremonial rituals activate and replay the deep symbolism embodied in the urban fabric. In London, for example, horse guards traditionally ride under the Admiralty Arch, reaching out to touch a brass nose protruding from one of its walls that resembles a Robert Gober artwork—according to urban myth, a cast of the Duke of Wellington's nose. Like rubbing a genie's lamp, it is a way of connecting the supernatural and historical content in the material fabric of the city to activate the urban present.

These are examples of the premeditated city-as-history designed to evoke precise forms of memory. But the larger argument is that any architecture is a form of materialized memory, acting as both witness to and evidence of societal experience. A house, for example, is both a house and a record of an era's ideas about domesticity and familial structure. Abstract social constructs like status, class, and value are embedded in its architectural form. Once built, architecture continues to perform these ideas, projecting them out into the world; its material memory continues to shape ideas about family and home. In other words, the material memory of architectural form continues to influence our imagination in the present.

Yet, architectural memory—like our own—does not remain static. The narratives embedded in the fabric of the city, like those inserted into our own gray matter, are in a continual state of flux. Like the brain, the city's form is also its content, and its ability to remember or to forget is embedded in its structure at any given moment. In this light, preservation is as much a device for shoring up architectural and urban memory as for historic restoration. It commits architecture to long-term memory while privileging certain architectural narratives within the maelstrom of urban growth. Indeed, what and how the city remembers is a highly charged political question. As a medium of memory, the city is central to acts of destruction and construction; its ability to remember can become the very reason why it must be erased. Equally, the act of construction can be a way of constructing new forms of memory. We see extreme assaults on the city as a repository of memory in wartime conflicts. Here, territory is contested as both strategic and symbolic, and the memory it holds can itself become the battleground.

The relationship of war to architectural memory was made explicit in the infamous Nazi Baedeker Blitz of 1942, which saw the Luftwaffe use tourist guides to identify targets. Nazi propagandist Baron Gustav Braun von Sturm declared, "We shall go out and bomb every building in Britain marked with three stars in the Baedeker Guide." The target here was not structures like shipyards or munitions factories but rather national history. By wiping out the cultural history of the

Construction kit of the Stari Most created by Aedes Ars, whose work specializes in the miniature reproduction of architectural monuments.

enemy, the theory went, you would demoralize them. As such, erasing the memory held in the city fabric is a means of forced amnesia. Reconstruction, then, is a way of resurrecting memory.

The same theory motivated the 1993 destruction of Mostar's Stari Most ("Old Bridge") by Croat forces during the Bosnian War. Blasted not for its strategic military value but as a cultural landmark, the sixteenth-century Ottoman bridge has now been reconstructed under the auspices of UNESCO; this new Old Bridge is both a historical reconstruction and a monument to its own destruction. The story of the Stari Most demonstrates the strange phenomena that begin to occur when destruction and reconstruction play with memory. Since the original act of the bridge's erasure, replicas have appeared in other formerly Ottoman regions, even as part of a suburban shopping center, for instance. It is as though the act of architectural repetition, like learning by rote, can prevent architectural amnesia. The bridge becomes committed to memory by the sheer multiplication of its original form, like so many ghosts haunting the landscape.

This scenario describes the whole of Dubrovnik, designated a UNESCO World Heritage Site in 1979. Inside the ancient city gates, there are two large maps affixed to a stone wall. One is a typical tourist-orientation map; the second shows the "damages caused by the aggression on Dubrovnik by the Yugoslav army, Serbs, and Montenegrins, 1991-1992." Black dots, triangles, and red bars littering the map indicate roofs destroyed by direct impact, burned by fire, or damaged by shrapnel and direct hits on the pavement. Dubrovnik's old town took 650 strikes during a seven-month siege, between October 1991 and May 1992, in the Croatian War of Independence. According to UNESCO observers, 55.9 percent of the buildings were damaged, 11.1 percent heavily damaged, and 1 percent burned down completely. The greatest losses were seven Baroque palaces, along with looted museums. Convictions for war crimes and devastation related to the siege—including attacks on civilians—were secured at the International Criminal Tribunal for the former Yugoslavia (ICTY), in The Hague. Yet this savage attack on the stones of the historic city was really an assault on its memory.

Restored under a program coordinated by UNESCO, Dubrovnik's fortified walls, marble-paved streets, cathedrals, and towers are now entirely reconstructed—almost too perfectly. There's something in the too-red roof tiles that lends an air of unreality, a frag in the trajectory of history that makes it more tangible and in higher definition than it should be. In other words, reconstruction is a way of writing a clearer memory into the present than ever existed before. Now Dubrovnik is both

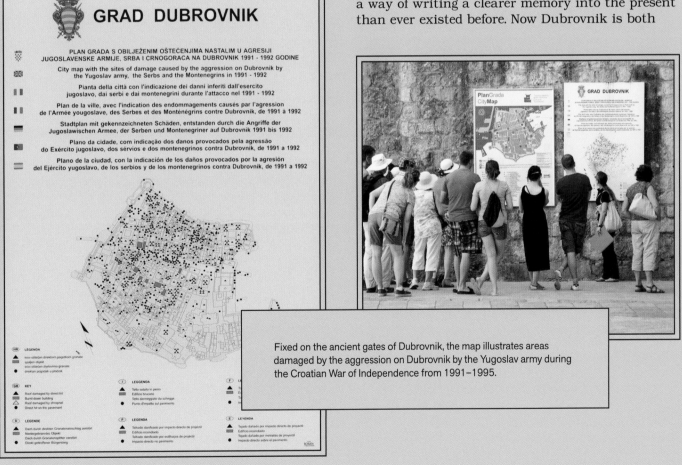

Fixed on the ancient gates of Dubrovnik, the map illustrates areas damaged by the aggression on Dubrovnik by the Yugoslav army during the Croatian War of Independence from 1991–1995.

View of the reconstructed Old-Town Dubrovnik, including its red roofscape.

historical and new, memory and forgetting at the same time. With giant cruise ships moored in the harbor, the city is flooded with a transient selfie stick-wielding population trailing around its fortified walls. The massive stone structures of the city, once attacked from the exterior, are now entirely hollowed out to house the infrastructure of tourism. In other words, it is just another typical summer in contemporary Europe.

Real history is hard though: all those abstract dates and obscure figures, those years of changing political regimes, religious wars, and cultural migrations are quite a challenge to get your brain around. Now in Dubrovnik you can experience a simulation of history without the homework. Capitalizing on the city's starring role in the HBO series "Game of Thrones," tours will take you to the site of King Joffrey's wedding, the Battle of the Blackwater, the Red Keep, and so on. The (real) reconstructed Dubrovnik is, for many of its visitors, made more real as (fictional) scenography. Is Dubrovnik's history more pliable because the mortar that holds its memory is not yet dry?

The problem of reconstruction is a hoary one. John Ruskin—from whom we can trace the philosophy of modern conservation—argued that "restoration" meant "the most total destruction which a building can suffer: a destruction out of which no remnants can be gathered: a destruction accompanied with false description of the thing destroyed." He adds, "It is impossible, as impossible as to raise the dead, to restore anything that has ever been great or beautiful in architecture." We might argue something different: thatthe conflicts over remembering and forgetting are an intrinsic part of the evolution of architecture and the city. The authentic Dubrovnik is not its original incarnation, but rather its material fabric as precipitated by event after event; it is formed as much by UNESCO reconstruction and HBO art direction as it is by rocket launchers or its time as the capital of the Republic of Ragusa. It is all of this at the same time.

Dubrovnik's experience of a history constantly in flux in the present, where memory and amnesia are tightly bound to the physical structure of the city, highlights architecture's roles in both remembering and forgetting. It also serves as a model of how memory is an active part of the

Until the mid-sixteenth century, Dubrovnik thrived as a wealthy, democratic state. Evidence of this episode of the city's distinguished past was erased by the devastating Earthquake of 1667 that nearly razed the entire city.

contemporary city and how close to the surface the politics of amnesia remain. Hallucination, fiction, and propaganda are the reality of its solid form, all acting on remembering and forgetting in particular ways. Just as with sample culture— exemplified by *Pump Up the Volume*—the city is not a consistent chronological record of history but rather an artificially assembled jump-cut collage of selected events. Through acts of construction, demolition, preservation, and reconstruction, the materialized memory of the city is constantly rewritten. As its physical fabric changes, so does its ability to remember and forget. Employing records as a site where new forms of memory can be constructed, sample culture reminds us of the possibilities of reassembling materialized memory.

It is not only history that is at stake here; memory and experience also act to shape our perception of the present. So the real issue in the conflicts over architecture's ability to remember is not the past, but the ways in which it can be reshaped to construct possible futures. As we gaze out over the city, we might feel the forces that struggle to maintain its topography as memory. We might feel its amnesiac crumbling and the shoring up of its foundations, the efforts to alter and retell the collective history of the city. But most of all, we should see it as the ground where the fictions of memory are contested in conflicts of remembering and forgetting that forge the future of the city.

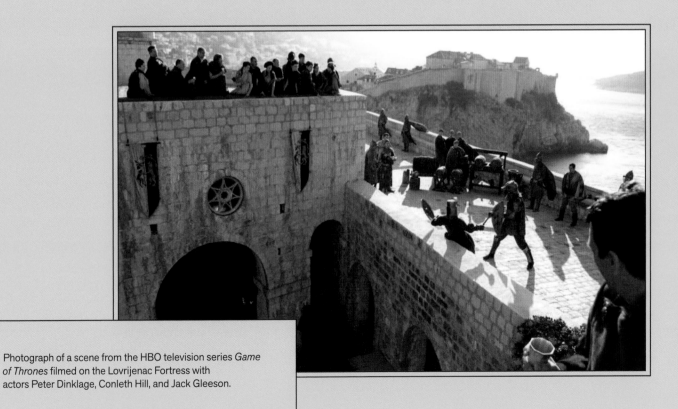

Photograph of a scene from the HBO television series *Game of Thrones* filmed on the Lovrijenac Fortress with actors Peter Dinklage, Conleth Hill, and Jack Gleeson.

Platonic Paradigms:
A Memory of the School of Athens

Anthony Vidler

Henri Labrouste, Bibliothèque Sainte-Geneviève, Paris, 1834–50. Entry hall.

Theuth said, "O King, here is something that, once learned, will make the Egyptians wiser and will improve their memory; I have discovered a potion (pharmakon) for memory and for wisdom." Thamus, however, replied, "O most expert Theuth [...] since you are the father of writing, your affection for it has made you describe its effects as the opposite of what they really are.

In fact, it will introduce forgetfulness into the soul of those who learn it: they will not practice their memory because they will put their trust in writing. [...] You have not discovered a potion (pharmakon) for remembering, but for reminding; you provide your students with the appearance of wisdom not the reality."
—Plato, Phaedrus[1]

An architect should know writing (*litteras*) so that he can produce a stronger memory in commentaries (*commentarii*).
–Vitruvius, *De Architectura*

Memory in Oblivion

There exists in architecture a form of memory that is neither a function of its monumental purpose, nor of its historical appearance through patina or ruin, but is shadowed by reference to textual or formal precedent. Established by means of spatial emulation or mythological connotation, this kind of memory has been, since the eighteenth century, understood as "typological." Beyond a simple genealogical relationship to common building types in history—the temple, the stadium, the church—this mnemonic filiation has a distinct position in the history of architecture: indeed, it relies precisely on the emergence of a self-consciousness of historical difference and its corollary, historical classification. The comparative tables of temple plans compiled by Julien-David LeRoy and the corresponding catalogs of institutional forms drawn up by Jean-Nicolas Louis Durand were attempts to provide diagrammatic codes for signifying at once an architect's homage to precedent and its obligatory transformation. Whether following Quatremère de Quincy's distinction between the "vague" type and the copied "model," or the more abstract, diagrammatic formulations of modernists from Le Corbusier to Louis I. Kahn, the trace of history was preserved within volumetric permutations that pointed to pre-existent paradigms while emphasizing their new and sometimes radical reformulations.

With the emergence of digital technology and the web in particular, this fragile link between architecture and its history has potentially been broken. As Antoine Picon points out in an evocative passage, "the relation between digital culture, memory, and history" has led to the paradoxical situation of a web which "is actually an archive" whose "tendency [is] to be oblivious of memory and history." The problem is exacerbated by the substitution of parametrical relations for the constructive elements of architecture, those parts that traditionally formed the syntax by which historical memory was evoked. The "smoothness" and continuity of parametric modulation, Picon concludes, "not only […] lead to forms that lack immediately recognizable scale; they are adverse to syntax-like tectonic expression."[2]

The question of the movement "from memory to oblivion," as Picon puts it, however, emerged in architecture long before the advent of the digital. Picon himself gives the example of Henri Labrouste's Bibliothèque Sainte-Geneviève, where the architect, responding to Viollet-le-Duc's declaration of the "death" of architecture at the hands of the book—the "book of stone" killed by the printed word—conceived of his facade as being made up of a series of panels emulating index cards displaying the names of celebrated authors whose books were stored in the library. The traditional "writing" *of* the walls, that last gasp of tectonic architecture embodied in the *architecture parlante* of Ledoux and Boullée, had, so to speak, been reduced to the literal writing *on* the wall.

Memories of Typology

On closer inspection, however, Labrouste's library embodies another, more traditional and highly tectonic form of memory in the distribution and form of its spaces. Indeed, his entire composition resonates with the spatial orders of a whole chain of historic libraries, stretching back to a certain antique library from the 4th century BC; we might see this as the memory of its "typological" history. This memory is set up on entrance. Entering through an arched "Etruscan" doorway flanked by burning torches, the visitor is introduced to this most urban of public libraries in a vestibule that emulates a garden. To either side, a mural simulates a high garden wall topped by a painted frieze of trees and vines from in front of which a group of ancient philosophers peer at the aspiring reader. Mounting the stairs to the reading room, the visitor is faced by a huge mural copy of Raphael's *School of Athens*. The reading room itself is a long rectangular double-vaulted space lined by reference shelves, above which light pours in from the arched windows.[3] Barry Bergdoll has observed that in an earlier scheme, Labrouste planned for the reading room to be spanned by a single vault.

Here, the reference to Étienne-Louis Boullée's celebrated project for the Bibliothèque Royale of 1784 is clearly stated. Boullée, in a much reproduced perspective, had proposed to roof the courtyard of the Bibliothèque Royale with a coffered Roman vault, forming, as he writes, "a vast amphitheater of books" lined on either side with stepped rows of stacks. In the drawing, readers in togas pour over volumes handed down by assistants from the terraced levels. Again, Boullée's reference is clear—indeed, he cites his source for the long perspective view in a long *mémoire* of 1785: "Deeply moved by the sublime conception of the *School of Athens* by Raphael, I sought to realize it: and I doubtless owe my success, if such I have obtained, from this idea."[4] Guarding the entrance, two huge Atlas figures hold up a globe of worldwide knowledge, standing in front of a blank facade, inscribed, as if a giant book, with mottos.

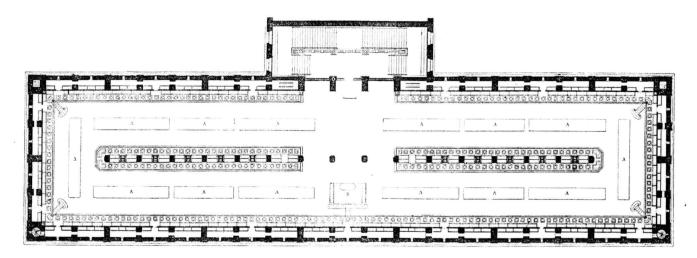

Henri Labrouste, Bibliothèque Sainte-Geneviève, Paris, 1839. Plan of the reading room.

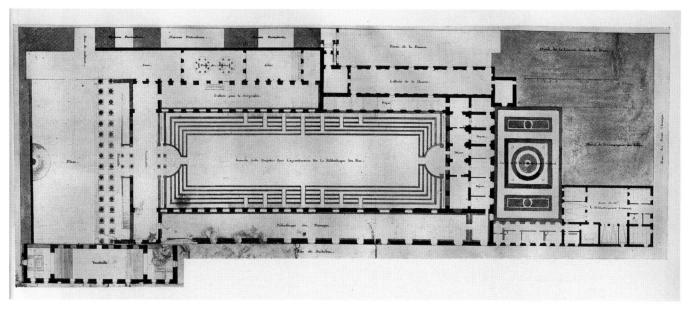

Etienne-Louis Boullée, Plan of the Bibliothèque royale, 1785.

This is the space intimated in Raphael's vision of *Philosophy*, later named *The School of Athens*. This fresco resides in the Stanza della Segnatura in the Apostolic Palace of the Vatican. It depicts a great vaulted hall, receding beneath several arches into the distance, and at the center, Plato, holding his book of the cosmos, the *Timaeus*, with finger held upwards toward the world of ideal forms. He stands beside his critical student Aristotle, who holds his own signature book, *Nicomachean Ethics*, with his hand palm down gesturing toward the practical world of things and people. Surrounding them are all the celebrated writers, mathematicians, and philosophers of antiquity, and, above, the huge overarching vault is inscribed with a traditional Greek meander.

Boullée's reference to Raphael's celebrated painting further returns us to another library image, also well-known in the late eighteenth century: that of Piranesi's engraving of another vaulted amphitheatrical library, this time half-ruined and looking out on a Roman city; that the image has been entitled "Ancient school built according to the Egyptian and Greek manners" only serves to connect the *School of Athens*, to its successor in Alexandria, and thus closes the link in this great chain of architectural bibliophilia to its origin in Plato's Athenian "School." What was commonly known later as Plato's "academy" thus emerges as the long-lost, original locus of this tradition of library building.[5]

Mythic Typologies

The precise layout of Plato's academy however, was unknown before the excavations of 1929 that began to uncover the foundations of the gymnasium said to house his school. Thus the "memory" of the *School of Athens* in the eighteenth century was based solely on later reports from Plutarch concerning the area named the "Akademia" outside the city, with a gymnasium and groves of trees. Plato was said to have inherited property nearby, and to have hosted students in his own house. Whether or not the later gymnasium was related in any way to his school is unknown. The building in *legend*, however, was more substantial: opened by Plato on his return to Athens in 387 BC, some twelve years after the death of his teacher Socrates, and set within a walled garden and olive grove, it was purported to be sacred to the legendary Academus (or, others claim, named after the former owner of the land), and his school was imagined as a gymnasium/library. The eighteenth-century author J. J. Barthélemy set the scene in his tale of the travels of Anacharsis, as described in ancient accounts:

> The Academy is only six *stades* from the town. It is a large site that a citizen of Athens named Academus had once owned. There you can see now a gymnasium and a garden surrounded by walls, ornamented by charming covered promenades, embellished by waters that flowed in the shade of plantains and many other kinds of trees. At the entry is an altar to Love and a statue of their god; inside are altars of many other divinities. Not far from there Plato had established his residence beside a small temple dedicated to the Muses, and in a part of the site that belonged to him.[6]

Giovanni Battista Piranesi, *Ancient School built according to Greek and Roman Methods*, 1750.

Thus within Plato's garden, in a building that was at the same time a gymnasium, a library, a place of study, a debating house, and a scriptorium, a new kind of imaginary space was developed—a space dedicated to philosophy. As "restored" in a plan by John Travlos, and in three dimensions by W. Hoepfner, the academy occupied the long, open, rectangular space of the gymnasium, surrounded on all sides by porticoes under which philosophers and their students would debate in the shade. As a "Temple of Knowledge," the Academy was furnished with statues of the appropriate gods (Athena or Apollo), and provided with side rooms for the storage of scrolls and the discussion of philosophic concepts.[7] This was, then, the site for the development of the series of dialogues couched in dialectical terms by a teacher, Plato, speaking in the voice of his teacher, Socrates, as he worked out his views of truth, justice, and the ideal constitution of the *polis* in the dialogue *Politeia* (the *Republic*), with an audience that included a motley population of Orphics, Eleatics, Sophists, Pythagoreans, Atomists, and Ionians, not to mention his often somewhat skeptical students, among whom was Aristotle.

Recounted and re-imagined, by Plato, these conversations were relayed to Plato's audience, thence to be re-enacted by the students as the first philosophic dramas. Finally, and despite Socrates/Plato's distrust of writing, they were recorded on wax tablets, re-transcribed on papyrus scrolls, and later stored in the library of Alexandria for the benefit of Hellenistic and neo-Platonic scholars. In this way, Socrates' voice and Plato's ideas are merged so that most of what we know of Socrates and almost all we know of Plato resides in the interior of dialogues where Plato himself never appears.[8]

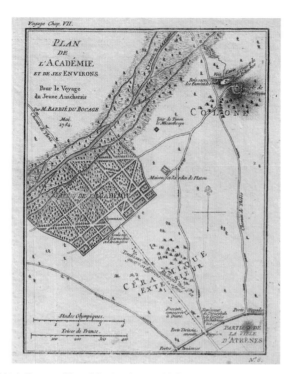

Barbié du Bocage, *Plan of the Academy and it Surroundings*, 1784. Published in J.J. Barthélemy, *Voyage du Jeune Anacharsis en Grèce* (Paris, 1787).

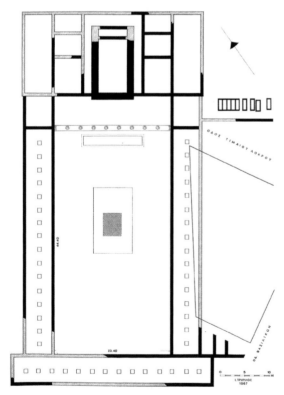

Plan of the Gymnasium on the site of the Plato's Academy, Athens.

Remembering a City

It has often been noted that Plato's dialogues were texts of remembrance—veritable feats of memory, as Plato recounted the discussions of Socrates with his interlocutors, often themselves recounted by Socrates, who, in turn, remembered accounts of former discussions of myths and fables, and who listened to his companions' own remembrances. This is especially the case of the paired dialogues, *Timaeus-Critias*, where Plato's account is developed as a succession of memories, reaching back to the foundation of the earliest cities. The *Timaeus* opens with Socrates asking his listeners to remember their discussion of the day before, and to remember "all the subjects he had assigned to them to speak on" as a follow-up. He was then called on to remind them of their discussion, repeating in outline his ideal political constitution for a polis that, for all intents and purposes, resembled the scheme that was developed in the *Republic*. He then asked for "repayment" in the form of three discourses that would, he said, furnish a more lifelike picture of the ideal city than that simply described in words: "My feelings are like those of a man who gazes upon magnificent looking animals, whether they're animals in a painting or even actually alive but standing still, and who finds himself longing to look at them in motion or engaged in some struggle or conflict that seems to show off their distinctive physical qualities" (*Timaeus*, 19b). The ensuing speeches, delivered by Timaeus and Critias, are accordingly framed to depict the city in action, "in a contest with other cities," competing for prizes, waging war, and putting its theoretical constitution into practice. Beginning at the beginning, Timaeus described the origin of the universe, the fabrication of the world by the Demiurge, and the birth of mankind; Critias followed with an account of the oldest foundation of Athens, and its triumphal contest with the empire of Atlantis, ending with the destruction of both, and their disappearance from Athenian memory.

It is here, in Critias' detailed descriptions, that the "recall" of what he calls a "true" history is elaborately fabricated, endowing what in reality is no more than a Platonic pastiche—an invented "myth"—with such veracity that it has persuaded generations of historians, archeologists, and treasure hunters ever since. The evidence of the former existence of Ancient Athens and Atlantis, was, Critias claims, passed down from the Athenian lawgiver Solon to his great-grandfather and thence to his grandfather, who told it to the ten-year-old Critias who, with some difficulty, but finally perfectly, remembered the whole story to tell to Socrates. The chain of memory goes further back, however, for Solon had heard it from an old priest of the city of Sais in Egypt, who himself had learned of these ancient cities from studying the thousand-year-old inscriptions on the temples, that in turn recorded events 9,000 years previously. Remembering the story he was told so vividly that, as Critias states, it has "all the indelible markings of a picture with the colors burnt in," he was earlier able to recount to Timaeus and Hermocrates, and is now ready to "translate" the city Socrates described "in mythical fashion" to the "realm of fact," placing it before their eyes "as though it is ancient Athens itself." As John Sallis has noted:

> In the *Timaeus,* the entire Socratic discourse on the city is a remembrance, and not only in the sense that it recalls what was said yesterday. To remember is to bring back before one's vision something that, as past, is—and remains—absent. In a more radical sense, to remember is to bring and hold before one's vision things that in and of themselves pass away, things that are always already past as soon as they come to presence, things that are not just singularly past but rather are determined as such by their becoming past, things that even before becoming singularly past are already stamped by their pastness. In the Platonic texts such remembrance is thought of as a vision of the *eidos* (to see).[9]

Monumental Memories

In Critias's adumbration of remembering, we should note, and despite Socrates' and Plato's suspicion of writing, the original account of Ancient Athens and Atlantis was, as the Egyptian priest testified, preserved by the survival of ancient antiquities: "all the events reported to us, no matter where they've occurred, if there are any that are noble or great or distinguished in some way or another, they've all been inscribed here in our temples" (*Timaeus,* 23a).[10] In this way, the myth of a city in Plato's account, acts as a "recollection" that established the potential of the polis for renewal. Monuments that had been consigned to oblivion were reconstituted as forceful exemplars for the future.[11] Socrates, the son of a stonemason, and by legend himself trained in sculpture, was here remembered by Plato as invoking the memory of monuments as guarantees of a past that might be repeated in the future.

The monuments that served to inscribe this memory "like a picture with the colors burnt in" were described in vivid detail. Ancient Athens was set in a fertile plain, surrounded by densely forested mountains; its widely spreading acropolis housed the warrior-guardians, living in common in their winter quarters to the north of the sanctuaries of Athena and Hephaestus, in tasteful houses built without ostentation, while the artisans and farmers lived on the lower slopes—a perfect "picture" of the society described in the *Republic*. The sea-girt island of Atlantis, on the other hand, required more elaborate defenses. Divided like the Athens of Cleisthenes into ten districts, and surrounded by circular rings of water, its monuments were constructed of many colored stones. At the center was the temple of Poseidon, clad in silver and gold with a roof of ivory, standing beside a magnificent palace; these were buildings that had "something barbaric in their appearance" (*Critias*, 113–117). It was perhaps as much the memory of these descriptions, as that of any traces of color still clinging to the ruins of the Acropolis, that inspired Labrouste and many other students of the École des Beaux-Arts to render so many colorful "restorations" as exercises in imagination and draftsmanship.

Erasing Memory

Critias's speech ends abruptly, however, before the subsequent history of Athens—its decline, fall, and recovery, could be recounted in detail. But the mythical saga was continued in Plato's account of the hypothetical construction of a real city on the island of Crete. In the *Laws*, a visitor from Athens converses with two older Cretan philosophers during a walk from Cnossos to the sacred cave of Zeus. Over the span of hundreds of pages and no doubt many days of walking, the outlines of a new colonial foundation were sketched, and its potential siting, layout, zoning, and the intricacies of its constitution were discussed in detail. If the ultimate ideal was the city of "Ancient Athens," the pre-historical antecedent of the city worked out in the *Republic*, then that of the *Laws* was, as Plato admitted a "second best city," as good as might be attained in reality. It is perhaps no accident, as scholars have noted, that this "second-best" resembles in many respects the former city of Atlantis, and it would not be stretching Plato's argument to propose that the mythical struggle between Atlantis and Ancient Athens represented in some way that between the real and the ideal, the second-best that must always keep striving towards the best, and, as with Atlantis, often fail in the attempt. Indeed, in the *Republic*, Plato has already depicted this conflict, in terms that come close to modeling a typical design process.

Designing the Ideal

Towards the end of the long conversation that investigated the nature of the just city of the *Republic* from every conceivable point of view, at the close of the interminably long dinner-party-without-dinner that he has had to undergo, Socrates arrives at a moment when he admits

School of Douris, *Seated Boy with Wax Tablet*, Red-figure vase painting, c. 500 BC.

that, whatever he (or Plato) may desire, the ideal city will eventually have to be "designed"—hopefully along the lines and "imitating" the universe as described in the *Timaeus* and with the topography and architectural forms of the Ancient Athens of the *Critias*.

Following the model of the Demiurge, Socrates claims that the best qualified designer would be one "who is most highly qualified in philosophy," he who "has his thoughts directed at what exists," "imitates and models as far as possible" those "things he sees which are regulated, always internally consistent, that do no wrong and are not wronged by each other, that are orderly and rational." And when "some compulsion comes upon him to put into practice what he sees in the divine realm in the private and public lives of men," such a model needs to be "portrayed" by "artists" in order for it to be successful. For "a city will never know happiness unless its outline has been traced by these artists-painters who work according to the divine model." Accordingly, when asked "What sort of a plan/portrayal/sketch/outline does he speak of?" Socrates then lays out the process of ideal design: "They would take the city, and the characters of human beings, as if it were a wax tablet, and, first in line, they would wipe it clean, which would be far from easy." (*Republic* 500e–501a)

That is, surprisingly, the instrument par excellence of writing, a wax tablet or *diptych*, which would now be employed in the active design of the new polis. But first, the existing polis would be looked upon as a writing tablet, inscribed in the wax as a set of existing conditions. The wax thus formed the ground on which to sketch the ideal. But, since the polis adopted for this redesign was already in existence, and far from ideal, the writing tablet, already containing it, needed to be wiped, or scraped clean: because these perfection-bound artist-urban designers were "unlike other reformers" and "immediately differing from other people" were "not content" "to deal with either an individual or a state, or even draft laws," unless "given a clean surface to work on." (*Republic* 501a)

Socrates completes his lecture on design by comparing the method to that of a painter mixing his colors: "And in this way they'd mix and blend the various ways of life in the city until they produced a human image based on what Homer called the 'divine form and image'." Plato uses the word "grinding" (*andreike-lon*) as if to accentuate the difficulty of combining all the different human traits into a single model figure.[12] Indeed much more scraping and erasing is needed to develop the painting to perfection: "they would rub out and redraw some parts until they had made human characteristics as much and as far as possible dear to the gods." (Jones-Preddy), or, as another translation has it, they would more directly, "rub out and redraw," or even "efface certain traits" and "design new ones" (*Republic* 501b).[13] The result would be a finest sketch or outline, a very beautiful painting of the constitution—one that would persuade even the most resistant citizen of its virtue and justice.

For all this rubbing and scraping of the wax was, in Plato's terms, equivalent to the polishing of the soul itself and endowing it with memory. It is in the *Theaetetus* that Socrates proposes the analogy:

Please assume, then, for the sake of argument, that there is in our souls a block of wax, in one case larger, in another smaller, in one case the wax is purer, in another more impure and harder, in some cases softer.

Let us, then, say that this is the gift of Memory, the mother of the Muses, and that whenever we wish to remember anything we see or hear or think of in our own minds, we hold this wax under the perceptions and thoughts and imprint

them upon it, just as we make impressions from seal rings; and whatever is imprinted we remember and know as long as its image lasts, but whatever is rubbed out or cannot be imprinted we forget and do not know. (*Theaetetus*, 191 c–e)

Designing the perfect polis is, then, the process of erasing existing memory and replacing it with the beautiful forms of the ideal. As Socrates' replies to Adeimantus at the close of the *Republic*:

Perhaps, there is a model (*paradeigma*) of it in heaven, for whoever wishes to gaze upon it, and following this vision, look at it and to make himself its citizen on the strength of what he sees. It makes no difference whether it is or ever will be some-where, for he would take part in the practical af-fairs of that city and no other. (*Republic*. IX, 592b)

Despite Socrates' admission that his ideal republic would perhaps never be realized, Plato's written account of his memory of Socrates recounting the long conversation at Piraeus that produced the dialogue of the *Republic*, has, paradoxically enough, exerted enormous power as a memory of an ideal city that never existed and might nev-er exist; as a paradigm, from Saint Augustine to Thomas More; as a spatial and social model to architects like Alberti and Filarete; as a prototype for anti-urban settle-ments for reformers like Ebenezer Howard and Patrick Geddes; as an anti-capitalist weapon for radicals like Guy Debord; as an enduring challenge to ethical thought for philosophers like Leo Strauss and Jacques Derrida (not to mention Alain Badiou who has recently delivered his own idiosyncratic retranslation).

But if Plato's city was recollected in the varied forms of utopia and the garden city; in architecture, it was the memory of the academic garden and its gym-nasium-like reading, writing, and speaking place that has endured—at least until recently. Not far from the Austerlitz railroad station in Paris, stands a new library. Its plan is now familiar: a long rectangle, its corners marked by four L-shaped glass towers; entered up steep flights of steps that lead to an upper plaza, from which the library itself is accessed. The architect Dominique Perrault has not been oblivious to centuries of architec-tural signification, a fact that was no doubt important in, as Boullée had it, his "success, if such he had ob-tained." The four towers stand as four monumental open books—empty enough signs in an age of their imminent disappearance, in a library dedicated to the eventual total digitization of the written word and casual enough toward real books in a transparency that quickly had to be obscured inside with wooden panels to protect them from the light.

Boullée's amphitheatrical stairs are now inverted, left outside as if signaling a ritual ascent to knowledge, made difficult enough in winter's ice and rain. Once the symbolic *temenos* has been reached, access to the library leads downwards again into a *passage* (memory of nineteenth-century shopping?) that surrounds a central courtyard, that itself mimics in plan the gymnasium, amphitheater, or reading room of historic libraries, transformed into a garden. Again, symbolically, this space is entirely closed, inaccessible to readers, its trees standing in for Plato's olive grove, for visual relaxation only. Architecture, reduced to an empty symbolism that "speaks" no longer to a society engrossed in its iPads, has finally succeeded in forcing even this memory of the library into oblivion; and not only the memory of books. For, as W. G. Sebald has ironically noted, the most disturbing symbol of all, is the site itself: this library of total knowledge, programmatically to be emptied of books and eventually to be filled only with the virtual sites of the digital era, stands on an abandoned railway yard, itself once the site of a warehouse that served as the repository of the pillaged belongings of Jewish families. He writes: "on the waste land between the marshalling yard of the Gare d'Austerlitz and the Pont Tobiac where this Babylonian library now rises, there stood until the end of the war an extensive warehousing complex to which the Germans brought all the loot they had taken from the homes of the Jews of Paris."[14]

Notes

1   All quotations from Plato's dialogues are from Plato, *Complete Works*, edited by John M. Cooper (Indianapolis: Hackett Publishing Company, 1997) unless otherwise noted.

2   Antoine Picon, *Digital Culture in Architecture* (Basel: Birkhäuser, 2010), 135–137.

3   See Barry Bergdoll, *European Architecture 1750–1890* (Oxford: Oxford University Press, 2000), 181.

4   Étienne-Louis Boullée, *Architecture, essai sur l'art, texts compiled and edited by Jean-Marie Pérouse de Montclos* (Paris: Hermann, 1968), 126.

5   Though not without passing through many later examples of the genre, including Hadrian's library in Athens (AD 132), and Trajan's Bibliotheca Ulpia (c. AD 100) in Rome. The library of Hadrian, constructed to the north of the Roman Agora on the north of the Acropolis, followed the general plan that we have been describing—a large open courtyard with a fountain at the center, and a series of "library" rooms at the eastern end.

6   J. J. Barthélemy, *Voyage du Jeune Anacharsis en Grèce* (Paris: Didier, 1843 [1787]), 4 vols., Vol. 1, 202–209.

7   See K. Sp. Staikos, *Books and Ideas: The Library of Plato and the Academy* (Athens: Aton Publications, 2013), who summarizes Plato's sources while explaining what is known of the Academy in architectural terms.

8   In some of the dialogues Plato gives the memorization of Socrates to others—to Phaedo for example, where Plato has been thought to use his own voice to communicate Socrates' (almost) last thoughts to a group of Pythagoreans, or in the *Laws*, to an "Athenian Stranger;" as Catherine Zuckert points out, however, there is not a "shred" of evidence for this assumption.

9   John Sallis, *Chorology: On Beginning in Plato's Timaeus* (Bloomington and Indianapolis: Indiana University Press, 1999), 30.

10 See Luc Brisson, *Plato the Myth Maker*, translated by Gerard Naddaf (Chicago: University of Chicago Press, 1998), 22. Brisson outlines the various stages of memory involved in these complex myths, recounted by Plato to authorize Socrates' arguments.

11 In this mythical art of memory, Plato famously differed with Aristotle, whose *ars memoria* was more instrumental.

12 Plato, *Cratylus*, 424d, where Socrates is speaking of how to apply letters in combination to produce a resemblance: "It's just the same with painters. When they want to produce a resemblance, they sometimes use only purple, sometimes another color, and sometimes—for example when they want to paint human flesh or something of that sort—they mix many colors." Plato, *Complete Works*, ed. John M. Cooper (Indianapolis and Cambridge: Hackett, 1997), 141.

13 The Paul Shorey translation is even more explicit as to the painters' methods: "I take it, in the course of the work they would glance frequently in either direction, at justice, beauty, sobriety and the like as they are in the nature of things, and alternately at that which they were trying to reproduce in mankind, mingling and blending from various pursuits that hue of the flesh, so to speak, deriving their judgment from that likeness of humanity which Homer too called, when it appeared in men, the image and likeness of God." "Right," he said. "And they would erase one touch or stroke and paint in another."

14 W. G. Sebald, *Austerlitz*, translated by Anthea Bill (New York: The Modern Library, 2001), 288.

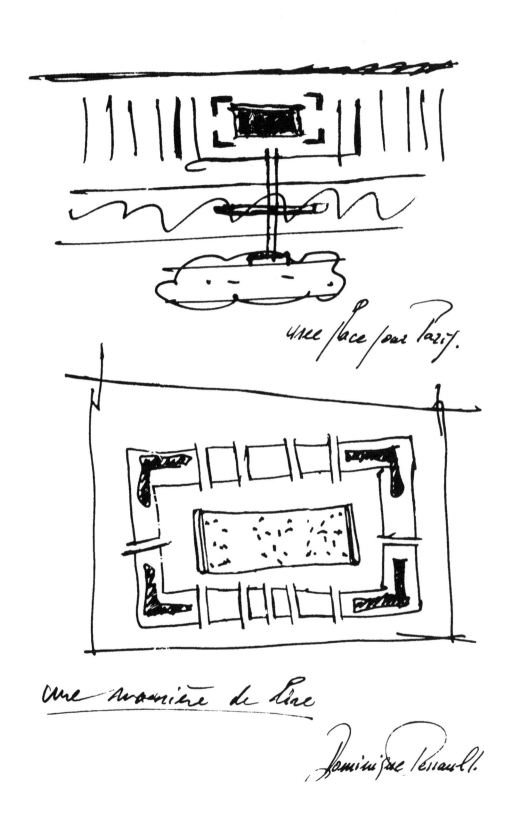

une place pour Paris.

une manière de Lire

Dominique Perrault

Dominique Perrault, Bibliothèque de France, Paris, 1989–1995. Parti sketch.

88

FROM THEATER OF MEMORY TO FRAMEWORK FOR MEMORIES:

JOHN SOANE'S MUSEUMS   *MARIA SHÉHÉRAZADE GIUDICI*

The idea of accumulating everything, of establishing a sort of general archive [...], the idea of constituting a place of all times that is itself outside of time and inaccessible to its ravages, the project of organizing in this a sort of perpetual and indefinite accumulation of time in an immobile place, this whole idea belongs to our modernity.
—Michel Foucault[1]

The "place of all times"—the museum—is a paradigmatic expression of the modern obsession with memory. As much as modern society is concerned with the idea of evolution, it is equally haunted by the need to record, store, display, and share memory. The cult of progress, so central to contemporary western culture, depends on historical continuity and recollection of the past—a fact that makes the museum a crucial institution in the construction of modern subjectivity. While evoking individual experience, memory can be seen also as a social product, and as such is a historically placed construct. The concept of memory that prompted the need to build a "general archive" arose in response to the emergence of a new urban class that had lost its fundamental link to the traditional family structure and a place of origin. Freed from the hierarchies of agrarian society, the new urban subject lacked a fixed ethical background, making it potentially volatile from a political and economic point of view. This issue affected society at every level—from the intellectual elite, which was forced to construct new narratives of beauty, to the working class, which belonged nowhere, had no past and no motivation to carry on a meek, ordered, productive life, a situation portrayed well by nineteenth-century writers like Balzac and Dostoyevsky. History at large, and individual memory in response to the passing of historical epochs, sought to address this lack of fixed references. Anything could have meaning as long as it could be seen as part of a large-scale historical, or teleological, dynamic. The museum became a key pedagogical institution precisely because it gave physical representation and increased accessibility to what had been an abstract concept for most of the population.

This institution was, therefore, an expression of nineteenth- and twentieth-century western culture in the midst of significant changes. While the museum originally represented memory through the physical presence of unique artifacts, its function has changed dramatically in the last decade. The development of today's *digital* archives threatens to supplant that idea of memory with one based on an infinitely accessible and expandable collection of digitized data. However, we could argue that the museum and the digital archive are not opposite paradigms, but rather two steps of the same process: the commodification of

PREVIOUS SPREAD Sir John Soane, The Soane House, London. The Picture Room. All photographs by Tommaso Franzolini.

The Soane House, London.

memory. Today, memory has become a crucial cog in the mechanisms of production and consumption; we buy memories (in the form of experiences) and memory (in the sense of storage space). Our experiences define who we are: this cliché seems innocent enough, yet it sustains an industry that has become monstrously powerful. The artificial production of experience, from tourism to spectacular architecture, has existed ever since pilgrimages have been recognized practices. The experience was traditionally supposed to be the final goal, the endpoint of the process, but the possibility to *record* this experience has transformed what was an action into a solidified, reified product. Part of this process is undeniably linked to market needs, but architecture has also played a part in the reification of memory, through the emergence of specific building types devoted to the conservation of memory, such as libraries, archives, and museums. The first half of the nineteenth century was a crucial moment in this process of intense typological experimentation. The shift from a traditional culture of memory (personal, intransmissible, and borderline magical) to a modern one (teleological and increasingly reified) can perhaps be read most clearly in the work of John Soane, an architect who explored both sides of the issue by building the last of the cabinets of curiosities and the first modern museum.

Born in 1753 to a humble family, Soane rose to become one of the most preeminent figures of his time.[2] He designed many works, including the first purpose-built public art gallery in the United Kingdom, the Dulwich Picture Gallery, and his personal *Wunderkammer*, at Lincoln's Inn Fields, in London. These two buildings are indices of a revolution in the western conception of memory. In a few decades, a series of technical advancements, such as the invention of photography and the emergence of industrial pulp mills for the production of cheap paper,[3] would make memory a quintessential commodity in the European economic system. In Soane's time, however, the reproduction and storage of data was still a nascent, unsystematic, and expensive process, heightening the symbolic value of collections such as the one he amassed, between 1809 and his death, in 1837. Nicéphore Niépce fixed his first photographic image in 1826, and by the end of Soane's life, the daguerreotype had gained popularity. At the same time, the main museums of England[4] became freely accessible to the general public, transforming memory from an upper-class privilege into an aspirational product that would become increasingly affordable to a larger portion of the population.

Soane's museums were created precisely at the dawn of this new culture of memory and contributed immensely to its construction by influencing the evolution of the museum and the development of a peculiar architectural language, "unshackled"[5] from the classical orders but bound to history by a critical relationship. During his lifetime, Soane was often criticized for his cavalier use of classical motifs, which he inserted with complete disregard to the accepted proportions of the orders—a fact that still prevents us from labeling him as a "neoclassical" architect, like his contemporaries.[6] In fact, his critical reinterpretation of the classical language could be read precisely as a refusal to conceive of architecture as timeless and static—a concern visible in Joseph Gandy's portrayals of Soane's buildings as ruins. The Chelsea Hospital Infirmary, whose exterior walls feature a bas-relief of brick arches, was attacked with unusual violence by Soane's own son, who wrote that "disproportion is the most striking feature in the works of this artist; he plunders from the records of antiquity things in themselves absolutely good, but which were never intended to meet in the same place."[7] However, the blind arches of the infirmary suggest neither a value-free pastiche nor the *ante litteram* postmodernist attitude criticized by Soane's son; instead, it points to an attempt to distill and simplify the classical language into a more abstract system of pure geometrical forms. This abstraction was not meant as a search for a new absolute, but rather as a way to produce a building that would belong to its own time. A similar attitude is visible in the Dulwich Picture Gallery. The Soane house, however, does not follow this line of experimentation; on the contrary, it refers back to an older idea of memory that did not rely on historical narrative. It is useful to compare these two museums today in the midst of another moment of positive crisis, both as far as memory itself is concerned and with regard to the social role of the museum.

The white-box model, which has its origin in the Dulwich Picture Gallery, has been challenged in recent years by a genealogy of museums that emphasize the idiosyncratic nature of its architecture as made up of elements that should have some sort of friction with the art exhibited. From the exuberant protagonism of Frank Gehry's Bilbao Guggenheim and the narrative pathos of Daniel Libeskind's Berlin Jewish Museum to OMA's ironic deconstruction of modernism in the Rotterdam Kunsthal, architecture often takes the foreground and the aura of the artifact diminishes proportionally to the strong characterization of the space. Architects are not entirely responsible for this trend, which is a political issue rather than an artistic one. City administrations often want to have one or more museums that they view not only as necessary containers of artwork, but also as economic engines and forms of pedagogical welfare. This desire existed long before Bilbao and can be

The Soane House, London.

traced back to the invention of modern memory in Soane's time. The Rotterdam case is particularly interesting because it does not mask the nature of the museum's public infrastructure: the lecture hall and bookshop are just as important as the galleries, and the promenade through the building is a voyage in itself, even in the absence of artifacts. Paradoxically, the most content-rich museums often conform to the white box, as demonstrated by Herzog & de Meuron's renovation of the Tate. Commercial art galleries, perhaps the real birthplace of the white cube, continue to conform to the model, as illustrated by the recently opened Marian Goodman Gallery in London, where David Adjaye created an extremely even setting of white walls and beautiful detailing aimed at the complete erasure of the building to the advantage of the artwork. In both architectural approaches, however, the result is the same: the *experience* of the visitor is increasingly important. Curating one's preferences and memories has become a primary concern. Ironically, a close analysis of Soane's buildings reveals that this contemporary attitude might actually be closer to the traditional language of the Wunderkammer than to that of the "modern" gallery.

MEMORY AS THEATER

Soane bought No. 12 Lincoln's Inn Fields in 1792. Between 1808 and 1809 he acquired the neighboring building and connected it to his house through a top-lit gallery. The houses are the typical London terraces built by commercial developers throughout the seventeenth and eighteenth centuries. The speculative nature of this type is clearly readable in the even distribution of the party walls, which act as both load-bearing structure and property division. These terraces represented the most efficient and rational way to subdivide a plot of land into equal parcels and were highly standardized, not only in terms of size and facade language, but even in their interior distribution, as visible in the original plan and detailing of Soane's house. Soane despised the repetitive character of the terrace and attempted to change both the interior and the facade.[8] As soon as he acquired the first terrace, he recorded his intention to create a "Plaister Room [sic]"[9] containing casts of architectural details and models of ancient monuments. As the collection grew, Soane bought a third house to expand his personal museum, which represented not only his hard-earned social status, but also his goal of introducing his sons to architecture. The Plaister Room was a repository for memory as the instrument of self-legitimation and as a tool for education. Starting there, Soane collected a substantial number of artifacts, which he rearranged several times in a warren of rooms of various sizes and shapes.

93

The main exhibition area, at the back of the house, is composed of a sequence of spaces that can be synthesized as the juxtaposition of one triple-height room (the Dome), a space divided into two floors and marked by a rhythm of columns (the Colonnade), and a room equipped with folding panels for the storage of paintings and engravings (the Picture Room). The Dome defines a cylinder of space that pierces through the ground floor down to the cellar, framing the centerpiece of the collection, an Egyptian sarcophagus.[10] The house museum was considered an "evocative setting that would transport the viewer to other times and places."[11]

When Soane bequeathed the house to the state, he insisted that nothing in its disposition be changed[12]—that it not be turned it into a museum tout court.[13] This bequest underlines the continuity between Soane's collection and the tradition of Renaissance house museums[14] and *studioli*, a type that evolved in the seventeenth century as the cabinet of curiosities, or Wunderkammer. The cabinet of curiosities was a private collection put together on the basis of the owner's taste containing objects of various kinds—from stones and plants to objects crafted by man. If Renaissance *studioli* had been a privilege of the aristocracy, seventeenth-century cabinets belonged to a new class of intellectuals, doctors, and scientists, such as Athanasius Kircher and Ole Worm, who did not see the Wunderkammern simply as private pastimes but as sources of legitimation for their own work. The more complete the collection, the more authority the owner would have; and here completeness is not a quantitative parameter but an ability to *order* a set of objects so as to reveal the order of the universe.

The idea of cataloguing the whole of reality in a room requires an implicit narrative,[15] though not necessarily a historical one. While the museum links memory to the temporal structure of history, the Wunderkammer ties the idea of remembering to an ability to mentally reconstruct the totality of things in their spatial order. Nineteenth-century museums were organized chronologically, as most large collections still are; the spatial diagram followed a historical narrative without any pretense to compose an overall picture with its own geometry. On the contrary, the Wunderkammer presents a strong compositional tension by the way in which the objects are arranged, as visible in the engravings of famous cabinets such as Ferrante Imperato's Palazzo Gravina, in Naples. Wunderkammern are microcosms,[16] and the objects they contain are memorabilia—extraordinary pieces to be remembered as exquisite or bizarre anomalies that offer a complete image of the universe recapitulated inside a room. On the contrary, the modern museum bears the hallmarks

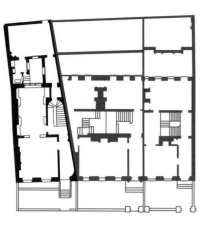

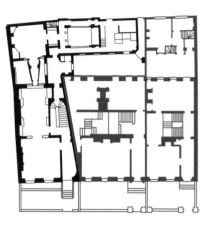

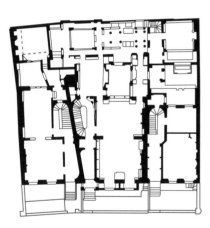

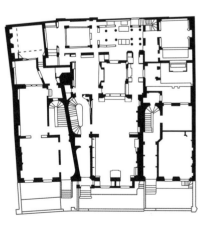

The Soane House, London.
Plans illustrating the acquisition and modification of neighboring properties.
OPPOSITE The Soane House, London.
Egyptian sarcophagus beneath the Dome.

94

of separation, fragmentation, and discontinuity.[17] There is no pretense to recompose a consistent cosmos in a museum: the objects collected should instead remind us of an elsewhere from which they were severed in the first place.[18] The Wunderkammer works by analogy, the museum by metonymy. The Wunderkammer mirrors the universe, while the museum is an *espace autre*[19] where physical fragments stand in for times and places we cannot access. The two mechanisms tackle the issue of memory in fundamentally different ways. Analogy likens things that, while different, share some kind of *structural* similarity:[20] it draws links between the known and the unknown, between what we remember and what we want to remember. Analogy was the backbone of the mnemonic method attributed to the Greek poet Simonides; it was the basis of the art of memory as developed by orators up until the Renaissance. Simonides's method worked through a *spatial* analogy: the physical order of spaces in a known building would become the *fil rouge* allowing the orator to recall a speech.[21] The order of the "visited" spaces was crucial to this art of memory, which read the building as pure *sequence*.[22]

Soane used this mechanism at Lincoln's Inn Fields. The dramatic variations in scale and proportion emphasize the differences between the rooms, and the building becomes an idiosyncratic filing system where every object has a specific place. In this respect, the Soane house museum is close not only to a Wunderkammer but to a "theater of memory."[23] Developed most notably by Giulio "Delminio" Camillo around the mid-sixteenth century, the "theater of memory" (of which there are no extant architectural prototypes, only written descriptions) was an interior space that served as the ideal template on which to exercise Simonides's method.

On the other hand, modern museums work through synecdoche, a type of metonymy in which the object exhibited is a fragment of a larger, absent whole. In comparison with analogy, metonymy lessens the possibility of misinterpretation; its message, or transmitted memory, is easier to share. In a museum, objects are bearers of memory not because of their symbolic, analogical relationship to what they stand for, but as a result of a direct and unambiguous physical contiguity. The Wunderkammer and Delminio's theater both frame memory as the individual's reading of an immanent order, while the museum presents memory as the link between subject and society—a tie established through history and its constant collective reelaboration.

Soane's collection recreates a cosmos by scripting the visitor's path through the house. In this respect, the house museum adopts the analogical model by becoming an inhabitable

The Soane House, London. The Dome.

Wunderkammer that spatializes the narrative of human life as a path from darkness to light, from death to rebirth.[24] The construction of the house museum was a piecemeal operation that lasted thirty years. Soane eventually opened the collection to a wider audience[25] and, since his sons refused to follow in his footsteps,[26] finally bequeathed the house to the state in 1833. The "museum" straddled the thin line between traditional cabinet of curiosities and modern educational institution, targeting a very specific audience. A newspaper described it as "a model-house, intended for architects, artists, and persons of taste." The place was "intended more for the benefit of a class, than for the use of the public indiscriminately."[27] Ultimately, the house-museum was constructed as a material trace of the existence of the architect-collector. It is the analogue of the cosmos via Soane's works and philosophy; it is a theater that preserves the memory of Soane's life through its spatial arrangement.[28] However, as memory shifted from the realm of the sacred to one of magic, and from a form of privilege to a commodity, institutions and practices evolved in response. Wunderkammern gradually disappeared, printed memory became accessible to a greater number of people, and museums endeavored to serve, educate, and control a wider population.

TOWARD THE WHITE BOX

When Soane started his Plaister Room, no building in Britain had been constructed as a public art gallery. In 1811, the task of designing such a building fell on Soane. The Dulwich Picture Gallery, which opened in 1815,[29] became the most representative example of Soane's architectural style[30]—executed in a simplified language, it was deemed by Emil Kaufmann as the "English parallel" of Claude-Nicolas Ledoux's work.[31] The top-lighting, the repetition of regularly shaped rooms, and the disappearance of the classical orders embodied in the Dulwich museum would have a lasting influence; art galleries would become blank frameworks, delegating the narrative power of the collection to the exhibited objects themselves.

The Dulwich Picture Gallery introduced an abstract, nonnarrative "styleless" kind of architecture that reflected a larger shift toward rationalization in western cities. From the late eighteenth through the nineteenth century, the European city became a matter of scientific inquiry, as seen in Pierre Patte's engineering diagrams and Ildefonso Cerdá's statistic tables. The ambitions to monumentality and theatricality that had ruled the Baroque city gave way to a concern for smooth circulation, the optimization of resources, and an exploitation of real estate values. As a consequence, the new urban landscape of the industrial city became as repetitive as Haussmann's boulevards and the systematized grids of Barcelona and Manhattan. This scientific approach to urbanism was accompanied by the emergence of a new subject: romantic art and literature have portrayed it, for example, as Friedrich's *Wanderer above the Sea of Fog*, but more prosaically, we could define it as the bourgeois self. A product of this new abstract and featureless urban environment, the bourgeois subject has neither a background history nor an established set of values, and thus craves the "identity" it essentially lacks. It craves novelty and the possibility to be different in reaction to the progressive systematization of the landscape and the city. This reaction is visible in the eclectic character of the architecture of that era, from Augustus Pugin's faux Gothic houses to Charles Garnier's overly decorated classicism. Private architecture offered an antidote to the progressive reification of the metropolis by turning toward issues of memory, identity, differentiation, originality, and fashion.[32]

From the Dulwich Picture Gallery onward, museums were treated as public infrastructure, conforming to the simplification and rationalization of the city rather than to personal eclectic taste and experimentation. They began to act as hosts, or backgrounds, for objects that were no longer parts of a generic natural cosmos but had acquired their own specific history. The "character" of these spaces was no longer in the cabinets themselves but in the individual objects on display. In the age of analogical thinking, architecture was necessarily loaded with symbolism. The construction of a collective form of memory, together with the cult of originality, required architecture to produce a suitable *background*. The two kinds of memory that emerged relate to radically different political conditions. Until the eighteenth century, memory was a form of power and validation that strengthened the political hierarchy upon which absolute monarchies were based. On the contrary, in a capitalist system, the issue becomes how to *share* memory.

Sharing memory means linking individuals to a collective sense of history and time, creating new values, and constructing a sense of responsibility toward one's descendants. This ethical framework, based on a new sense of history, began to replace the traditional—and by now defunct—ethical system, based on unquestionable hierarchies. Constructing such a framework was crucial in Soane's time[33] because the ruling elite was concerned with the need to "civilize" the mass of proletarians moving into the city to work in the new industries.[34] A civilized proletariat was less prone to drinking and unrest; it was more productive and efficient and had more reasonable demands. Collective memory is a civilizing

The Soane House, London. The Dome.

mechanism in that it links man to a history of civilization. Having (and leaving) a memory means that actions have significance beyond their immediate results. While the pedagogical task of the museum may be seen as neutral, cultural institutions of the time were conscious of their potential to shape new subjectivities.[35] In a less politically motivated way, art connoisseur Francis Bourgeois shared this pedagogical ambition when he donated his collection—partly inherited from his friend Noel Desenfans—to Dulwich College. Bourgeois hired Soane to build a mausoleum for Desenfans in 1807, and in his will, he asked Soane to reconstruct another for himself and the Desenfans family in addition to the new gallery spaces at Dulwich.

The funds were barely enough since Bourgeois had envisioned only a remodeling of the existing spaces rather than a new building. But while content with refashioning a domestic environment for his own collection, Soane insisted that the artworks at the Dulwich Picture Gallery be displayed in proper exhibition spaces. He developed several options in order to convince the College Board of the necessity for new construction. As built, the gallery completes the preexisting complex with a new wing composed of five rooms centered symmetrically around the mausoleum for Desenfans and Bourgeois. The building is bold and simple; the dangerous honesty of the composition defies the proportions of orthodox orders and was much criticized at the time.[36] Today, however, it is viewed as a compelling attempt to retain the culture of classicism while casting aside the straitjacket of the classical orders.[37] The gallery has often been compared in its simplicity to other Soane buildings, such as the stables and infirmary of the Royal Hospital Chelsea,[38] but the top-lit spaces of Dulwich are probably closer to the commercial arcades of the period, such as the Burlington Arcade, or to auction rooms like that of Christie's.[39] Early art galleries and shopping arcades were also reciprocally influenced[40]—a fact that makes us reflect on the commodification of art and memory during the 1800s.

As the art market introduced itself to a bourgeois audience, memory was transformed into a salable good. Artwork became a tangible sign of the flow of history; its memory and commercial values collapsed into one. The museum became a place of education for both consumers and producers. Unshackled from traditional hierarchies, the romantic-era individual was no longer reliant upon the institutional narratives of previous generations. This prompted a paradigm shift in which all the crucial institutions of European society—from the monarchy to the church—ceased to be seen as absolute and natural. The cult of history[41] was born out of the paradox of modern subjectivity, one with no fixed point of reference. Values,

99

institutions, and ideals were understood as historical constructs rather than fixed and inalterable truths, so the romantic man sought reassurance and continuity in history as the source of all variations. Museums, therefore, address a historically situated kind of memory, related to the development of humankind and influenced by the rhetoric of progress.

In Soane's time, the standardization of infrastructure (where infrastructure stands for welfare provision and includes museums and mass housing) became the counterpart of eclecticism, and even sentimentalism, in the realm of architecture. As a typology, the museum gradually retreated from the subjective symbolism of the cabinet of curiosities to become an increasingly depersonalized space wherever a new culture of originality emerged. Even Soane gave in to the compensatory nature of eclecticism, but he never saw a contradiction between the critical abstraction of the *public* Dulwich museum and the stylistic extravaganza of the one at Lincoln's Inn Fields, which was conceived as a rebellion against the impersonal character of the London terrace.[42] In Soane's generation, one could still see this stylistic idiosyncrasy as a form of rebellion; however, the cult of originality would fall into a different category: fashion. In the end, the "Romantic" generation would serve the market it had initially criticized, by popularizing *novelty*, the powerful and enduring mechanism of consumption.

However, this relationship between Romantic values and commodity goes well beyond fashion; it is part of a wider socioeconomic dynamic, as discussed in a 1929 lecture by controversial jurist Carl Schmitt.[43] He argues that while the eighteenth century focused on issues of ethics and morality, nineteenth-century subjectivity centered on economic rationale. For Schmitt, the Romantic Weltanschauung precipitated a shift from morality to economy through the cult of aestheticism:

> *The aesthetic domain [...] is the surest and most comfortable way to the general economization of intellectual life and to a state of mind which finds the core categories of human existence in production and consumption. Romantic aestheticism promoted economic thinking.*[44]

Following this analysis, the evolution of the Wunderkammer to the blank framework of the museum seems quite logical. The rise of the "aesthetic domain" stresses the importance of the senses as the means by which we appreciate objects; it flattens any transcendental concern and makes a tabula rasa of the tradition of analogical thinking associated with the Wunderkammer.

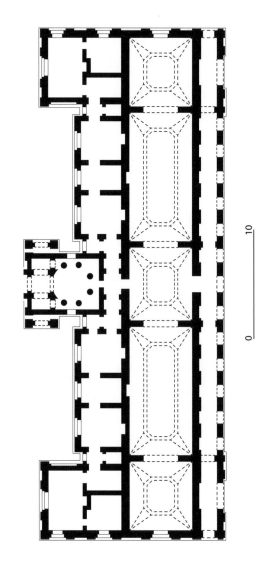

Sir John Soane, The Dulwich Picture Gallery, London.
Plan of the museum.

The architecture of the Dulwich Picture Gallery is a testimony to this transition. It rejects the classical orders and asks the visitor to simply perceive the space in an unprejudiced manner. Its "primitivism" is a device that wakes the senses of visitors and cleanses them of preconceived notions, making them more receptive to aesthetic impressions. It belongs resolutely to the "now": it is perhaps the first time that a building that declares itself *contemporary* is in clear opposition with the artworks it contains. On the other hand, the museum at Lincoln's Inn Fields asks the visitor to build experience-rich memory layer upon layer, to the point where it becomes impossible to *see* the Soane museum while you are immersed in its cosmos. Visiting does not mean taking notice of individual objects, but rather embarking on a journey within ourselves and *our* memories (in addition to Soane's). On the contrary, the neutral style of the Dulwich Picture Gallery aims to rid us of our previous "education" and open us to the pure, unmediated experience of art. Ironically, the unmediated experience contains a constellation of social constraints of a higher order, namely the

ABOVE   Perspective of the Soane House, 2015.
Drawing: Maria Shéhérazade Giudici.
BELOW   Perspective of the Dulwich Picture Gallery, 2015.
Drawing: Maria Shéhérazade Giudici.

not only for consumers in their everyday lives, but also for artists themselves as producers forced continually to seek the next big thing.

The museum as an institution is the offspring of this complicated condition, in which aestheticism and historicism helped trigger the development of a mature market economy. If the nineteenth century was the century of historicism and, as Germain Bazin said, the century of the invention of the museum[46] (and therefore history), we could also say that it was the century of the invention of memory as we conceive of it today. Interestingly enough, however, as the capacity to store and record life has become almost infinite, the issue of curating memory has become a widespread concern, from personal music playlists and social media to biennials and large museums. For this reason, the idiosyncrasies of Soane's house feel somewhat closer to our contemporary concerns than does the "progressive" agenda of the Dulwich Gallery. In fact, the resurgence of the Wunderkammer as an archetype applicable to today's digital sphere is widely accepted. In Soane's era, the "subject" of memory was the industrial worker, and its fabrication acted mainly as a civilizing tool, until its utility overstepped the boundary of production to influence consumption by triggering a renewed urge to consume. Today in the western world, the economy is based mainly on immaterial exchanges of knowledge and services. Workers no longer produce and consume goods; instead, they produce and consume ideas, social interactions, and cultural products. The museum as institution has to follow this shift just as it followed the previous one. It is no longer a place of memory and pedagogy, but an explicit instrument for the construction of our intellect, our ideas, and even our taste. In this sense, the ironic and perhaps pathetic culture of the "selfie," the torrent of snapshots that documents entire lives, is both nothing new (after all, on the Grand Tour, everybody had their portrait done) and something entirely unprecedented. The production of memory is no longer a matter of pure pleasure; it is a duty that contributes to the ultimate kind of production—of the self.

This return to the Wunderkammer is not without negative consequences: an emphasis on the individual has precluded the possibility for consensus or shared discourse. The dark side of this condition is the lack of a shared discourse, since the cabinet-of-curiosities model implies the impossibility of consensus and works, through the exacerbation of the individual. Interestingly, Rem Koolhaas attempted to tackle this issue in the 2014 Venice Biennale by returning to the "elements" of architecture itself, to questions that predate any discussion of style or even concept. The decision to use the biennial—perhaps the

ethos of a bourgeois society focused on economy as its main value. As the well-known adage goes:[45] in the age of biopolitics, more empowerment equals more exploitation. Institutions that are supposed to cater to the citizens are also mechanisms of control, perhaps none more explicit than the museum, which is the ultimate machine for the production of civilized subjects. The need to *have memories* becomes not only a strong push for the construction of a tamer citizen, but it unexpectedly builds a fetish of the new, which has its own accelerating impact on the culture of consumption. The constant search for the next step in historical narratives and the thrust toward finding new trends thus become totalizing conditions, most idiosyncratic, Wunderkammer-like format of the last few decades—is both striking and symptomatic. Unlike the museum, the biennial is a type of exhibition that gives a strongly characterized portrait of the moment through the biased manifesto-like lens of a curator. While biennials can be informative, they are not pedagogical vehicles per se. Koolhaas's exhibit, on the other hand, sought to be pedagogical in nature; the "elements" explored in the exhibition were discussed in terms of their historical development, in a method emblematic of the modern tradition that informed galleries, starting with Dulwich. Beyond the success or the failure of Koolhaas's attempt, perhaps most notable was its implicit perversion, or rejection, of the biennial as a Wunderkammer. Here the model is exploited to advance its opposite: an abstract framework for the reconstruction of a shared history and, perhaps, a possible common discourse. In this sense, Koolhaas's *Elements* could not but fail—heroically so—as it seems almost impossible to reconstruct such a framework in a decade that has seen the sudden and violent return of the fragmented Wunderkammer memory. This return is based on two key issues: first, the flattening of the idea of history and progress that has animated modern exhibition spaces from Soane to Koolhaas; and second, the fact that memory has been atomized to a level where the individual, rather than institutions, controls it. Both conditions are essentially premodern; the feeling of eternal present generated by having all of humankind's history at one's disposal equals the perpetual now possessed by peasants who lived the cyclical life of the fields, with no tomorrow and no yesterday. What still remains to be seen is how architecture will respond to this new shift in the social construction of memory.

While it is seductive to imagine a return to the Wunderkammer as a solution to our contemporary condition of curatorship, the 2014 Venice Biennale demonstrated that the architectural community regards this with a certain amount of unease. However, this apprehension predates the "eternal present" of social media and microcuratorial culture; it emerged with the demise of the white box in the 1990s and the rise of projects such as the aforementioned Guggenheim Bilbao. These projects refused to become mere backgrounds for objects, and in doing so, they not only lessened the value of the artifacts but also established themselves as "experiences" in their own right—as spectacle. They initiated a taste for narrative and anecdote through formal variations and bizarre circulation, just as the Soane museum had done two centuries earlier. The spectacle-museum forecasted a shift in the way we understand memory and experience that could only be accomplished in the next two decades as a result of the internet.

However, the two trends—the "narrative" museum and digital memory—should be seen as continuous rather than opposing: both further the same process of memory commodification that started in the nineteenth century. If one way to offer an alternative to the intellectual dispersion—and possibly exploitation—of the new Wunderkammern is to look for shareable categories, as Koolhaas tried to do in Venice, I would argue that we could also start by dismantling the two key categories that make these Wunderkammern possible: the idea that everything has to be remembered, and the concept that memory is both nonphysical and personal.

Not everything has to be remembered. In fact, forgetting has its virtues: not only does it allow new ideas to keep experiences fresh, but it also protects us—the citizens—and our lives from becoming infinitely and unendingly accessible.[47] As we have seen, there are many cases of architects trying to create an architecture of memory, but maybe there is no architecture for forgetting. If architecture cannot solve this issue of forgetting, then perhaps it can make it more explicit by taking care of all the structures that actually support and physically make possible our eternal present and our atomized landscape of personal curatorial projects. Because obviously, if we cannot forget, if we are allowed (or forced) to record in minute detail all the supposedly special details that make us who we are, it is only thanks to archives that are not immaterial at all. The archive is indeed one of the most important architectural types of today. Here is where another yet unexplored project for contemporary memory—and forgetting—could start: from the logistic center, the body of this unseen infrastructure. This is the place where, in a very material sense, our memories are still stored, the place where we as subjects and citizens are truly being shaped and constructed. After all, the truest expression of our increasing "originality" is an ultra-white box, or perhaps even a black box—the data center, its server quietly humming in a secluded location, a physical repository of a past that has become the inescapable present.

1. Michel Foucault, "Of Other Spaces," *Diacritics* 16 (Spring 1986): 26.

2. He was professor at the Royal Academy, architectural surveyor of the Bank of England, appointed at the Office of Works in 1791 and at the Office of Woods in 1797.

3. Although this invention lowered the price of paper, books remained a fairly expensive product throughout the century, as explained by Viktor Mayer-Schönberger in *Delete: The Virtue of Forgetting in the Digital Age* (Princeton, New Jersey: Princeton University Press, 2009), 40–41. On the other hand, the production and distribution of newspapers flourished around the same time.

4. Tony Bennett analyzes the democratization of access to the main British museum institution in *The Birth of the Museum: History, Theory, Politics* (London and New York: Routledge, 1995), 69–73. The British elite feared that unrestricted access to museums might prove dangerous for the safety of the artifacts; this attitude changed around the time of the opening of the South Kensington Museum (later the Victoria and Albert), in 1857. Sponsored by the board of education, it was the first institution targeted explicitly at the education of the masses.

5. "Architecture unshackled" is an expression that can be traced back to George Dance the Younger, the young Soane's employer and teacher and, later, friend. "We know Dance's innermost architectural thoughts only from the diarist Farington, who recorded a conversation with him in 1804 in which 'he derided the prejudice of limiting Design in Architecture within certain rules … [for] *Architecture unshackled* would Afford to the greatest genius the greatest opportunities of producing the most powerful efforts of the human mind,'" As reported by Jill Lever in her introduction to *Catalogue of the Drawings of George Dance the Younger (1741–1825) and of George Dance the Elder (1695–1768) from the collection of Sir John Soane's Museum* (London: Azimuth Editions, 2003).

6. Most notably Karl Friedrich Schinkel.

7. Extract from George Soane, "The present low state of the Arts in England, and more particularly architecture," *The Champion*, September 24, 1815. Reprinted in Ian Donnachie and Carmen Lavim, eds., *From Enlightenment to Romanticism: Anthology II* (Manchester: Manchester University Press, 2004), 195.

8. His interventions were not well received by the authorities; he had to argue his case in court to be allowed to change the facade. See James Gowan, *Style and Configuration* (London: Academy Editions, 1994), 55.

9. For a careful analysis of the conception of 13 Lincoln's Inn Fields, see Susan G. Feinberg, "The Genesis of Sir John Soane's Museum Idea: 1808–1810," *Journal of the Society of Architectural Historians* 43, no. 3 (1984): 225–37.

10. Acquired in 1824.

11. Feinberg, "Sir John Soane's Museum Idea," 235.

12. "The House and Museum of Sir John Soane," *Penny Magazine of the Society for the Diffusion of Useful Knowledge* 363, October 31–November 30, 1837, 458: "The house was a private house; *as a private house, it is intended to remain.*"

13. The transformation of Soane's private house into a public museum is discussed in detail by John Elsner in "A Collector's Model of Desire: The House and Museum of Sir John Soane," in *The Cultures of Collecting*, ed. John Elsner and Roger Cardinal (London: Reaktion Books, 1994), 157–59.

14. Feinberg, "Sir John Soane's Museum Idea," 225.

15. See Mieke Bal, "Telling Objects: A Narrative Perspective on Collecting," in *The Cultures of Collecting*, ed. John Elsner and Roger Cardinal (London: Reaktion Books, 1994), 101: "More often than not, chronology is mixed up in narrative."

16. "A large part of the justification for collections in the Renaissance was borrowed from medieval scholasticism, its ideas concerning the innate meaning of things and the nature of revelation,

and its vision of the relationship between microcosm and macrocosm." Anthony Alan Shelton, "Renaissance Collections and the New World," in ibid., 181.

17. "The existence of the whole that is a museum requires a great many things to be broken." Jonah Siegel, *The Emergence of the Modern Museum* (Oxford and New York: Oxford University Press, 2008), 4.

18. This condition has been challenged by made-for-museum art from about 1850 on, but it is still valid today for ancient art.

19. "There are also, probably in every culture, in every civilization, real places—places that do exist and that are formed in the very founding of society—which are something like counter-sites, a kind of effectively enacted utopia in which the real sites, all the other real sites that can be found within the culture, are simultaneously represented, contested, and inverted. Places of this kind are outside of all places." Michel Foucault, "Of Other Spaces," 22–27.

20. See Esa Itkonen, *Analogy as Structure and Process* (Philadelphia: John Benjamins, 2005).

21. Frances A. Yates, *The Art of Memory* (London: Routledge and Kegan Paul, 1966), 4.

22. Cicero says that for Simonides sight became the most important sense. See Yates, *The Art of Memory*, 4.

23. We refer here to "Renaissance Memory: The Memory Theatre of Giulio Camillo," in ibid., 129–59.

24. This narrative follows the standard logic of the Masonic initiation ritual as underlined in Donald Preziosi, "The Astrolabe of the Enlightenment," in *Brain of the Earth's Body: Art, Museums, and the Phantasms of Modernity* (Minneapolis: University of Minnesota Press, 2003), 89–90.

25. Pierre de la Ruffinière du Prey notices "the Portland stone façade, deliberately quasi-public in appearance." De la Ruffinière du Prey, *John Soane: The Making of an Architect* (Chicago and London: University of Chicago Press, 1982), xxi.

26. A detailed account of the making of 13 Lincoln's Inn Fields in relationship with Soane's private life can be found in Gillian Darley, *John Soane: An Accidental Romantic* (New Haven and London: Yale University Press, 1999), 208–15.

27. "The House and Museum of Sir John Soane," 458.

28. The pedagogical role attributed to architecture is readable in the importance Soane attributed to the Model Room, a collection of models that was moved several times in the attempt to find a fitting role for it in the overall narrative. Finally Soane decided to host it in the attic, where the visitor could also enjoy a view of the roofs of London.

29. In 1815, students of the Royal Academy were routinely admitted to study in the gallery. See *Repository of Fine Arts* 14 (1815): 340; and G.-Tilman Mellinghoff, "Soane's Dulwich Picture Gallery Revisited," in *John Soane*, ed. John Summerson, David Watkin, and G.-Tilman Mellinghoff (London: Academy Editions, 1983), 82.

30. "One of Soane's most individual buildings," as John Summerson wrote in *Sir John Soane* (London: Art and Technics, 1952), 34. Georges Teyssot wrote a sharp analysis of Soane's style, its origins, and its implications in "John Soane and the Birth of Style," *Oppositions* 14 (1978): 61–83.

31. Emil Kaufmann, *Three Revolutionary Architects: Boullée, Ledoux, Lequeu* (Philadelphia: American Philosophical Society, 1952), 474.

32. As Georges Teyssot wondered, "Is it not at the very moment that urban form becomes a 'matter of regularity and clarity […]' that the question of architectural style arises again?" See "John Soane and the Birth of Style," 65.

33. For instance, an illuminating essay on the public and the British Museum can be found in *Penny Magazine of the Society for the Diffusion of Useful Knowledge* 1 (1832), 13–14. Here the anonymous author scathingly quotes (and heavily criticizes) the following sentence taken from a

contemporary number of the *Quarterly Review*: "The characteristic of the English populace is their propensity to mischief. The people of most other countries may safely be admitted into parks, gardens, public buildings, and galleries of pictures and statues; but in England it is necessary to exclude them, as much as possible, from all such places."

34. "Repairing, improving, and beautifying" were the tasks imagined by Bourgeois in his will, in Edward Cook, ed., *Catalogue of the Pictures in the Gallery of Alleyn's College of God's Gift at Dulwich* (London: Darling and Son, 1914), 319.

35. "The museum and the department store […] were both formally open spaces allowing entry to the general public, and both were intended to function as spaces of emulation, places for mimetic practices whereby improving tastes, values and norms of conduct were to be more broadly diffused through society." Tony Bennett, *The Birth of the Museum: History, Theory, Politics* (London and New York: Routledge, 1995), 30.

36. "The roof unsham'd by slate or tile, / The brick with Portland dress'd, / The *stepless* door, the *scored* wall, / Pillars *sans* base or capital, / And curious antiques" read an ironic ode against Soane's Dulwich Gallery published in *Knight's Quarterly Magazine* in 1824, 461.

37. Soane warns his own students at the Royal Academy against the "prejudice of custom." See David Watkin, ed., *Sir John Soane: The Royal Academy Lectures* (Cambridge: Cambridge University Press, 2000), 160.

38. Giles Waterfield, "Dulwich Picture Gallery," in *John Soane Architect: Master of Space and Light*, ed. Margaret Richardson and Mary Anne Stevens (London: Royal Academy of Arts, 1999), 176.

39. Mellinghoff, "Soane's Dulwich Picture Gallery Revisited," 90.

40. Neil Harris, "Museums, Merchandising, and Popular Taste: The Struggle for Influence," in *Material Culture and the Study of American Life*, ed. I. M. G. Quimby (New York: W. W. Norton, 1978).

41. "History becomes the refuge of all the elements of society at variance with their own age, whose intellectual and material existence is threatened; and the refuge, above all, of the intelligentsia, which now feels disillusioned in its hopes and tricked out of its rights." Arnold Hauser, *The Social History of Art, Volume III: Rococo, Classicism, and Romanticism* (London and New York: Routledge, 2006), 162.

42. Although it is commonly referred to as the "Georgian" terrace, it is important to point out that the birth of the terrace predates the Georgian era.

43. Carl Schmitt, "The Age of Neutralizations and Depoliticizations," in *The Concept of the Political: Expanded Edition* (Chicago: University of Chicago Press, 2007), 80–96.

44. Ibid., 84.

45. Because we have to be willing to sell our labor power—and to buy goods—in order to be exploited by the market. Georg Simmel had already noted this dynamic in his 1903 text "The Metropolis and Mental Life," in *The Sociology of Georg Simmel* (New York: Free Press, 1950): "In addition to more liberty, the nineteenth century demanded the functional specialization of man and his work; this specialization makes one individual incomparable to another, and each of them indispensable to the highest possible extent. However, this specialization makes each man the more directly dependent upon the supplementary activities of all others."

46. Germain Bazin, *The Museum Age* (New York: Universe Books, 1967).

47. The "right to be forgotten" on Google was at the center of a groundbreaking legal case in 2014. See "EU court backs 'right to be forgotten,'" Guardian.com, accessed November 23, 2014, http://www.theguardian.com/technology/2014/may/13right-to-be-forgotten-eu-court-google-search-results.

The Ambiguity of Non-Finito Architecture: The Deceiving of Time

Marco Frascari

No redeeming architectural trends seem to surround abandoned constructions and building sites as they await futures that will never come. These building remains and construction relics are not ruins, because they were never actually completed; they are simply "unfinished buildings." In spite of their incompleteness, some of these neglected structures belong to an architectural *poiesis*, or making, that architectural historian and critic Bruno Zevi has labeled "the poetic of the non-finito."[1]

Originally, *non-finito* referred to a sculpting technique where the artist carves only a portion of the block, leaving the figure partially submerged within the original form of the material.[2] Applying this sculptural locution to architecture, we can similarly address those buildings that have been left, for any number of possible reasons, in an elegant but incomplete state by architects or builders. Although quite a large number of buildings are left uncompleted, the label "unfinished" is rarely attached to them by their occupants or by historians. The majority of individuals, in their quotidian association with these non-finito buildings, tolerate their incomplete presences without ever questioning the architecture's unfinished condition.

The Basilica di San Petronio, in the main square of Bologna, for instance, presents a facade that is an elegant example of the non-finito. The upper portion of the marble facade is clearly missing, yet if the occasional passerby were questioned about it, he would likely acknowledge the state of incompleteness with a certain degree of surprise, as if he had never noticed it before. The same is true for the extension of the **Duomo di Siena**, which was never completed. Its unique state of non-finito results in an odd urban parking space that is neither fully within nor without.

A

the survey made by Ottavio Bertotti Scamozzi, in his monumental opus devoted to Palladio's architecture.[3] This drawing shows the facade as a complete construction, but clearly visible on the right are stone tenons that suggest a planned continuation of the facade. Similar exercises of editing out irregularities to show completed buildings appear in many old drawings of Alberti's Palazzo Rucellai. Only in modern representations do we see the irregular edge of the stonework on the left side of the facade.

In 1964, when Bruno Zevi cocurated the exhibition *Michelangiolo Architetto*, he claimed that while the poetics of the non-finito had been subject to multiple interpretations within the domains of sculpture, its ramifications for architectural phenomenology had yet to be fully investigated:

None of Michelangelo's buildings were ever completed: the Laurentian library does not have the triangular-shaped space planned at the end of the reading room, and the Roman Palace of the Senate is missing a canopy. In addition, the design of the Campidoglio was distorted in the uniform cadences of lateral volumes; the massive building of the Farnese family was left without its rear facade and without its planned connection to the other side of the Tiber River. St. Peter's was split with an extension of an aisle that subverted its stereometric system. [...] No longer do I believe that those are fortuitous events. Instead, they are consequences of a specific creative attitude, a poetic mystery whose real motivation we can recover today.[4]

Many parts of the **Basilica di Sant'Andrea**, in Mantua, have similarly been left unfinished. The topmost part of the main facade remains bare, and the pronaos of the north transept is an incomplete replica of the one its architect, Leon Battista Alberti, built on the front of the cathedral. In fact, Alberti never finished many of his buildings—such as the Chiesa di San Sebastiano, in Mantua, the Tempio Malatestiano, in Rimini, and the Palazzo Rucellai, in Florence, to name a few. These incomplete buildings have sparked endless debates among architectural historians as to how Alberti was planning to complete them, and it is exactly their state of non-finito that makes them particularly provocative prompts for creative speculation.

The titleholder for the most instances of non-finito architecture, however, is Palladio. Countless are his unfinished palaces and villas, such as **Villa Porto**, in Molina di Malo, as well as **Palazzo Porto**, Palazzo del Capitanio, and **Casa Cogollo**, all in Vicenza. Each of these buildings is a clear example of the non-finito, though none have ever really been acknowledged as such. Such a blind spot demands that we take a closer look at the difference between merely incomplete, inelegant buildings and elegant non-finito architecture.

Palladio's **Casa Cogollo** is a small townhouse on Corso Palladio, the main urban axis of the city. The front of the house has always been accepted and presented as a complete facade by formal studies and analyses. The fundamental graphic reference is

Antoni Gaudì's **Sagrada Familia**, in Barcelona, embodies the same poetic mystery: an unfinished edifice that cannot be expressed simply as a work in progress, it exists at a deeper stage of an elegant process and derives its value from being incomplete.

The non-finito is interactive; it involves the visitor in the creation of mental images driven by cognitive completion. The essence of the building is there, yet its unfinished state allows a sense of infinite evolution for those contemplating it. Thus, these uncompleted buildings are ruins not of the past but of the future. The architectural non-finito is a process rather than a state, immersed in the eternal Heraclitean *panta rhei*. Many of these non-finito edifices were not hastily left unfinished but were brought to and left at a certain state of completion. Therefore, the temporality of non-finito buildings is different; they do not belong to the building-in-time stipulation that dominates the modern era of construction. Non-finito architecture is not ruled by pecuniary processes based on dates of completion and punch lists; it belongs, instead, to a process of building-outside-time.

When construction stops, many buildings built within the financial constraints of contemporary market requirements, and within the artificial time advances of contemporary technology, become just incomplete artifacts for which time has run out. But the time frame governing the non-finito simply pauses when construction stops. For non-finito architecture, temporality is no longer just a neutral or secondary factor; it is an epistemic condition that implicitly affects our experience of the built environment. Through subjectivity, change, and selection, our architectural understanding of the non-finito becomes a fluid, imbricate process in which time plays a central role.

Non-finito edifices were intentionally left in suspended, ambivalent formal and temporal states because the ambiguity of the non-finito is essential. It must be unfinished enough to offer several solutions, all of equal validity, as to how the structure might be completed. There is no right answer to the architectural puzzle offered by non-finito edifices. This ambiguity is the architectural sleight of mind that redirects your attention, temporarily altering reality, to make a building eternally provocative. Thus, an elegantly incomplete edifice takes on a life of its own—one with real staying power. The simple yet thoughtful construction of what is there gives the missing pieces their surprising power, as absence becomes just as important as presence. Completeness in the built realization becomes unnecessary since the non-finito relies on the tantalizing power of suggestion generated by what is not yet there.

Notes

1   Bruno Zevi, *Saper Vedere L'architettura* (Turin: Einaudi, 1964), 163.

2   The technique was pioneered by Donatello and popularized by Michelangelo's uncompleted sculptures.

3   Ottavio Bertotti Scamozzi, *Le Fabbriche e i Disegni di Andrea Palladio, Raccolti ed Illustrati da Ottavio Bertotti Scamozzi* (Vicenza: Alec Tiranti, 1968).

4   Bruno Zevi, "Mostra su Michelangiolo Architetto," accessed June 25, 2011, http://www.fondazionebrunozevi. it/19551964/frame3/pagine3/mostrami-chelangiolo.htm.

In Memoriam: Marco Frascari, 1945–2013.

Images

A   Basilica di San Petronio, Bologna.
B   Chiesa di San Sebastiano, Mantua.
C   Tempio Malatestiano, Rimini.
D   Palazzo del Capitanio, Vicenza.

They Too Were Silent

Kyle Dugdale

In the opening pages of his monumental *Spheres* trilogy, Peter Sloterdijk suggests that modernity's characteristic disorientation is accompanied by a form of "willful ignorance."[1] In this he is building on a text by Friedrich Nietzsche, in which he, too, writes of modernity's disorientation. Sloterdijk's "willful ignorance" corresponds to a condition that psychiatry might today describe as a form of "dissociative amnesia." For if Sloterdijk does not immediately address the pathology of this disorder, a reading of Sloterdijk's assessment alongside Nietzsche's text would suggest that modernity's amnesia is in fact a response to a violent trauma: a trauma associated with memories of wiping blood from knives, that leaves the guilty party searching for adequate means of atonement. This diagnosis may usefully be compared to that offered by the psychiatrists, who note that the primary cause of amnesia is trauma, and who observe that, in its extreme forms, the disorder is accompanied by "perplexity, disorientation, and purposeless wandering."[2] But in this instance, the act of violence also concerns the architect; for if, in the absence of atonement, amnesia offers an alternative means of dismissing the trauma, the discipline of architecture is nonetheless left to deal with the side-effects of a lingering disorientation that cannot be fully dispelled.

Sloterdijk's statement introduces a text that is presented as a "late-twentieth-century bookend" to the work of Martin Heidegger,[3] claiming to supplement "Heidegger's existential analytics of time" with a corresponding and overlooked analytics of space prescribed as medication for "the existential blindness to space in conventional thought."[4] Indeed, it is clear that modernity's disorientation is by definition a spatial problem, perhaps even an architectural problem. It would not be remarkable to suggest that modernity's architecture reveals symptoms of that disorientation; some architects would doubtless argue that contemporary practice is disoriented as never before. But if that lack of orientation is to be understood, in some regard, as a disorder, it is also related to more elusive conditions, less readily diagnosed but evidently just as painful: to the alienation of the individual within the modern city, to the transience of modernity's historical situation, or perhaps, more broadly still, to the transcendental homelessness of the human condition. Such language, too, is familiar to today's architect, who has learned to be suspicious of any architectural assertion that seems too secure in its occupation of space.[5] Indeed, Sloterdijk's own analysis turns frequently to architecture, as a mere glance at his illustrations will indicate. But what, then, is this "willful ignorance" of which he writes? And what is the implied relationship between disorientation and amnesia?

Sloterdijk's diagnosis is offered within the context of a discussion of a familiar passage from Nietzsche's 1887 *Gay Science*—the section that begins with the words "The madman." It is a narrative elaboration of what he describes elsewhere as "the greatest recent event—that 'God is dead'; that the belief in the Christian God has become unbelievable."[6] In his account Nietzsche not only points to human complicity in the death of God, he also draws the connection to the disorientation of modernity. "Where is God?" cries the madman:

I'll tell you! *We have killed him*—you and I! We are all his murderers. But how did we do this? How were we able to drink up the sea? Who gave us the sponge to wipe away the entire horizon? What were we doing when we unchained this earth from its sun? Where is it moving to now? Where are we moving to? [...] Aren't we straying as though through an infinite nothing? Isn't empty space breathing at us? [...] God is dead! God remains dead! And we have killed him! How can we console ourselves, the murderers of all murderers! [...] Who will wipe this blood from us? With what water could we clean ourselves? What festivals of atonement, what holy games will we have to invent for ourselves? Is the magnitude of this deed not too great for us? Do we not ourselves have to become gods merely to appear worthy of it?[7]

This is the very passage that Heidegger would subject to critical exegesis in his essay "The Word of Nietzsche: 'God Is Dead,'" first published in 1950 but composed some years earlier.[8] And if Heidegger's commentary may seem, to many, to do more to broaden than to sharpen the focus of Nietzsche's text, he too writes of disorientation. "If God as the suprasensory ground and goal of all reality is dead, [...] then nothing more remains to which man can cling and by which he can orient himself."[9] In a newly godless world, deprived of prior hopes of metaphysical security, humanity finds itself reliant on its own ingenuity to articulate an otherwise featureless void.

Heidegger in turn ties Nietzsche's text back to G.W.F. Hegel's 1802 *Faith and Knowledge*, an essay that itself attempts to come to terms with society's multidimensional alienations—the believer's alienation from the gods, man's alienation from nature, and the individual's alienation from the community.[10] In his effort to address this existential disorientation Hegel turns, of course, to philosophy. But to read Nietzsche, Heidegger, and Sloterdijk with an eye to architecture is to come to terms with the spatial and architectural implications of Nietzsche's "infinite nothing" and of Sloterdijk's "yawning abyss"[11]—that cold and empty space that assumes the place of an absent God. Indeed, architecture, for all its purported physicality, is unquestionably among the disciplines that attempt to fill the metaphysical void. As Heidegger insists, "the empty place demands to be occupied anew and to have the god now vanished from it replaced by something else."[12] Into that space, he suggests, step other ideals: the authority of reason, a faith in historical progress, a commitment to earthly happiness, an enthusiasm for a culture possessed of sufficient power to shape mortal existence. These ideals are certainly familiar to the historian of modernity's architecture. More broadly, if more tentatively, it might be imagined that in a world lacking in metaphysical goods the value of architecture should be expected to rise. For it can readily be observed that once promises of goods "beyond this world" have been removed from circulation, equivalent demands will instead be made of more worldly goods. And among these are the products of architecture. In a universe stripped of other opportunities for transcendence, security, permanence, and redemption, architecture takes on a new significance.

But the architectural implications run deeper still, for the prime protagonist in this re-occupation of vacant space is none other than the human *creator*. "Creativity, previously the unique property of the biblical god, becomes the distinctive mark of human activity."[13] The role of the architect, that is, takes on a new authority. As Nietzsche notes of *the greatest recent event*, "Do we not ourselves have to become gods merely to appear worthy of it?" The figure of God as architect (*deus architectus mundi*) is replaced by something resembling the figure of the architect as God, with the world itself understood as the ultimate work of art–*Gesamtkunstwerk Erde*–and the task of architecture understood to extend far beyond the construction of buildings.[14] After the death of God, the world must create for itself new values; and that process of creation is, fundamentally, an artistic act, an aesthetic praxis. After all, the term *architectus secundus deus* can be interpreted in more than one direction: both as a pious confession of the architect's subordination to a creator God, and as an assertion, less pious, of the architect's newly independent status in a world deprived of superior creative authorities. But there are more troubling associations too. Heidegger's essay, developed in lectures delivered between 1936 and 1943, speaks also of the assertion of power. Such assertion must be read against the background of a period in history when Germany's temporal leader could be proclaimed, without any sense of irony, as the supreme architect of the Third Reich. "Man finds himself [...] set before the task of taking over the dominion of the earth."[15] And yet, in a different but not unrelated sense, this is also a feature of modernity more broadly, an age marked by "the struggle for mastery of the earth."[16]

It is a struggle closely comparable to that of which Nikolaus Pevsner would write in 1936, when arguing that the architecture of modernity must be contrasted with that of an earlier, more pious age, the age of the Gothic cathedral, an age that was focused on otherworldly speculation. "In the thirteenth century," he argues, "all lines,

Lyonel Feininger, *Architecture of a new faith*, 1919. Cover illustration to Walter Gropius, *Bauhaus Manifesto*, 1919.

functional though they were, served the one artistic purpose of pointing heavenwards to a goal beyond this world." But the new architecture, he insists, glorifies the "creative energy" of a new world that "we want to master, a world of science and technique, of speed and danger, of hard struggles and no personal security."[17] Pevsner's lines point to the architecture of Walter Gropius as a paradigm for such an approach; and they, too, were written in 1936, at a moment when that new world's appetite for speed and danger would soon be fully indulged in the struggle for mastery.

Pevsner's text does not refer directly to the death of God. But there had been moments in prior years when architects were acutely conscious of that event. One of these moments coincided, perhaps predictably, with the birth of architectural modernism. Oskar Schlemmer's manifesto of 1923, composed to accompany the first Bauhaus exhibition in Weimar, is an artifact closely comparable to Gropius's more familiar Bauhaus manifesto of 1919. It is worth remembering that the image chosen for the cover of Gropius's declaration was Lyonel Feininger's woodcut of a new cathedral, conceived in anticipation of "the new structure of the future" that would one day rise toward heaven "like the crystal symbol of a new faith."[18] Gropius's rising tower, like Feininger's, is a surrogate cathedral, the architectural embodiment of a new faith that is designed to replace an obsolete order. In its energetic verticality, it offers a new point of reference, a new landmark that will dispel modernity's disorientation. It is a monument best appreciated, perhaps, in the light of the death of God.

But if Gropius's manifesto has survived as a monument of modernist aspiration, Schlemmer's manifesto proved short-lived. For it was promptly deemed too dangerous for circulation. Its most offensive sentence, often tied to the image of Feininger's earlier woodcut, is typically assumed to be the following:

> The Staatliche Bauhaus, founded after the catastrophe of the war, in the chaos of the revolution and in the era of the flowering of an emotion-laden, explosive art, becomes the rallying point of all those who, with belief in the future and with heaven-storming enthusiasm, wish to build the cathedral of Socialism.[19]

But Schlemmer continues, making it clear that the motivation for the construction of this new heaven-storming cathedral is tied to the perception of a spiritual void:

> The triumphs of industry and technology before the war and the orgies in the name of destruction during it, called to life that impassioned romanticism that was a flaming protest against materialism and the mechanization of art and life. The misery of the time was also a spiritual anguish. A cult of the unconscious and of the unexplainable, a propensity for mysticism and sectarianism originated in the quest for those highest things which are in danger of being deprived of their meaning in a world full of doubt and disruption.[20]

The words are thickly assembled into a closely printed block of accumulated significance, marshaled into a rigorous geometric order as if to counteract the palpable disorientation of the historical context. And there is more, rising in a veritable paroxysm of undeveloped aphorisms and Goethean references. *Die Baukunst türmt Utopien auf Papier* [...] "Architecture piled Utopian schemes on paper. Reversal of values, changes in point of view, name, and concept result in the other view, the next faith. [...] Reason and science, 'man's greatest powers,' are the regents. [...] Calculation seizes the

transcendent world."[21] *Reversal of values*: already Nietzsche's voice can be heard. And where do such pronouncements lead? They culminate in a brief, bald statement that dismisses one authority while neatly substituting the rational faculties of another:

> Religion is the precise process of thinking, and God is dead.[22]

There is little space provided in which to flesh out the implications of those last three words, inserted casually into the running text. God is dead [...] I AM WHO I AM is no longer; God's eternal will is obsolete, the creator of the universe no longer active. But again, Nietzsche's word seems apt: "God is dead! God remains dead! And we have killed him! [...] Is the magnitude of this deed not too great for us? Do we not ourselves have to become gods merely to appear worthy of it?"[23] Schlemmer seems conscious of the gravity of this condition, noting that "Germany, country of the middle, and Weimar, the heart of it, is not for the first time the adopted place of intellectual decision. What matters is the recognition of what is pertinent to us, so that we will not aimlessly wander astray. [...] Thus we become the bearers of responsibility and the conscience of the world."[24] This is a heavy responsibility—and one that the architect might, with good reason, be reluctant to assume. But as if in response, at the foot of Schlemmer's page, the reader finds an exclamatory declaration of self-assertion, printed in widely spaced capital letters:

WE ARE! WE WILL! AND WE CREATE![25]

Schlemmer's text is less familiar today than Gropius's manifesto. For if Feininger's woodcut left room for ambiguity, Schlemmer's manifesto, which appealed to the "creative forces" of the arts, was immediately recognized as being overly explicit. Intended as part of another four-page pamphlet, but printed before it had received Gropius's approval, it was rapidly withdrawn from circulation, and most copies were destroyed.[26] The death of God was to be neatly excised from this portion of modernism's

DAS STAATLIC

ist die erste und bisher einzige staatliche Schule des Reichs —
Kunst aufruft zu wirken während sie lebendig sind und zugleich m
Verbindung und fruchtbare Durchdringung erstrebt mit dem Ziel
wiederbringen, die in einem versackten Akademikertum und eine
ziehung aufs Ganze wiederherstellen und in einem höchsten Sinn
jedoch immer wieder neu; die Erfüllung ist der Stil und nie war
Geister und Begriffe macht, dass Kampf und Streit um sein We
wird als die neue Schönheit. — Eine solche Schule, bewegend
schütterungen des politischen und geistigen Lebens der Zeit und

D. Staatliche Bauhaus, gegründet nach der Katastrophe des Kriegs, im Chaos der R
Kunst, wird zunächst zum Sammelpunkt derer, die zukunftsgläubig-himmelstürmend die
und Technik vor dem Krieg und deren Orgie im Zeichen der Vernichtung währenddess
war gegen Materialismus und Mechanisierung von Kunst und Leben. Die Not der Zeit
ein Hang zu Mystik und Sektiererei entsprang dem Suchen nach den letzten Dingen,
zu werden drohten. Der Durchbruch der Bezirke klassischer Ästhetik verstärkte die Grenz
der Neger, Bauern, Kinder und Irren Nahrung oder Bestätigung fand. Der Ursprung k
erweitert. Eine Inbrunst der Ausdrucksmittel entstand wie auf den Bildern der Altäre. Do
vollen Werte flüchten. Als Höchstleistungen individueller Übersteigerung, fessellos und u
heit des Bildes selbst, alles schuldig bleiben. — Das biedere Handwerk tummelt sich

Die Umkehrung der Werte, Wechsel von Standpunkt, Name und B
Ball mit Paradoxen und macht die Atmosphäre frei und leicht. A
dem Mondschein und der Seele, so schreitet mit Eroberergeste
die Regenten und der Ingenieur ist der gelassene Vollstrecker der
und Macht und Geld die Diktatoren der modernen Phänomen
der Materie, Organisation des Unorganischen erzeugen Wunder
der Natur, gegründet auf die Macht des Kapitals ein Werk des M
Nutzen zum Maßstab aller Wirkung und die Berechnung ergreift
ein Leben nach dem Tode, im Monument des Würfels und im Farbqu
und Vollkommene, von jeder Puppe an Exaktheit übertroffen, ha

ethe: „Wenn die Hoffnungen sich verwirklichen, dass die Menschen
vereinigen und voneinander Kenntnis nehmen, so wird sich ereignen,
schaffen, wir erschaffen seine Welt." Es ist die Synthese, die Zusamme
idee der Mitte, fern von Halbheit und Schwäche, verstanden als Wage
der Mitte, und Weimar, Herz in diesem, ist nicht zum ersten Mal Wahls
mäss ist, um uns nicht ziellos zu verlieren. Im Ausgleich der polaren G
Anarchismus abgewandt; vom Selbstzweck, Einzel-Ich im Anmarsch au
wir zu Trägern der Verantwortung und zum Gewissen der Welt. Ein Ideal
dringt und einigt und der in Forschung — Lehre — Arbeit wirkt, wird
Gleichnis ist. Wir können heute nicht mehr tun, als den Plan des G
W I R   S I N D !   W I R   W O L L E

I N   W E

...HE BAUHAUS

...nn nicht der Welt — welche die schöpferischen Kräfte bildender
...r Errichtung von Werkstätten auf handwerklicher Grundlage deren
... Vereinigung im Bau. Der Baugedanke soll die verlorene Einheit
...erbosselten Kunstgewerbe zugrunde ging; er soll die grosse Be-
...s Gesamtkunstwerk ermöglichen. Das Ideal ist alt, seine Fassung
... Wille zum Stil mächtiger als eben heute. Aber die Verwirrung der
... ist, das aus dem Zusammenprall der Ideen heraus sich bilden
... in sich selbst bewegt, wird ungewollt zum Gradmesser der Er-
...eschichte des Bauhauses wird zur Geschichte gegenwärtiger Kunst.

...tion und zur Zeit der Hochblüte einer gefühlgeladenen explosiven
...edrale des Sozialismus bauen wollen. Die Triumphe von Industrie
...efen jene leidenschaftliche Romantik wach, die flammender Protest
...uch die Not der Geister. Ein Kult des Unbewussten, Undeutbaren,
... einer Welt voll Zweifel und Zerrissenheit um ihren Sinn gebracht
...igkeit des Fühlens, die in der Entdeckung des Ostens und der Künste
...rischen Schaffens wurde ebenso gesucht wie seine Grenzen kühn
...der und immer wieder Bilder sind es, in die sich die entscheidungs-
...t zugleich, mussten sie der proklamierten Synthese, ausser der Ein-
...tischer Lust am Stoffe und die Baukunst türmt Utopien auf Papier.

...ergibt das Gegenbild, den nächsten Glauben. Dada, Hofnarr in diesem Reiche, spielt
...anismus auf Europa übertragen, die neue in die alte Welt gekeilt, Tod der Vergangenheit,
...egenwart einher. Vernunft und Wissenschaft „des Menschen allerhöchste Kraft" sind
...egrenzten Möglichkeiten. Mathematik, Konstruktion und Mechanismus sind die Elemente
...s Eisen, Beton, Glas, Elektrizität. Geschwindigkeit des Starren, Entmaterialisierung
...ostraktion. Gegründet auf Naturgesetze sind sie das Werk des Geistes zur Bezwingung
...en gegen Menschen. Tempo und Hochspannung des Merkantilen machen Zweck und
...anszendente Welt: die Kunst ein Logarithmus. Sie, ihres Namens längst beraubt, lebt
...t. Religion ist der präzise Denkprozess und Gott ist tot. Der Mensch, der Selbstbewusste
...f die Resultate der Retorten, bis sich die Formel auch für „Geist" gefunden . . . .

... mit allen ihren Kräften, mit Herz und Geist, mit Verstand und Liebe sich
...an jetzt noch kein Mensch denken kann — Allah braucht nicht me...r zu
...sung, Steigerung und Verdichtung alles Positiven zur starken Mitte. Die
... Gleichgewicht wird zur Idee der deutschen Kunst. Deutschland, Land
...geistiger Entscheidung. Es geht um die Erkenntnis dessen, was uns ge-
...sätze; fernste Vergangenheit wie fernste Zukunft liebend; Reaktion wie
... Typische, vom Problematischen zum Gültigen und Festen — so werden
...s der Aktivität, der Kunst und Wissenschaft und Technik umfasst, durch-
...Kunst-Bau des Menschen aufführen, der zu dem Weltgebäude nur ein
...n zu bedenken, Grund zu legen und die Bausteine zu bereiten. Aber
...! U N D W I R S C H A F F E N !

...I M A R

Oskar Schlemmer, "The other view, the next faith" a retracted manifesto published in conjunction with the first Bauhaus exhibition in Weimar, 1923.

documentary history. And yet a handful of copies had already reached the school's critics, strengthening prior convictions that the Bauhaus was ideologically dangerous. Ten years later, similar accusations would prompt the school's closure under the Nazi regime. Today a copy of Schlemmer's manifesto is held by Yale's Beinecke Rare Book & Manuscript Library, listed among the contents of the Eisenman Collection; but for some time it too has been inaccessible to readers, temporarily unavailable—as if the death of God were after all best forgotten.

Sloterdijk refers to Heidegger, who draws on Nietzsche, who turns to Hegel. All speak of disorientation, and all speak of the death of God. And Sloterdijk, Heidegger, and Hegel all refer back to different passages in Blaise Pascal's *Pensées*. Pascal, too, acknowledges the terror of infinite space (*Pensées* 205), and he in turn refers back to Plutarch's extraordinary account in *De defectu oraculorum* of the death of Pan, the Greek god (*Pensées* 695).[27] Sloterdijk, Heidegger, Nietzsche, Hegel, Pascal, Plutarch: it is a remarkable genealogy of thoughts and thinkers. But it is left to others to insist that the concept of the death of God is already present, albeit in a different sense, in the very Christian belief that Nietzsche describes as having become unbelievable. There too it provokes incredulity; and there too it is embedded in a narrative that is consistently elaborated in architectural figures. In the biblical account the first appearances of architecture are, precisely, reactions to the terror of open space. If the fig leaves of Genesis 3 can be understood to perform a proto-architectural function, as a provisional response to an unsettling consciousness of exposure, and if Adam's presumed primitive hut is typically imagined as a response, equally provisional, to the boundless space outside Eden, rendered hostile by the alienation of nature, by the "thorns and thistles" of Genesis 3:18, it is in the figure of Cain's archetypal city in Genesis 4 ("and he built a city, and named it Enoch"[28]) that architecture emerges with full insistence. And it emerges precisely as a response to a violent trauma that leaves the guilty party searching for adequate means of atonement.

For his representative act of fratricide Cain is condemned to being "a fugitive and a wanderer on the earth," exacerbating his existing alienation from Eden.[29] If Adam and Eve are in a sense already homeless, expelled for their sin from the presence of God, Cain's sin renders him doubly homeless. The narrative of Genesis 4 reinforces this point: "Then Cain went away from the presence of the Lord, and settled in the land of Nod, east of Eden."[30] Biblical commentaries annotate the name Nod with the words "location unknown," while noting its relationship, in Hebrew, to the term for "wandering." And just as it is clear that the opening chapters of Genesis deal with humanity as a universal condition, with Adam—whose name in Hebrew means "man"—standing as a type for humanity, so a similar logic applies to Cain, perpetrator and projected victim of reciprocal violence. It is as if Cain's experience describes a permanent condition, the permanent alienation of man living apart from God. To Adam and Eve's alienation is added a further, social alienation—one that prompts, as the reader of Genesis soon discovers, a turn to architecture. And thus the opening of Genesis anticipates the full range of Hegel's multidimensional alienations: alienation from the gods, alienation from nature, and alienation from the community.

The account of Cain's city leads on to further architectures—most immediately, perhaps, to that of Babel, of which a hint is offered in the genealogy at the very end of Genesis 4. That in turn is part of a longer genealogical trajectory. For the same narrative leads on to other architectural figures: to the ark, the tabernacle, and the temple in Jerusalem, City of Peace—architectures reportedly built according to the specifications not of the human but of the divine creator, architectures that anticipate a more permanent resolution of humanity's alienation. And within Christian doctrine the account can be continued through the New Testament, past the great event of the death of God, itself tied to earlier architectural motifs, and on to the very end of Scripture, where Paradise is itself described as a city: the New Jerusalem, a city shaped both by the presence of God and by the absence of violence.

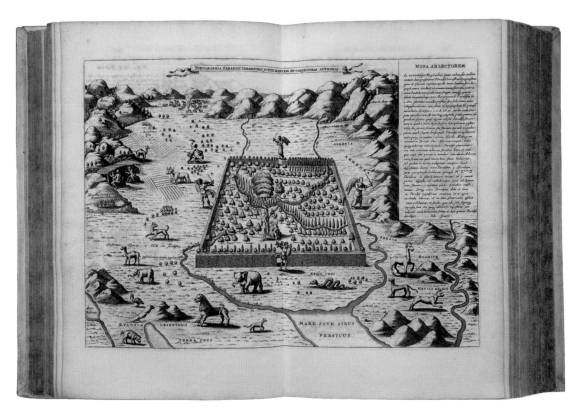

Anthanasius Kircher, "Topographia Paradisi terrestris," *Arca Noë* (Amsterdam: 1675). Alienation, violence, and architecture: in the center, a walled Eden; at left, Adam and Eve's primitive hut; to its right, Cain's act of fratricide, and below it, Cain's city; at upper right, the redemptive architecture of Noah's ark.

This is doubtless, to contemporary ears, a strange account. The very suggestion that the narrative of redemption might be inscribed in architectural figures is disconcerting. It did not always sound so strange, and the histories of architecture—even of the Bauhaus era—echo with its memories. After all, the very "heaven-storming enthusiasm" of Schlemmer's manifesto recalls not only the story of Prometheus but also the account of Babel. But in the context of modernity such accounts have become increasingly unbelievable, and increasingly forgotten. More familiar are the various attempts made by the architects of modernity to respond to the demands of Gropius, of Schlemmer, or of Pevsner. Those manifestos, those statements of belief, have themselves grown less believable over the intervening years; so subsequent histories must trace new efforts to identify viable replacements. What remains stubbornly predictable is the attempt to deny Schlemmer's "world full of doubt and disruption," to mitigate that characteristic disorientation, to banish the alienation that has preoccupied architecture since the opening chapters of Genesis. For if modernity has exacerbated the disorientation and intensified the alienation, it has also provoked equal and opposite attempts to offer architectural responses: responses that present themselves as nothing other than provisional coping mechanisms, as traces of a collective amnesia that can never succeed in resolving the underlying disorder.

If it is true that the task of the architect in a modern world can be held to differ from that of the architect in a pre-modern world, it is also true that the status of the architect in a universe that is godless is distinct from that of the architect who must practice in subordination to an eternal creator. Architecture after the death of God is an endeavor radically different to that which went before. And yet this is hardly a well-recognized fact. As a discipline architecture has largely failed to confront the death of God, and most schools of architectural thought do not go out of their way to train their students to discriminate between the competing claims of such esoteric debates, instead focusing their creative energies on more tangible material constructions. And so the field of such architectural discrimination remains, in many respects, unfamiliar territory, echoing with a resounding stillness. One might argue as to whether this answers to the "willful ignorance" of a culture that refuses to confront the terror of empty space, preferring instead, as Sloterdijk suggests, to "drown the questions of Nietzsche's chief witness" in the material comforts of modernity—to which architecture itself may be expected to contribute.[31] Is this not, after all, a mere rehearsal of the disconcerted silence that greeted Nietzsche's madman? Approaching its conclusion, the narrative hesitates:

The madman fell silent and looked again at his listeners; they too were silent and looked at him disconcertedly. Finally he threw his lantern on the ground so that it broke into pieces and went out. "I come too early," he then said; "my time is not yet. This tremendous event is still on its way, wandering; it has not yet reached the ears of men."[32]

I am indebted to others for reactions and amendments to this essay: to Karsten Harries, Karla Britton, Eric Dugdale, and my colleagues Surry Schlabs and Justin Hawkins. The remaining infelicities, unfortunately, are all mine.

1 Peter Sloterdijk, *Spheres*, vol. 1, *Bubbles: Microspherology*, trans. Wieland Hoban (Los Angeles: Semiotext(e), 2011), 27.

2 American Psychiatric Association, *Diagnostic and Statistical Manual of Mental Disorders*, 5th ed. (Arlington, VA: American Psychiatric Association, 2013), s.v. "Dissociative Amnesia." This is the standard psychiatric diagnostic reference.

3 "*Bubbles*: *Spheres* Volume I," *Semiotext(e)*, accessed June 11, 2012, http://semiotexte.com/?p=1025.

4 See the programmatic excursus on "Heidegger's Doctrine of Existential Place" in Sloterdijk, *Spheres*, 1:333–42, here quoting 333 and 338.

5 For an examination of the gradual exacerbation of modernity's estrangement, a disorder marked by symptoms that are both spatial and temporal, "leading to historical amnesia," see the introduction to Anthony Vidler, *The Architectural Uncanny: Essays in the Modern Unhomely* (Cambridge, Massachusetts: MIT Press, 1992), 3–14. Opening with the "fundamental insecurity" of a people "not quite at home in its own home," Vidler ties his narrative to the assessment by Heidegger, among others, of "the (lost) nature of 'dwelling'" under the conditions of modernity, concluding that "estrangement and unhomeliness have emerged as the intellectual watchwords of our century."

6 Friedrich Nietzsche, *The Gay Science*, ed. Bernard Williams, trans. Josefine Nauckhoff (Cambridge: Cambridge University Press, 2001), 199.

7 Nietzsche, *Gay Science*, 119–20.

8 Martin Heidegger, "The Word of Nietzsche: 'God Is Dead,'" in *The Question Concerning Technology and Other Essays*, trans. William Lovitt (New York: Harper Perennial, 1977), 53–114; for Heidegger's comments on dating, see the translator's preface.

9 Heidegger, "Word of Nietzsche," 61.

10 See Walter Cerf, "Speculative Philosophy and Intellectual Intuition: An Introduction to Hegel's *Essays*," in Georg Wilhelm Friedrich Hegel, *Faith and Knowledge*, trans. Walter Cerf and H. S. Harris (Albany, New York: State University of New York Press, 1977), xi–xxxvi.

11 Sloterdijk, *Spheres*, 1:26.

12 Heidegger, "Word of Nietzsche," 69.

13 Heidegger, "Word of Nietzsche," 64.

14 For the world as a work of art see, for instance, the quotation from Nietzsche in Heidegger, "Word of Nietzsche," 85.

15 Heidegger, "Word of Nietzsche," 96–97.

16 Heidegger, "Word of Nietzsche," 92.

17 Nikolaus Pevsner, *Pioneers of the Modern Movement: From William Morris to Walter Gropius* (London: Faber and Faber, 1936), 207.

18 Walter Gropius, "Programme of the Staatliches Bauhaus in Weimar," trans. Wolfgang Jabs and Basil Gilbert, in *Programs and Manifestoes on 20th-Century Architecture*, ed. Ulrich Conrads (Cambridge, Massachusetts: MIT Press, 1970), 49.

19 Oskar Schlemmer, "The Staatliche Bauhaus in Weimar," translated in Hans M. Wingler, *The Bauhaus: Weimar Dessau Berlin Chicago*, trans. Wolfgang Jabs and Basil Gilbert, ed. Joseph Stein (Cambridge, Massachusetts: MIT Press, 1969), 65. I have omitted the inverted commas added by the translators around the term "cathedral of Socialism," as they are absent in the German. I have also adjusted the translation to read "heaven-storming" in lieu of "sky-storming," better reflecting the Promethean significance of the German *himmelstürmend*. For the German text see Oskar Schlemmer, "Die erste Bauhaus-Ausstellung in Weimar Juli bis September 1923," transcribed in *Das Staatliche Bauhaus in Weimar: Dokumente zur Geschichte des Instituts 1919–1926*, ed. Volker Wahl (Cologne: Böhlau Verlag, 2009), 297–98.

20 Schlemmer, "Staatliche Bauhaus in Weimar," 65.

21 Schlemmer, "Staatliche Bauhaus in Weimar," 65–66.

22 Schlemmer, "Staatliche Bauhaus in Weimar," 66. For a discussion of the figure of the cathedral in light of the recognition that "Schlemmer's new faith is a humanist one that presupposes the death of God," see Karsten Harries, *The Ethical Function of Architecture* (Cambridge, Massachusetts: MIT Press, 1997), 335.

23 Nietzsche, *Gay Science*, 120.

24 Schlemmer, "Staatliche Bauhaus in Weimar," 66.

25 Schlemmer, "Die erste Bauhaus-Ausstellung," 298; my translation. The standard rendition into English fails to communicate the biblical weight of "Wir sind!" and the Nietzschean weight of "Wir schaffen!" in the expression "Wir sind! Wir wollen! Und wir schaffen!"

26 For more on this story, see for instance Karen Koehler, "The Bauhaus Manifesto Postwar to Postwar," in *Bauhaus Construct*, ed. Jeffrey Saletnik and Robin Schuldenfrei (London: Routledge, 2009), 13–36.

27 In a further twist, Pan's death was once commonly associated (to the ridicule of subsequent critics) with the life of Christ, the end of one era thus coincident with the start of another.

28 Genesis 4:17 (NRSV).

29 Genesis 4:12 (NRSV).

30 Genesis 4:16 (NRSV).

31 Sloterdijk, *Spheres*, 1:27.

32 Nietzsche, *Gay Science*, 120.

Crossing front lines in eastern Congo is tense but usually quiet. The interface between enclaves sees a trickle of silent civilians carrying vegetables on market day. Or in more active conflict areas, displaced populations carry their lives on their shoulders, their women laden with children. A villager's acid glance at a rebel sentry speaks volumes. Communities are severed; infrastructures end. Sometimes you have to walk for twenty minutes through no man's land, down a muddy path past ambush foxholes, abandoned huts, or entire villages in a state of being reclaimed by the jungle.

Civilians build provisionally here, anticipating future evacuation. Axes separating territories under the control of armed groups and the Congolese national army shift often, disrupting communities and forcing families to relocate, often in a hurry. In search of safety, many resort to camps for displaced people. Others flee farther into the jungle. They are all forced to rebuild.

I was struck most of all by the sculptural form of these humble structures. Cannily built, they express vernacular creativity in the face of extreme hardship and instability. Many of these huts are quite tiny; it is hard to imagine a family living within. Over time I began to make a series of prosaic portraits of these architectural forms. I hope that these deadpan compositions allow the attention to detail and situation of each building to speak for itself.

This gesture was made in dialogue with Bernd and Hilla Becher's typological photographs of industrial architecture. Seriality and the grid were central themes in the clinically detached realism of their documentary approach to postwar Germany. The Becher's insistent hyperfocal attention to subtle variations in anonymous architectural forms renders a meticulous gaze on the constructive aspects of German society. The repetition evokes a mnemonic, a pattern or rhyme, to aid recollection—or in this case to speak of blocked or repressed memory.

I wanted to bring a playful and less monolithic, in some respects inverse, variation in this approach to the architecture of eastern Congo as a way of examining the region's rhythm of displacement—the constant cycle of abandonment and rebuilding—and of meditating on the elusive traces of this conflict on the equatorial landscape, a central problem for the documentary photographer.

According to writer W.G. Sebald, in *On the Natural History of Destruction*, Germans in the post-WWII era trained themselves not to look at certain things, namely the wreckage of their urban landscape. Sebald describes riding on a train and watching his fellow travelers studiously ignore passing scenes of the apocalypse visible through the carriage windows. Discussing his own architectural photographs of Germany's urban landscape, Thomas Struth called Dusseldorf "a city that's embarrassed about its past." In his images you can almost read this embarrassment on the unremarkable facades of buildings that could be in any German city that has been rebuilt after the war.

The buildings I was drawn to photograph in eastern Congo don't seem embarrassed. Indeed there's an uninhibited joy in their design, a puzzle of efficiency. While making this series, I associated the form of the huts with a composition by Steve Reich titled *Come Out* (1966). This extremely minimal piece of music is an early example of Reich's technique of "phasing" multiple sampled recordings using cassette tapes to create intense patterns of repetition and difference through stereo playback. The result is an austere form in which the voice slips out of sync to multiply into many voices that repeat, elide, and reform.

Come Out was made from a historical document. It samples a recording of a victim of racially motivated police violence, a member of the Nation of Gods and Earths, who was involved in the Harlem riot of 1964. Reich's composition focuses on the single phrase "come out to show them," taken from the longer sentence "I had to like open the bruise up to let the bruise blood come out to show them." I was especially drawn to the ambivalence and tension this statement evokes, as the victim of racial violence is basically admitting that he manipulated evidence by opening up old wounds to prove he was attacked. This reminds me of Werner Herzog's "ecstatic truth" and speaks a great deal about the basic problem involved in documentary forms: the difficulty in showing or revealing a trace of conflict upon a landscape whose history or memory has been lost, destroyed, buried, disavowed, or forgotten.

That was the challenge for me in attempting to adequately represent the clash in eastern Congo. The nature of the conflict is sporadic, remote, and nomadic. It is hidden beneath the jungle's canopy. Where postwar German artists dealt with history's repression, the civilians of eastern Congo face being forgotten. The systematic cycles of Congo's "vicious little wars" are conveniently overlooked through the amnesia of global consciousness.

The traces of war in eastern Democratic Republic of Congo are not as obviously written on its architecture as they tend to be in most places. Its signs are difficult for the camera to communicate concretely since the architecture is often designed to be temporary. Displacement and transience are figured into the lives of many civilian populations in eastern Congo, and the modest architecture here speaks of how these people have learned to live around the conflict, abandoning and rebuilding.

Open Architecture as Adventure Game:
John Hejduk in a Noncitizen District
Esra Akcan

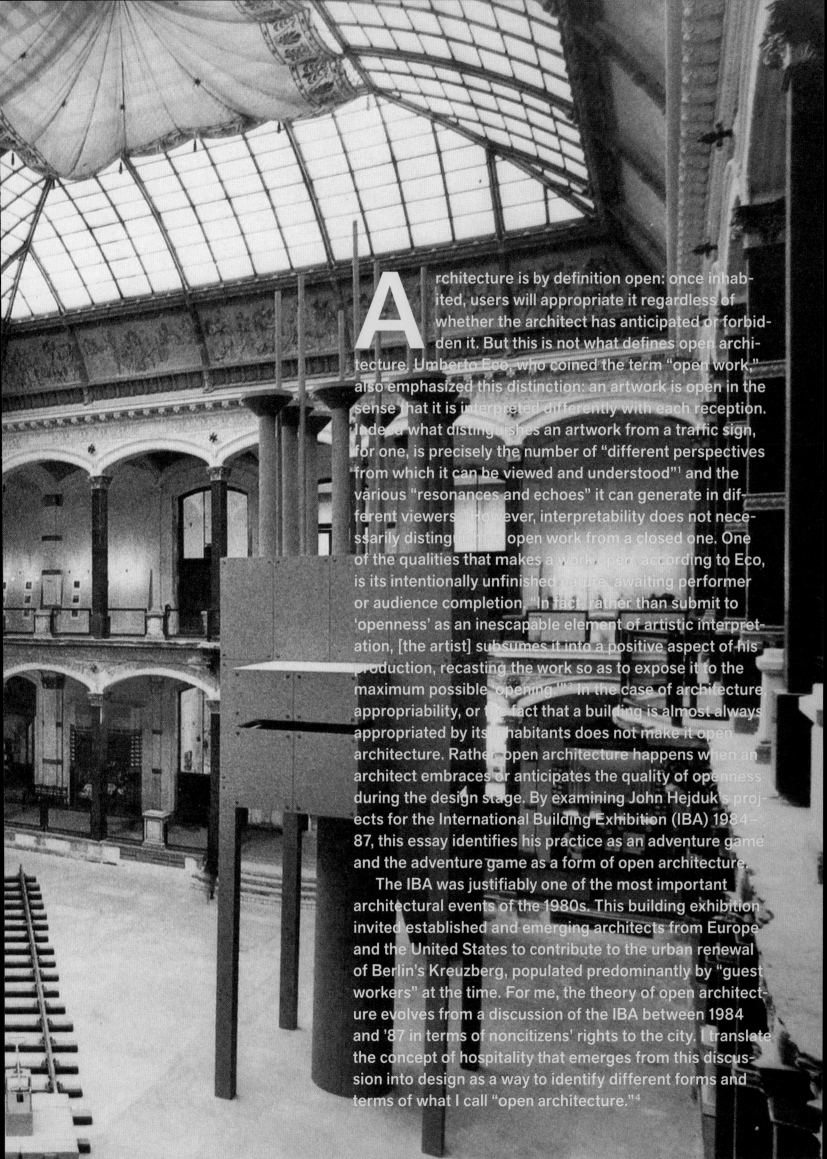

Architecture is by definition open: once inhabited, users will appropriate it regardless of whether the architect has anticipated or forbidden it. But this is not what defines open architecture. Umberto Eco, who coined the term "open work," also emphasized this distinction: an artwork is open in the sense that it is interpreted differently with each reception. Indeed what distinguishes an artwork from a traffic sign, for one, is precisely the number of "different perspectives from which it can be viewed and understood"[1] and the various "resonances and echoes" it can generate in different viewers.[2] However, interpretability does not necessarily distinguish an open work from a closed one. One of the qualities that makes a work open, according to Eco, is its intentionally unfinished nature, awaiting performer or audience completion. "In fact, rather than submit to 'openness' as an inescapable element of artistic interpretation, [the artist] subsumes it into a positive aspect of his production, recasting the work so as to expose it to the maximum possible 'opening.'"[3] In the case of architecture, appropriability, or the fact that a building is almost always appropriated by its inhabitants does not make it open architecture. Rather, open architecture happens when an architect embraces or anticipates the quality of openness during the design stage. By examining John Hejduk's projects for the International Building Exhibition (IBA) 1984–87, this essay identifies his practice as an adventure game and the adventure game as a form of open architecture.

The IBA was justifiably one of the most important architectural events of the 1980s. This building exhibition invited established and emerging architects from Europe and the United States to contribute to the urban renewal of Berlin's Kreuzberg, populated predominantly by "guest workers" at the time. For me, the theory of open architecture evolves from a discussion of the IBA between 1984 and '87 in terms of noncitizens' rights to the city. I translate the concept of hospitality that emerges from this discussion into design as a way to identify different forms and terms of what I call "open architecture."[4]

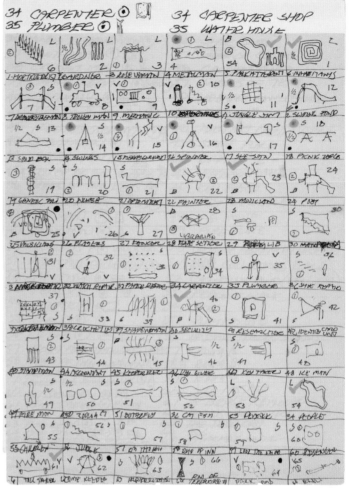

fig. 1 (previous spread)
John Hejduk. *Studio for a Musician* and *Studio for a Painter*, as they were exhibited in IBA's Idea Process Experience exhibition, Berlin, 1984.

fig. 2 (above, left)
John Hejduk, *Victims: sketches of structures*, 1984.

fig. 3 (above, right)
John Hejduk, *Victims: table and list of characters and structures*, 1984.

fig. 4
John Hejduk, page from *Berlin Masque* sketchbook, c.1982. Sketch of snake with caption "Berlin", and envelope containing postcards with views of Porta Pia, Rome, and Largo San Mauro, Solopaca, Italy.

Open Architecture and the Emancipated Spectator

Of all the North American architects who participated in the IBA, none was perhaps as enigmatic and unordinary as John Hejduk (1929–2000). Not having built anything in the conventional sense, except for the three buildings for the IBA (the Wall House was built posthumously), Hejduk was an influential educator (as dean of the School of Architecture at the Cooper Union for twenty-five years) and an architect who designed through freehand drawings, brightly colored paintings, and laconic poems. A shift in Hejduk's design practice took place just as he was preparing his projects for Berlin—one that has since been analyzed as a shift from langue to parole, from structure to meaning, and from non-representation to narrative.

Each of Hejduk's two competition projects for the IBA, the Wilhelmstrasse and the Prinz-Albrecht-Palais competitions, was conceived as a "Berlin Masque," where freestanding sculpture-like objects were scattered throughout a hedge-enclosed site.[5] Masques emerged in sixteenth- and seventeenth-century Europe, flourishing especially in England, as a form of theater usually with no beginning, end, or fixed plot. It could involve singing, dancing, acting, pantomime, and improvisation performed within an elaborate stage design. In the vernacular version, players with masques would call on the nobles to participate, and spectators could join in the dancing. In Hejduk's 1981 Wilhelmstrasse project, the list of proposed structures included a reading theater, a pantomime theater, a public theater, a house for the eldest inhabitant, an observation tower, a clock tower, a conciliator, a neighborhood physician's unit, a crossover bridge, a bell tower, a watch tower, a water tower, a mask tower, a wind tower, a book market, a lottery kiosk, guest towers, and shopping booths (fig. 2). If this design had won the competition and been subsequently built, the site would have been filled with randomly placed buildings that stimulated one's imagination in search of metaphors: theaters with tails, facades with eyes, towers like umbrellas, bridges like geometrized caterpillars, kiosks like medusa heads on bad-hair days, booths like tents, and houses like robots on wheels (fig. 3). Seen from above, a hedge would have proclaimed "Berlin Masque" in a squarish stylized font. The "Berlin Masque" sketchbook contained enigmatic representations of the project, such as poems and stories, sketches of Medusa heads, and pictures of fallen angels. Freehand drawings and texts on different papers, as well as photographs of existing Berlin buildings, envelopes with postcards inside, and other such wonders were glued to the delicate yellow pages of this unique sketchbook (fig. 4).[6] The detailed studies for the "Studio for a Musician" and "Studio for a Painter" were added in 1982, and their full-scale models were constructed in 1984 for the IBA's *Idee, Prozeß, Ergebnis* ("Idea, Process, Experience") exhibition, in Berlin (fig. 1).

The project for the Prinz-Albrecht-Palais competitions in 1984, which Hejduk named "Victims," was located on the site used for torture by the Nazis during the Second World War and where the Topography of Terror museum stands (fig. 5). If Hejduk's design had been chosen, sixty-seven objects—each with a name, a picture, and a story—would have been placed within the borders of the site to activate the emerging Holocaust memory debate in Germany.[7] Hejduk continued to prepare many more masques until he passed away in 2000, including several for Venice, Berlin, Lancaster/Hanover, Riga, and Vladivostok.[8] For the "Lancaster/Hanover Masque" (1982–83), he designed sixty-eight objects—many of them the same as in "Victims"—for as many subjects, about whose lives he wrote stories: a widow's house that would change inhabitants each time a woman was widowed in the community; an old clothes-man's wagon pulled by a horse; a retired actor with a low voice who occasionally performed pantomimes; a Ferris wheel that completed a circle every twenty-four hours, with a timekeeper's place (this timekeeper had previously watched another Ferris wheel collapse, leaving a dead child in each seat); a reaper's house with a private library full of books about the history of reaping; a place for the reddleman referred to by Thomas Hardy; and a house of suicide, among others.

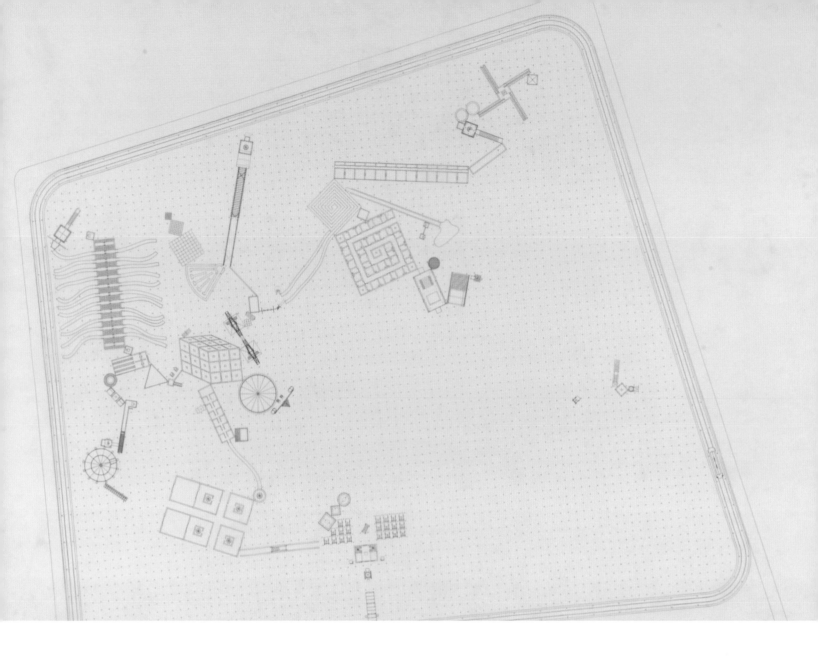

fig. 5
John Hejduk, Project for IBA 1984/87 Prinz-Albrecht-Palais
competition ("Victims"), 1984. Partial site plan.

There were intertextual relations in Hejduk's oeuvre as well. The buildings and characters moved between different masques; they could appear for the first time in a masque for one city and be transferred to another. Just as actors could embody different characters in multiple plays, the painters' studio in Berlin was cast as the old farmer's house in the "Lancaster/Hanover Masque," and the musician's studio as the widow's house. After a while, as in the masques for Russian cities, the objects even inherited wheels to travel freely. This inspired Anthony Vidler to name Hejduk's practice as "vagabond architecture," not only because his objects were on wheels but also because they stood for a nomadic ethic as opposed to an institutionalized architecture, not unlike Gilles Deleuze and Felix Guattari's characterization of the nomad space in contrast to the state space. The vagabond was the utmost antidote for the sedentary.[9]

Of the many possible interpretations that Hejduk's work calls for,[10] I would like to entertain the idea of an adventure game—an intersubjective play, to delineate a rapport that opens an individual to a stranger—on the one hand, and a happening that evolves over time, on the other. If Hejduk's "Berlin Masques" were built, a visitor could have visited the site/stage, circled around the structures without any predefined order, entered into the houses, climbed the towers, crossed the bridges, and shopped at booths and kiosks. Reading Hejduk's accompanying texts, the visitor could have joined the dots in multiple directions both within and across writing as well as physical space. A set of characters allegorized in these built structures could have generated an indefinite number of stories in each visitor's imagination.

Overall Hejduk's oeuvre is like an adventure game where players wander either physically or virtually with their minds in between the objects, from one masque to another, from one character's life to another, decoding messages and finding clues in each step until a story is revealed, even if it is a different one for each of us. The whole process is like a puzzle-solving and empathic exploration, an adventure game that is predicated on an intersubjective experience.

In an adventure game, players transport themselves into a new world that is free from existing memories. They have to look around for clues in an environment where they have never been before, as if waking up to a world of which they remember nothing. Unlike their daily routines, they open every drawer, lift every book, check every corner, and collect every possible clue in the hopes of solving the mystery of the game. Players are asked to engage with the artifacts of this artificial universe by succumbing to amnesia, leaving behind the symbolic system and know-how of their daily lives. The decoding of Hejduk's intertextual masques is a similar experience. While they invite us to a world without memories, they are not meant to make us forget permanently. On the contrary, they offer an alternate way of remembering something—as in "Victims"—that is beyond representation with one's familiar symbolic system. Theodor Adorno was the first to point out this unrepresentability when he said that there could be no "poetry," in the conventional sense, after Auschwitz;[11] and Hejduk's "Victims" reinvents commemoration by acknowledging the incommensurability of that which needs to be remembered with an established dictionary or a closed system of architectural meanings.

Hejduk's naming of his own works as *masques* invites us to discuss architecture through the lens of theater and performance studies. The objects of his projects are highly personal, enigmatic, impenetrable, and uninterpretable with any level of certainty, but they are not the musings of an isolated mind. Unlike classical stages, which place the theatrical play in a separated frame before the audience, Hejduk's objects invite audience participation in the theater, just like masques do. The hidden meanings and secret codes in his masques activate the meaning-construing spectator. The intersubjective experience of the adventure game may involve a one-to-one relationship between the architect and the viewer (as in interactive art), or it may require many people to activate a social practice (as in participatory art). In "Victims," for instance, the city's inhabitants would have decided on the placement of each of the sixty-seven objects in a span of sixty years. This must be why Hejduk represented it using an ensemble drawing for which the ground plan of each structure was cut out and stitched to the site plan with temporary tape. The architectural work in Hejduk's masques is less a finished building and more an evolving, performative stage; the architect less an all-defining author and more a co-producer of a play; and the inhabitant less a user expected to live the life determined by the all-knowing architect and more an active, participating audience.

There is something similar in this scenario to what Umberto Eco identified as "openness" in Luciano Berio's and Karlheinz Stockhausen's musical compositions. According to Eco, these resembled "the components of a construction kit" that the composer hands to the performer, as if he were "unconcerned about the manner of their eventual deployment"[12] (fig. 6). During

fig. 6
John Hejduk, *Berlin Night*, c.1980.

Left to right

a. Canal Bridge, End of Night Structure, Security Bureau, Astronomy Observatory, Building Department, Theater Studios, and Custom House.

b. Building of Time, Museum of Japanese Armor, End of Night Structure, Structure for the Study of Dürer's Etchings, and Museum of Teutonic Armor.

c. Building Department, Clock Tower, the Senate and Council, and Jurist Stadia.

d. Ministry of Communications, Record Keeper, Central Archives, and Cemetery.

the peak of poststructuralist thinking, Eco and Roland Barthes explained a new era in artwork's reception as a historical necessity rather than a random choice, in their texts "Open Work" (1962) and the "Death of the Author" (1968) respectively. Several chronological markers, including the emergence of the modern subject and the collapse of theological meaning, brought along a "sharpening awareness of the concept of the work as susceptible to many different interpretations," in Eco's words. For Barthes, the death of the author brought along "the birth of the reader," and it is precisely this acknowledgment of the reader's empowerment over the meaning of the text that allows for the emergence of the open work.[13] The concept of the emancipated audience has retroactively inspired scholars to try to understand the ability of the visual arts to construct a communal space of collective and political engagement. For example, re-reading the history of modern and avant-garde art throughout the twentieth century from the perspective of performance studies, Claire Bishop pointed out that the "desire to activate the audience in participatory art is at the same time the drive to emancipate it from a state of alienation induced by the dominant ideological order—be this consumer capitalism, totalitarian socialism, or military dictatorship."[14] Today the idea of an emancipated spectator in participatory performance continues to inspire thinkers as a model for fruitful relations between aesthetics and politics, rather than a situation where one is subordinated under the other. Positing the theater as an "exemplary community form" in his book *The Emancipated Spectator* (2008), Jacques Rancière spoke about the possibility of realizing a "theater without spectators," and of challenging the separation between viewing and acting, stage and auditorium, and seeing and doing so that the spectator is not simply seduced by images but becomes an active participant. "The less the playwright knows what he wants the collective of spectators to do, the more he knows that they should, at any rate, act as a collective, transform their aggregation into community."[15] Whether or not Hejduk intended for his masques to embody the intellectual and political potentials I ascribe to them through performance and participatory art theories, his work invites a discussion of the future of open architecture in these terms.

Berlin Tower Housing and the Politics of the Stateless

Hardly any project could have been as far from the requirements outlined in the IBA's Wilhelmstrasse competition brief as Hejduk's proposal.[16] The IBA directors sought to align the whole event with the public-housing tradition in Germany but against the postwar planning values, which they criticized for reducing the city into a function of vehicular transportation. They also significantly distanced their urban-renewal policy from postwar large-scale housing projects, including the IBA 1957 Hansaviertel, where existing buildings were torn down and replaced with freestanding prismatic blocks. The IBA-Neubau director Josef Paul Kleihues cited Wolf Jobst Siedler's *Die gemordete Stadt* and Aldo Rossi's *L'architettura della Città* as his most important intellectual sources.[17] Both books raised consciousness about the merits of what Kleihues referred to as the "historical city," as opposed to the high Modernist values of functional zoning and detached blocks on a tabula rasa. While Siedler criticized the impact of postwar housing on Berlin's existing urban fabric, Rossi inspired a sharp break in architectural design by calling architects to respond more attentively to the collective memory, the historical typology, and the morphology of the city.[18] The IBA proposed to "critically reconstruct" and "carefully repair" the inner city "as a place to live," rather than demolish Berlin's urban fabric for the Modernist cause.

Kleihues argued that this critical reconstruction would be possible by preserving the "ground plan," which he defined as the "gene structure of the city."[19] It soon became clear that the perimeter block—a group of buildings that encircle a block's borders to concretize street edges in the front and courtyard gardens (*Hof*) at the back—was the "gene" of Berlin (fig. 7). In his introduction to the Wilhelmstrasse competition brief, Kleihues noted that "our imagination will complete the ground plan" and directed the competitors to the late nineteenth century (Kaiserreich era, 1871–1918) as the most "decisive period," when the area "took its characteristic architectural" morphology.[20] However, Hejduk's competition projects neither fulfilled any of the IBA's programmatic requirements nor were reminiscent of what was perceived as Berlin's typological qualities.

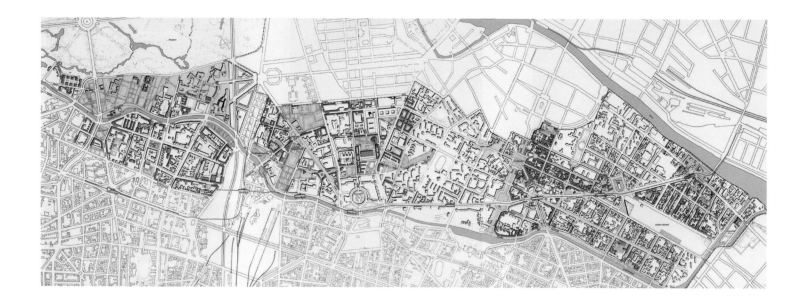

fig. 7
IBA 1984/87 (Internationale Bauausstellung-Berlin) city plan showing IBA buildings. Directors: Josef Paul Kleihues (Neubau-West Kreuzberg), Hardt Waltherr Hämer (Altbau-East Kreuzberg).

While Hejduk's Wilhelmstrasse project might have been a far stretch from the IBA's values and competition requirements, it was more conceivable that "Victims" could win the Prinz Albrecht Palais competition, which called for a more lyrical memorial. But Hejduk's project was not chosen for the first prize, and Kleihues explained the reason as follows: Hejduk's project "won the jury's sympathy right from the start, though the enigmatic nature of his sublimated, intellectually complex aesthetic, charged with literary references, [which] appeared obscure to many. [...] His work was comprehensible to children, animals, and metaphysicians. But it proved difficult to relate to a place charged with guilt."[21]

Even though he did not win any of the competitions, Hejduk must have inspired Kleihues to such an extent that the IBA thereafter looked for a site to build the assimilated versions of his projects. Hejduk was the architect of an urban villa in Tegel, the Berlin Tower housing in Block 11, and the Berlin Gatehouse, in a tiny infill slot on the Wilhelmstrasse competition site. The Berlin Tower housing, at the corner of Charlotten and Besselstrasse, is a midway between Hejduk and Kleihues. It is not a perimeter block but rather two parallel five-story buildings staging a fourteen-story tower in between, all with metal-clad bright green balconies, awnings, and window frames on a grayish stucco surface. The buildings enclose a green area and a playground, secluded from the street by its setback location but completely open to public access (fig. 8).[22] The adventure game was partially closed, so to speak, due to its appropriation in relation to the IBA's urban-design principles. Cooper Union graduate Moritz Müller was the contact architect in Berlin and must have helped significantly in meeting the mandatory German housing standards and securing the precision of the constructed buildings. Once the residents moved in, however, Hejduk's buildings regained their lives as masques and the inhabitants took on extended roles in shaping their built environment, thereby amplifying the project's character as open architecture.

The intellectual sources of open architecture can be traced back to Barthes and Eco or, more recently, to Rancière, but it is Giorgio Agamben's revisiting of Hannah Arendt's text "We Refugees" that helps us come to terms with noncitizen participation.[23] The still prolific refugee continues to expose the limits of modern institutions in handling statelessness. The refugee is stateless, and the guest worker is in between states. Both are noncitizens with barely any citizenship rights in either country, and therefore "in a condition of *de facto* statelessness." The stateless exposes the very limits of human rights defined under the precondition of being a citizen of a state in the first place. "The paradox here," Agamben wrote, "is that precisely the figure that should have incarnated the rights of *man par excellence*, the refugee, constitutes instead the radical crisis of this concept."[24] When citizenship rights disappear, so do certain human rights.

fig. 8
John Hejduk, Berlin Tower Housing, Kreuzberg, Berlin, 1984–87.
General view.

Before the IBA took shape, the Berlin Senate and landlords used the lack of noncitizen's human rights in quite opportunistic ways. Civil-society advocates at the time reported that landlords and housing bureaus consistently turned down rent applications by foreign families, who were subsequently pushed to the rundown buildings in Kreuzberg. "The apartment will not be rented to foreigners" was a common clause in newspaper advertisements in Berlin.[25] Taking advantage of the lack of noncitizen rights, landlords neglected legal maintenance measures and foreign families could hardly make official complaints about the decaying state of their apartments. This sort of ghetto making was seen as an efficient way to initiate a large-scale architectural development from scratch by managing public support to destroy rundown neighborhoods. Similarly there was a proposal for Kreuzberg to build an autobahn with a massive junction that crossed over Oranienplatz, made easier by the fact that noncitizens were so much easier to displace. By renewing Kreuzberg rather than rebuilding it from scratch, the IBA aborted these calculations, but its own immigration policies were complicated by the discriminatory housing laws of the time. Between 1975 and 1978, the Berlin Senate passed a series of regulations meant to address the "foreigner problem." The "ban on entry and settlement" (*Zuzugssperre,* 1975*)* prohibited the movement of additional noncitizen families to Kreuzberg, Wedding, and Tiergarten; the desegregation regulations (1978) mandated that only ten percent of residential units could be rented to foreigners in West Berlin. Justified as an "integration of guest workers" into German society by their forced dispersal evenly throughout the city, the restrictions were received with contempt among noncitizens as they were meant to prevent them from forming social networks.[26] To be precise, the Berlin Senate, the IBA's employer, had assessed that there were too many noncitizens from Turkey living in

IBA's areas, so the urban-renewal project was a new form of social control that would decrease the noncitizens' chances of moving into the IBA-Neubau buildings, and thereby regulate a sort of forced desegregation. These housing laws were transposed into the functional program of the IBA-Neubau buildings, including the Wilhelmstrasse competition program, by controlling the percentage of flats that would be fitting for the stereotypically large guest worker family.[27]

In this context, a critical historiography would engage with the voice of the stateless, which was meant to be erased through the acts of history. Indeed the questions of open architecture are not dissimilar to those of architectural research, as long as a scholar seeks to give voice not only to the architects and policymakers, but also to stateless residents. I propose to raise this voice through a genre inspired by oral history and storytelling, as opposed to the methods of sociology and ethnography that have conventionally been used to record the experience of the "user" in architecture.[28] Out of the infinite possible ways an inhabitant could play the adventure game in Hejduk's IBA buildings, let me illustrate one of the resident appropriations—one that is unavoidably contingent and partial, as is any storytelling. This contingency and partiality acknowledges the necessarily open nature of architectural history itself.

Having grown up in Dortmund as the daughter of two Turkish immigrant teachers, Yeliz Erçakmak lives with her husband in one of the duplexes in Hejduk's Berlin Tower (fig. 9). Working in Türkische Gemeinde Deutschland (TGD)—one of the biggest and by far the most politically influential civil organizations protecting noncitizen rights—she is well aware of the discrimination that is still prevalent. "I do believe that there is a certain level of discrimination in all state buildings, such as kindergartens or public housing. The ad-hoc research also adds up to this conclusion. […] In Germany it is common that they will not rent a vacant apartment based on the name of the applicant. This has happened to a friend of mine."[29]

Erçakmak must have adopted the role of mediator as a child, ever since she was singled out as the only Turkish kid in school who was not placed in the class for foreigners. When she was growing up, anti-immigration campaigns had penetrated even the universities, as exemplified by the Heidelberg Manifesto, signed by university professors in 1982, which demanded that foreign students not take classes with Germans as it "threatened" German culture.[30] She still remembers the juvenile fights during breaks, when German and Turkish kids threw apples at each other, and how she, as the only Turkish kid in the German class, acted like "a ping-pong ball" trying to stop the dispute.

Erçakmak was not fixed on living in Kreuzberg and had never imagined herself in Hejduk's building. "When I saw this building from the outside, I never expected to live here. On the contrary, I told myself that this is an uninhabitable building. It is a bit gray, a bit green; it does not look like a house. I also found it weird that the building is standing in the middle of the site, without a *Hof*. When I walked along the street, this building always caught my eye; I found it odd. I was curious about the side façade that looks like a smiling face, but I never followed up with my interest. It was rather a coincidence that I moved here, but I am really glad I did." (fig. 10)

The appropriations in the apartment suggest that it is perhaps not the original design that she likes but her own version of it. The Erçakmaks do not use the second floor of the apartment as an open space, as Hejduk intended; instead they have divided it into several private rooms. Hejduk's daughter and the architectural students who have since visited the apartment have informed Erçakmak about the architect's original intention, but she still prefers the divided space as a more appropriate setup for modern couples. She explains this as an empowered resident, which does not necessarily diminish her respect for the architectural community. On the contrary, she empathizes with the groups of ten to twenty architecture students who often appear on her doorstep without prior notice, expecting to be invited in, a request she always accepts even when she thinks the apartment is too messy to receive visitors.

Other spaces of curiosity in Hejduk's adventure game are the small square balconies. Erçakmak knew that the two balconies were rather unusually small before moving in, but she eventually found them quite functional and sufficient. Imagining that the man and woman of the house would each sit in one of the balconies, her husband joked about bridging the two by suspending a wooden platform in the air between the two balustrades. The Erçakmaks now use only one of the balconies for outdoor activities and are amazed that the small space accommodates not only two chairs and a coffee table (even if it is the smallest on the market) but also their bicycle. They had to reserve the second balcony for their satellite dish, which barely fits. Like many other immigrants from Turkey, whose apartments are easily identifiable because of their large satellite dishes, they use the device to watch Turkish TV channels. It was only after a Turkish immigrant family won its appeal to the German Federal Constitutional Court in 1993 (207 C 171/93) that the residents gained legal permission to have their satellite dishes, as part of the constitutional right for the freedom of information. The number of satellite dishes has since exploded in Germany: visual cacophony according to some, symbols of the freedom of information to others, these satellite dishes are a testimony to the lived-in forms of the IBA buildings. While expanding noncitizens' rights, these satellite dishes also stamp their houses as territories of the stateless (fig. 11). The satellite dishes scattered

fig. 10
Berlin Tower Housing. Side view of the apartment block.

fig. 11
Satellite dishes on the facade of the Berlin Tower Housing.

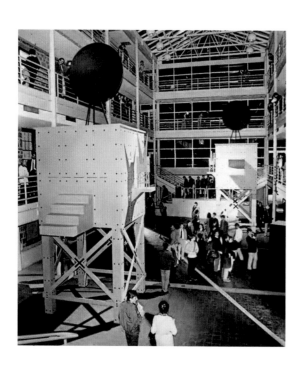

around Hejduk's housing complex, along with other signs of socially imposed absurdities, remind visitors of the architect's original masques. In a historical coincidence, Hejduk used satellite dishes in one version of his "Subject/Object" installation in 1987 (fig. 12).

One of the most idiosyncratic features of Hejduk's tower is the set of transparent bridges that must be traversed to reach the small towers on the sides (fig. 13). A kitchen, a bathroom, a laundry room, and a reading room are placed in each tower room of Erçakmak's apartment, which is no bigger than a mere six square meters. She smiles with a sense of tolerance at the unorthodox transparent bridge that connects the living space to the bathroom. "It requires undressing and dressing completely in the bathroom," she jokes. "And one needs to stay constantly on the watch for those looking inside the bathroom door." She likes the other three tower rooms much more. She can quickly finish the household chores in the minimal yet efficient kitchen and enjoy the rest of the day; and the laundry is conveniently detached from the rest of the house in another tower room. She appreciates how the act of crossing the bridge to the reading room creates the feeling of leaving the house, how that detachment allows her to feel as if she is in another world if she chooses to close the door or to stay informed about the inside by leaving the door open, and how that ability to choose to be inside or outside emancipates her as a resident.

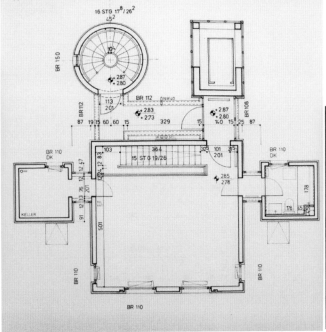

The Call for Open Architecture

Before ending, I must clarify why it is important to explore open architecture today: open architecture is predicated on the welcoming of a distinctly other mind, or a group of minds, into the process of architectural design. It is the translation of the ethics of hospitality into architecture.[31] For Rancière, the emancipation of the spectator is a strategy against the overbearing impotency that comes with the constant critique of the society of spectacle, which "generates a kind of anti-democratic discourse and the incapacity of the masses for any political intervention and, [...] it nurtures a discourse on the uselessness of any kind of artistic practice because it says everything depends on the market. [...] But it's necessary to get out of this discourse [...] of impotence."[32] Similarly for an architectural discourse too willing to boost or to condemn the starchitect in this society of spectacle, for an architectural determinism too confident about the architect's authority over the lives of residents, and moreover in a global practice too content with its own neocolonialism, the mobilization of open architecture may have added importance.

Hints toward an open architecture have so far taken on different forms. For example, participatory architecture (namely design that is shaped in relation to democratic communal meetings, like the ones in the IBA's Altbau section) is one form of open architecture, but there are others. Collective urban design, or the collaboration of nonhierarchically positioned architects in a given urban setting, might evolve into another form of open architecture. So can the anticipation of change, of user appropriation, and of the unfinished or ongoing nature of a work. A significant form of open architecture involves seeing the inhabitant as a subject rather than an object, required to behave in a predefined way by the author-architect. Still another difficult but worthy form of open architecture for the global present involves the welcoming of noncitizen participation in design—the introduction of individual architects to the stateless and the opening of architectural discourse to the immigrant and geographical "other."

Part of the reason I have chosen Hejduk to illustrate open architecture is because he disrupts many formulaic categories that would have frozen this discussion in bipolarities, such as the individual vs. collective, aesthetic vs. political concerns, complex vs. simple communication with the audience, egoistic vs. collaborative architect, and top-down vs. typological urban planning. Some of these binaries produced an increasingly wide gap between the IBA's Neubau and Altbau sections, for instance, foreclosing the possibility of thinking of more options that could emerge in between or out of the two. Instead of picking sides in these bipolarities, Hejduk's initial, highly individualized the IBA projects were examples of open architecture, even if they did not commit to the IBA's collaborative typological urban design or to the reconstruction of collective memory, and even if they were indeed closed, so to speak, by the proponents of this approach. Nonetheless, the residents activated the open nature of the built work after they moved in. At each stage of Hejduk's work—from initial design and construction to habitation—active spectators charged his architecture with new layers of openness.

Notes

1   Umberto Eco, "The Poetics of the Open Work," in *Open Work,* trans. Anna Cancogni (Cambridge, Massachusetts: Harvard University Press, 1989), 3.

2   "Hence, every reception of a work of art is both an interpretation and a performance of it, because in every reception the work takes on a fresh perspective for itself." Eco, "Open Work," 4.

3   Eco, "Open Work," 5.

4   This article is part of a broader research project that will culminate in a book, provisionally titled *Open Architecture and the Noncitizen: Urban Renewal of Berlin-Kreuzberg with IBA'1984–87.* For fuller treatment of the themes that are summarized here and a more comprehensive bibliography on the IBA, see Esra Akcan, "A Building with Many Speakers: Turkish 'Guest Workers' and Alvaro Siza's Bonjour Tristesse Housing for IBA-Berlin," in *The Migrant's Time,* ed. Saloni Mathur (Williamstown, Massachusetts: Sterling and Francine Clark Art Institute, 2011), 91–114; Esra Akcan, "Immigration, Participation and IBA 84–87," in *25 Jahre Internationale Bauausstellung in Berlin 1987: Ein Höhepunkt des europäischen Städtebaus,* ed. Harald Bodenschatz, Vittorio Magnago Lampugnani, Wolfgang Sonne (Dortmund, Germany: Deutsches Institut für Stadtbaukunst, 2012), 57–74; Esra Akcan, "Can the Immigrant Speak? Autonomy and Participation in IBA 1984–87," in *The Death and Life of the Total Work of Art,* ed. Chris Dähne, Rixt Hoekstra, Carsten Ruhl (Berlin: Jovis Verlag, 2014); Esra Akcan, "Exit Implies Entries Lament: Open Architecture in John Hejduk's IBA'1984–87 Immigrant Housing," in *Notes on Critical Architecture: Praxis Reloaded,* ed. Gevork Hartoonian (London: Ashgate, forthcoming in 2015).

5   Drawings can be found at Landesarchiv, Berlin, and the John Hejduk Archives at the Canadian Centre for Architecture.

6   "Berlin Masque Sketchbook," John Hejduk Archives at the Canadian Centre for Architecture, DR 1998:0098:001.

7   Drawings can be found at the IBA Prinz-Albrecht-Palais competition holdings, in Landesarchiv, Berlin, and the John Hejduk Archives at the Canadian Centre for Architecture, AP 145. S2. D55, DR 1998:0109:001, DR 1998:0109:002:001-037. Also see John Hejduk, *Victims: A Work by John Hejduk* (London: Architectural Association, 1986).

8   See, for instance, John Hejduk, *Lancaster/Hanover Masque* (London and Montreal: Architectural Association and Canadian Centre for Architecture, 1992); John Hejduk, *Berlin Night* (Rotterdam: Netherlands Architectural Association, 1993); John Hejduk, *Vladivostok: A Work by John Hejduk,* ed. Kim Shkapich (New York: Rizzoli, 1989); John Hejduk, "Evening in Llano," *A+U* 1 (1991): 127–8; John Hejduk, "Oslo Fall Night," *Columbia Documents of Architecture and Theory* 2 (1993): 7–35; John Hejduk, *Adjusting Foundations,* ed. Kim Shkapich (New York: Monacelli Press, 1995).

9   Anthony Vidler, "Vagabound Architecture," in *The Architectural Uncanny* (Cambridge, Massachusetts: MIT Press, 1992), 206–14.

10   See, for instance, the critics Hejduk inspired during his lifetime (in chronological order): Alberto Perez-Gomez, "The Renovation of the Body: John Hejduk and the Cultural Relevance of Theoretical Projects," *AA Files* 13 (1986): 26–29; William Firebrace, "John Hejduk: Lancaster/Hanover Masque," *AA Files* 21 (1991): 78–84; David Shapiro, "An Introduction to John Hejduk's Works: Surgical Architecture," *A+U* 1 (1991): 6–7; essays by Michael Hays, Detlef Mertins, Edward Mitchell, Peggy Deamer, Stan Allen, R. E. Somol, and Catherine Ingraham in *Hejduk's Chronotope,* ed. Michael Hays (New York: Princeton Architectural Press, 1996).

11   See also Saul Friedländer, ed., *Probing the Limits of Representation: Nazism and the "Final Solution"* (Cambridge, Massachusetts: Harvard University Press, 1992).

12   Eco, "Open Work," 4.

13   Roland Barthes, "The Death of the Author," in *Image Music Text,* trans. Stephen Heath (New York: Hill and Wang, 1977, original, 1968), 148.

14   Claire Bishop, *Artificial Hells: Participatory Art and the Politics of Spectatorship* (New York: Verso, 2012), 275.

15   Jacques Rancière, *The Emancipated Spectator,* trans. Gregory Elliot (London: Verso, 2009), 16.

16   Hejduk competed for Block 19 (3.29 hectares) in the Wilhelmstrasse competition, which also involved Blocks 9 and 20, against Helge Bofinger (Berlin), Douglas Clelland (London), Jasper Halfmann/Clod Zillich (Berlin), Friedrich Kurrent (Munich), and Jürgen Sawade (Berlin). The jury was composed of Carlo Aymonino, Werner Düttmann, Klaus Humbert, Josef Paul Kleihues, Christoph Sattler, and Anthony Vidler.

17   J. P. Kleihues, "Die IBA vor dem Hintergrund der Berliner Architektur- und Stadtplanung des 20. Jahrhunderts," in *Modelle für eine Stadt,* ed. Vittorio Magnago Lampugnani (Berlin: IBA, Siedler Verlag, 1984), 24–36.

18   Aldo Rossi, *The Architecture of the City,* trans. Diane Ghirardo and Joan Ockman (Cambridge, Massachusetts: MIT Press, 1982).

19   "It is the *ground plan* in particular that testifies to the spiritual and cultural idea behind the founding of a city." Josef Paul Kleihues, "Southern Friedrichstadt," in *International Building Exhibition Berlin 1987,* ed. Heinrich Klotz and Josef Paul Kleihues (New York: Rizzoli, 1986), 128.

20   IBA 1984, "Internationaler engerer Wettbewerb Berlin Südliche Friedrichstadt Wilhelmstrasse," Competition Brief, Berlin, May 1981, 8.

21   Josef Paul Kleihues, "A Non-Place: Competition Designs for the Prinz Albrecht Palais in Berlin," *Lotus* 42 no. 2 (1984): 101–10, quotation, 102.

22   The drawings can be found at the John Hejduk Archives at the Canadian Centre for Architecture; DR 1998: 0118 -120-140; DR 1998: 0118 -072-110, DR 1998: 0118 – 09-76.

23   Hannah Arendt, "We Refugees," *Menorah Journal* 1 (1943): 77. Giorgio Agamben, "We Refugees," trans. Michael Rocke, *Symposium* 49 no. 2 (1995): 114–19.

24   Agamben, "We Refugees."

25   Cihan Arın, Safter Çınar, Necati Gürbaca, Hakkı Keskin, M. Yaşar Öncü, and M. Niyazi Turgay, *Yabancıların Yabancılar Politikasına İlişkin Görüşleri/Stellungnahme der Ausländer zur Ausländerpolitik* (Berlin: IGI [Initiativkreis Gleichberechtigung Integration], May 1981), 24.

26   For more discussion, see Cihan Arın, "Analyse der Wohnverhältnisse ausländischer Arbeiter in der Bundesrepublik Deutschland—mit einer Fallstudie über türkische Arbeiterhaushalte in Berlin Kreuzberg" (PhD diss., Technische Universität, 1979).

27   Individuals from Turkey reportedly made up seventeen percent of the Wilhelmstrasse competition site, but the statistics were imprecise due to the difficulty of obtaining correct numbers in a rundown, noncitizen neighborhood. Once new apartments were provided, it would have been very likely that migrants would have wanted to move in as neighbors to their relatives and friends, who made up the majority population in East Kreuzberg. However, the Wilhelmstrasse competition mandated that seventy percent of the units would be studios or one/two bedroom apartments, hardly suitable for big "guest worker" families, and only five to ten percent were allowed for four-bedroom apartments. Hejduk's Berlin Tower eventually provided big, open lofts intended for artists, many occupied instead by bigger families and not used as studios. Wilhelmstrasse competition brief, 24, 46.

28   I would like to problematize not only the history but also the historiography of the noncitizen voice in urban space. In architectural research, the resident, called the abstract "user," is analyzed scientifically through sociological methods, by collecting sufficiently big samples, by distributing multiple-choice questionnaires, and by turning the results into quantifiable data. The positivist sociological methods are still the dominant mode of migration studies in Germany. On a parallel pursuit, ethnography has long inspired art and architectural history as a reflection of the Western concern with what it deems to be primitive. (One can think of Gottfried Semper, Alois Riegl, Heinrich Wölfflin, and many others here.) The residues of early ethnographic premises must still be so pertinent today that any research on immigrant or non-Western city districts is immediately cast as ethnography. In my own work I try to keep a distance from sociological and ethnographic-centered architectural research and to propose an alternative by configuring the individual noncitizen voices through a narrative genre inspired by oral history and storytelling. Oral history, which has no claims to representability or objectivity as it relies on one witness, is one of the few channels to the voice of noncitizens in the absence of official documents. In translating these oral histories into writing, I entertain the idea of storytelling as a format that mobilizes the voice of both the historian-author and the resident-architect. Walter Benjamin characterized storytelling as an experience that is passed from mouth to mouth, as opposed to a novel with an isolated author or the ever-speedy information highway, and the storyteller as the mediating author who conveys "counsel woven into the fabric of real life." A storyteller of architecture alternates back and forth between the roles of historian and resident to perform an open format of writing; a storyteller recognizes that the fabric of everyday life unfolding in an individual's experience of a space is also part of its history. The contingency and partiality of storytelling acknowledges the necessarily open nature of architectural history.

29   Esra Akcan, interview with Yeliz Erçakmak, spring 2012, in Berlin, video and audio recording in author's collection (in Turkish).

30   "Heidelberg Manifesto," *Frankfurter Rundschau,* March 4, 1982.

31   The concept of hospitality from Kant and Emmanuel Levinas to Derrida and beyond has evolved into a very rich and complex discourse in literary and political theory that is impossible to summarize here. For my position about its place in architecture, please see Esra Akcan, *Architecture in Translation: Germany, Turkey, and the Modern House* (Durham, North Carolina: Duke University Press, 2012), especially the Introduction and chapter 5.

32   Jacques Rancière interviewed by Gabriel Rockhill and Alexi Kukuljevic, "Farewell to Artistic and Political Impotence," *The Politics of Aesthetics,* ed. and trans. Gabriel Rockhill (London and New York: Bloomsbury, 2004), 77–78.

Ruin Count:

Le Corbusier
and European Reconstruction

Stanislaus von Moos

1   Should Our Cities Survive?

La mort est le sacrement de la vie.

Sans mort, la vie n'a pas de sens.

La mort implique un délai, l'étape,

le cycle, l'entier, l'œuvre.

D'un coup tout disparaît.

Pourquoi ne veut-on pas conduire au

Père-Lachaise les œuvres humaines :

les outils.

les maisons.

les villes.

Fixer les délais, ne plus léguer son

résidu, puisqu'on ne lègue pas son

corps.

Le Corbusier, "Death is the sacrament of life," in *La Ville Radieuse* (Paris: Vincent Fréal, 1933).

"A disaster—and an opportunity," in Gwilym Gibbon, *Reconstruction* (London: The Architect and Building News, 1943).

Up until 1939, except for the fatality of earthquakes, forest fires, tsunamis, and the many violent moments of urbanization and urban renewal in the nineteenth and twentieth centuries, the tabula rasa in architecture and urbanism was primarily a thought model, a rationalist *idée fixe*, perhaps an ideal, and sometimes a joke. Neither Le Corbusier nor his contemporaries appear to have been particularly preoccupied by the ominous foreshadowing of the 1934 proposal for the cleaning-up and rebuilding of Paris, just a few years before the first deadly air raids of World War II devastated Warsaw, Rotterdam, and London: "Indeed it seems that the bell was struck for the general reform of cities: it is the very program of the present age."[1] In fact, like the Plan Voisin (1925), and as if conceived in a military command center, the 1934 plan proposes the elimination of practically the entire city center between the Louvre and the Marais, except for the Louvre itself and a selection of consecrated historic monuments.

According to modernism's agenda for urban recovery, to demolish and cleanup is synonymous with bringing a better life to the urban masses, even though those who end up moving into new premises are often not the ones who were evacuated. In 1924, the Swiss avant-garde journal *ABC* carried an ad by a construction firm that offered "demolitions of all sorts, executed by the most modern methods": what may look like a joke is, of course, entirely consistent with the journal's agenda.[2] In Paris, at about the same time, Le Corbusier couldn't help but feel great as he saw the seventeenth- and eighteenth-century houses go down to make room for the Boulevard Haussmann.[3] "One demolishes? Yes, indeed, every day. […] What is important is that one demolishes well and firmly and following a healthy program." For "death is the sacrament of life. […] Without death, life makes no sense," he continued.[4] Why, therefore, should we not admit that cities, like people, cannot live forever? "Why don't we send the man-made works to the Père Lachaise Cemetery? Fix the dates! Forget about making a legacy of your corpse."[5]

In light of such lofty perspectives, architects almost inevitably saw the ruins of World War II more as an opportunity than a disgrace, to paraphrase Winston Churchill's famous phrase that served as a caption to the first page of Gwilym Gibbon's book *Reconstruction*.[6] At first sight, the British appear to be the European avant-garde in their no-nonsense approach to ruination. By 1941, only a few months after the first German air raids on London and Coventry, *The Architectural Review* began to publish lavishly illustrated reports on the damages of

1   "Il semble bien que l'heure sonne de la réforme générale des villes: c'est le programme même de l'époque présente. "*Le Corbusier: Oeuvre Complète, 1934–1939*, 46. Draft versions of the present essay have been presented in lecture form at Yale, in Berlin, at Rice University, at Roma Tre University, and elsewhere, and I am grateful for the comments I received from students and colleagues. Beyond that, it is heavily indebted especially to two recent books: Emmanuel Rubio, *Vers une Architecture Cathartique (1945–2001)* (Paris, Editions Donner Lieu, 2011); and Jean-Louis Cohen, *Architecture in Uniform: Designing and Building for the Second World War* (Montreal: Hazan/Canadian Center for Architecture, 2011), as well as to recent

discussions in literature and comparative studies that I refer to mainly by implication. See in particular W. G. Sebald's Zurich lectures (*Luftkrieg und Literatur:* Züricher Vorlesungen, (Frankfurt: Fischer, 2000); and Andreas Huyssen, "Authentic Ruins: Products of Modernity," in *Ruins of Modernity*, ed. Julia Hell and Andreas Schönle (Durham, North Carolina: Duke University, 2010), 17–28.

2   For example, "Abbrüche jeder Art: Abbruch Honegger," in *ABC*, no. 2, Zurich, 1924.
3   Although planned since the 1850s, this boulevard was completed only after 1925. Le Corbusier, *Urbanisme* (Paris: Cres & Cie, 1925), 247ff.
4   Le Corbusier, *La Ville Radieuse* (Paris: Vincent Fréal & Cie, 1933 [1964]), 203.
5   Ibid.
6   Gwilym Gibbon, *Reconstruction* (London: The Architect & Building News, 1943). Both the frontispiece and the caption often reappeared in the architectural press; see, for example, Hans Bernoulli, "Der Wiederaufbau in England," *Das Werk*, no. 7 (1944): 6.

war bombing and the opportunities they represented for reconceptualizing urbanization throughout the country.[7] In the advertisements, new factories, schools, and housing complexes were shown about to spring from the ruins, reflecting the long dormant functionalist dreams of many modernists. As to the pragmatism of the Germans, on whose turf the war began, it does not have the gentlemanly aura of the British approach. Here architects were perpetrators, Niels Gutschow notes, not merely victims of the military strategy of urban demolition. In many places, their dispositions anticipated, and ultimately legitimized, Himmler's orders.[8] Already by 1941–42, Adolf Hitler and Albert Speer openly discussed the positive effects that could result from Allied retaliations in response to the blitz, as "the bombing of Berlin would alleviate the need for extensive demolition, not to mention the displacement of tens of thousands of Berliners."[9] Though military realism did not always coincide so neatly with social policy, as it did in the case of Speer, the episode nevertheless resonated with the careers of many German architects, especially when these retaliations began to take effect. Most, if not all, German architects shared Speer's conviction that the nineteenth-century city was fundamentally dysfunctional, and worse, corrupt. According to Gutschow, frustration with the evils of the nineteenth-century—overcrowding, filth, crime, and moral degeneration—was so visceral that by 1943 some greeted the spectacle of the firestorms caused by Allied bombing in Hamburg and other cities with dark fascination. They experienced it as a fatality that allowed the "World Spirit" to "unleash extraordinarily powerful energies" to the effect that "the outline of a better, 'New City', capable of bringing about salvation," could appear on the horizon. Some even fostered a desire "for apocalyptic annihilation."[10]

From the planner's viewpoint, demolition and rebuilding have always been the obvious medicine against the miseries of damp, narrow streets and traffic congestion. Ruins were as integral to the work of Bramante ("*il ruinante*") in fifteenth- and sixteenth-century Lombardy and Rome as they were to Baron Haussmann in nineteenth-century Paris or to Robert Moses in twentieth-century New York. In *La Ville Radieuse*, Le Corbusier argues that one of the purposes of contemporary urbanism will be to prevent ruination from ever happening in the future—except, of course, for the bulldozing that is necessary to arrive at that ideal state.[11] Note that the official

CIAM "manifesto" on urbanism, published by José Luis Sert in 1941, in the United States, demonstratively exposes densely populated cities as the origin of contemporary social and human ills, while the survival of urban civilization is seen as depending on the freeways that will ultimately help it explode (*Can Our Cities Survive?*). Also note that Sert's book was originally titled *Should Our Cities Survive*, sufficiently ominous for the cover of a book that was about to appear the very year the United States entered the war.

Nor was the synergetic blur of military and urbanistic plans a German specialty, as is exemplified by American planner Edward J. Logue. During the war, Logue served as a bombardier in the air force, surveying and targeting cities in southern Italy. After the war, at the service of a singularly radical form of urban renewal, he continued to survey and target urban forms in New Haven, Connecticut. Later when he became the development administrator for the Boston Redevelopment Authority, Logue was able to operate at a scale Le Corbusier could have only dreamed of.[12] Of course, the destructive impulse of the military strategist does not necessarily coincide with the goals of the social engineer: is there a more aggressive way of conceptualizing the power of the artist-urbanist-engineer than by declaring entire urban areas disposable? Furthermore, should architects' dreams of extinction be seen as reflections or as movers of hegemonic power instincts?[13]

"The Parthenon stood for the triumph of the human spirit over darkness," advertisement in *The Architectural Review* (no. 354, 1941).

7   "The End of Last Time: The First Installment of a Survey of Bomb Damage to Buildings of Architectural Importance," *The Architectural Review* 90/535 (1941): 7–25. The survey was continued in the subsequent issues of the journal. See also J. M. Richards, "Planning and Reconstruction," ibid., 117–88; "What Happened Last Time," ibid., 3–5; and "Towards a Planning Policy," ibid, 38–9. As is well known, the British MARS Group's planning for a new London began as early as 1937 and became a blueprint for postwar reconstruction throughout Europe.

8   Niels Gutschow and Barbara Klain, *Vernichtung und Utopie: Stadtplanung Warschau 1939–1945* (Hamburg: Junius, 1994), 10. Gutschow, Germany's foremost historian of urbanism in the 1930s and '40s, knows what he is talking about because his father, Konstanty Gutschow, was responsible for the reconstruction plans drawn for Hamburg under Hitler and Speer. Among Gutschow's many writings on the subject, see also Werner Durth, *Träume in Trümmern* (Munich: DTV, 1993) and "Europa, verbrannte Erde und Zukunft," in *Krieg, Zerstörung, Aufbau*, Schriftenreihe der Akademie der Künste, vol. 23, ed. Jörn Düwel, Werner Durth, Niels Gutschow, and Jochem Schneider (Berlin: Henschel Verlag, 1995), 176–94. Gutschow is also co-responsible for what is probably the most encompassing anthology of recent studies on planning in Europe between 1940 and 1945: Ibid., with Jörn Düwel, eds., *A Blessing in Disguise: War and Town Planning in Europe 1940–1945* (Berlin: Dom Publishers, 2013).

9   Johann Friedrich Geist and Klaus Kürvers, "Tatort Berlin, Pariser Platz," in *1945: Krieg, Zerstörung, Aufbau, Architektur und Stadtplanung 1940–1960*, ed. Jörn Düwel, Werner Durth, Niels Gutschow et.al. (Berlin: Akademie der Künste/Henschel Verlag, 1995), 55–118; especially 107–9. See also Elias Cannetti, "Hitler, nach Speer," in *Das Gewissen der Worte* (Frankfurt: Fischer, 1981), in particular 172; and Walead Beshty and Eric Schwab, "Stumped," *Cabinet* (Winter 2005/06).
10   The quotations are from Niels Gutschow and Ernst Düwel, *Fortgewischt sind alle überflüssigen Zutaten: Hamburg 1943– Zerstörung und Städtebau* (Berlin: Lukas Verlag, 2008).
11   Le Corbusier, *La Ville Radieuse*, 60ff., 171. See Jean-Louis Cohen, *Architecture in Uniform: Designing and Building for the Second World War* (Montreal: Hazan/Canadian Centre for Architecture, 2011), 141–50 et passim.

12   D. W. Dunlap, "Edward Logue, Visionary City Planner, Is Remembered," *New York Times*, April 23, 2000; quoted by Rubio in *Vers une Architecture Cathartique*,88.
13   See Horst Bredekamp, "Modernität und Einsturz," in *Sankt Peter in Rom und das Prinzip der produktiven Zerstörung* (Berlin: Verlag Klaus Wagenbach, 2000), 121–22.

Ruin
and Beginnings

Urbanists and their fantasies imply ruin and ruins as their very condition. Yet part of the deal is their absolute invisibility. Architects, in turn, are obsessed with the *looks* of ruins. "Look at a building after it is built," Louis Kahn reminded an interviewer. "Each part that was built […] tries to say when you're using the building, 'Let me tell you about how I was made.' Nobody is listening because the building is now satisfying a need." Only as time passes, when the building begins to fall apart, does "the spirit of its making come back. It welcomes the foliage that entwines and conceals. Everyone who passes can hear the story it wants to tell about its making. It is no longer in servitude; the spirit is back."[14] No wonder many of Kahn's built works in India and Bangladesh have the pathos of construction sites arrested in time, and thus of "ruins in reverse."[15] Kahn's interest in ruins as essential figurations

Louis Kahn, Indian Institute of Management, Ahmedabad, c.1970. Construction photograph.

of structure stands in a tradition that goes back to Choisy and Viollet-le-Duc. John Soane famously demonstrated the structural makeup of the Bank of England by having it rendered as a ruin.[16] As for Le Corbusier, no fewer than 29 out of 150 illustrations in *Vers une Architecture* (1923) show ruins of the Parthenon: their purpose is to illustrate architecture's nature as "pure creation of the spirit." By nature abstract—that is, divested of the meanings that were once part of what their viewers saw in them—the role of those ruins is to invite a new conception of architecture, either based on the raw play of horizontals, verticals, and volumes, or on the primitive beauty of the "chassis," as in the ruins of imperial Rome.[17]

A "ruin" is a fragment of something that no longer exists, a building whose life cycle has come to an end. A construction site, in turn, implies something that is still in the making. The sculptor Robert Smithson thus spoke of "Ruins in Reverse." What he had in mind was the rubble, the rusting pipes, and the steel brace work of an old bridge he found scattered along the river of his hometown in New Jersey. He defined them as "the opposite of the 'romantic ruin,' for the buildings don't fall into pieces after having been built, but they rise to the status of ruins before being built."[18] "Has Passaic Replaced Rome as the Eternal City?" Smithson asks in the title of his essay. Whether he had Piranesi on his mind, we don't know; neither do we know if, in his view, Chandigarh would have qualified as yet another "Eternal City." What does seem clear, however, is that Piranesi's engraving entitled *View of the Remains of the Walls of Paestum* actually represents ruins, whereas, for example, Ernst Scheidegger's picture of the High Court Building at Chandigarh, as seen through the scaffolding of the Secretariat Building in 1955, represents a construction site, and thereby literally a "ruin in reverse". All this would be no more than a play on words were it not for the twin nature of the ruin: its simultaneous implication of the past as well as the future—in short, its contradictory relation to the course of time inscribed in the very notion of the ruin as it has existed in western architectural culture for centuries.[19] Were it not for this dual character of Piranesi's antiquity, Kahn would hardly have decided to hang Piranesi's *Campo Marzio*— a print in which Rome is present both as witness to its own decay *and* in its second nature as an idealized vision of the polis—on the wall of his office in Philadelphia. For

14   Heinrich Klotz and John W. Cook, *Conversations with Architects* (New York and Washington, D.C.: Praeger, 1973), 183. For an inspiring discussion of the ruin as a paradigm in post–World War II architecture, see Kurt W. Forster, "Die Ruine als Nachklang, Vorbild oder Zukunftsbotin," in *Ruinierte Oeffentlichkeit: Zur Politik von Theater, Architektur und Kunst in den 1950iger Jahren*, ed. Claudia Blümle and Jan Lazardzig (Zurich and Berlin Diaphanes, 2012), 182–206.
15   On Kahn and ruins, see Vincent Scully, "Louis Kahn and the Ruins of Rome," in *Vincent Scully: Modern Architecture and Other Essays*, ed. Neil Levine (Princeton, New Jersey: Princeton University Press, 2002), 298–319. On the concept of "Ruins in Reverse," see below.

16   *John Soane Architetto* (London/Vicenza/Milano: Royal Academy of Arts/Centro Internazionale di Studi di Architettura Abdrea Palladii/Skira, 2000).
17   See Jean-Louis Cohen, "La 'Leçon de Rome,'" in *L'Italie de Le Corbusier*, ed. Marida Talamona (Paris: Fondation Le Corbusier/Editions de la Villette, 2010), 50–61; and Francesco Passanti, "Rome," in *Le Corbusier Before Le Corbusier*, ed. Stanislaus von Moos and Arthur Rüegg (New Haven/London/New York: Yale University Press/Bard Graduate Center, 2002), 188–93.

18   Robert Smithson, "The Monuments of Passaic: Has Passaic Replaced Rome as the Eternal City?" *Artforum* 6, no. 4 (Winter 1967); reprinted in *Robert Smithson: The Collected Writings*, ed. Jack Flam (Berkeley: University of California Press, 1996), 68–74. For a discussion of the concept, see Stanislaus von Moos, "'Ruins in Reverse': Notes on Photography and the Architectural 'Non Finito,'" in *Chandigarh 1956*, photographs by Ernst Scheidegger, (Zurich: Scheidegger & Spiess, 2009), 45–66.

19   Ruins have been a symbol of human hubris and of vanitas since biblical times, and long before Diderot's phrase "Il faut ruiner un palais pour en faire un objet d'intérêt" (*Salons*, vol. 3 [Paris, 1767]: 227; a comment on a painting by Hubert Robert), the ruin has fascinated architects as a metaphor of transition or a way of understanding structure and tectonics in building. For a good recent survey on the place of the "ruin" and the "fragment" in modern architectural thought, see Barry Bergdoll and Werner Oechslin, eds., *Fragments: Architecture and the Unfinished, Essays Presented to Robin Middleton* (London: Thames & Hudson, 2006).

Kahn, it went without saying that architecture must be defined between these two poles of ruin and utopia.[20]

Though Kahn's discovery of Rome's ruins occurred a few years after World War II,[21] the war probably had no share in this epiphany. Richard Zorn, who lived and worked in Hamburg, is a different story. During the weeks and months following the deadly air strikes of 1943, which killed some 30,000 people within a few hours, he wandered among the debris photographing the damages. What Zorn discovered was not so different from what Kahn had found on the Palatine Hill or in Ostia Antica: the power of architecture, a true apotheosis of its stripped-down essence, revealed in the ruins of the city. "Is this a ruin?" He asks in view of the geometric splendor of an isolated wall and its shattered windows. "No," he concludes. "With more pride than ever, the building dominates its ruined surroundings." Elsewhere the debris of another building reveals "bourgeois architecture in the best possible sense," a perfection that makes "the cheap panopticon-architecture next door" (obviously dating from the nineteenth century) look even more "depressing."[22]

Just as Rome inspired Kahn's architectural ontology, the ruins of Hamburg unleashed Zorn's explorations in the fundamentals of classicism. For others, the war experience appears to have triggered the discovery of the ruin's unexpected productive potential for social redemption and community building. By the logic of geopolitics, Alvar Aalto was the first architect within CIAM to be immediately touched by the experience of ruination through war and to draw lessons from it. At the end of 1939, quite possibly encouraged by the brutal German invasion of Poland, Soviet troops invaded parts of Finland. By 1941, Aalto was invited to Switzerland to develop his ideas about reconstruction.[23] He started, as an ethnographer would, by describing a group of women who had returned to their abandoned homes a few months after the war had begun only to find them in ruins. After moments of panic at the sight of the devastation, the women began to reconstruct their lives by baking bread in the chimneys of the ruined houses. Though the circumstances of Aalto's wartime revelation of the hearth and

chimney as the fundamentals of building might not have been as benign as his rather staged photographs would suggest, it is tempting to juxtapose them against a rather more dramatic painting by Franz Radziwill (*Flanders*, 1947). The discovery, apart from suggesting the potentially liberating possibilities of bricolage opened-up by ruins, also reminds one of the permanence of life embodied in the form of the chimney. Among the images brought to mind are Frank Lloyd Wright's Prairie Style houses, and the way they are nestled around a fireplace.[24] Or Philip Johnson's Glass House, in New Canaan, Connecticut, with its cylindrical service core, that opposes it to the Miesian model. Irritatingly enough, Johnson himself refers to some ruined houses he saw in Poland when he visited the country in the aftermath of the Nazi invasion, in 1939.[25] One may also think of the Weekend House in Upper Lawn, England, by Alison and Peter Smithson that is arguably nothing but a chimney—or even some of Robert Venturi's early house projects whose disproportionately large chimneys resonate with snapshots from 1968 that show the architect and his partner and wife, Denise Scott Brown, in front of a burned-out fireplace of some forgotten house in Las Vegas.[26]

Hamburg after an allied bombing raid, in Jörn Düwel and Niels Gutschow, *Fortgewischt sind alle überflüssigen Zutaten* (Hamburg: AS Verlag, 2008).

20   On Kahn and ruins, see note 15 and Neil Levine, "The Architecture of the Unfinished and the Example of Louis Kahn," in Bergdoll and Oechslin, *Fragments*, 323–42.
21   Kahn was a Fellow at the American Academy in Rome in 1951–52.
22   Richard Zorn, "Gebautes Hamburg in Schutt," in Gutschow and Düwel, *Fortgewischt*, 112–20.
23   Alvar Aalto, "Der Wiederaufbau Europas stellt sie zentralen Probleme der Baukunst unserer Zeit zur Diskussion," in *'Der Magus des Nordens': Alvar Aalto und die Schweiz*, ed. Teppo Jokkinen and Bruno Maurer (Zurich: GTA Verlag, 1998), 117–87; ferner Red. (Alfred Roth), "Wiederaufbau: Stadtplanung–Altstadtsanierung," *Werk*, 33 (1946): 101.

24   Note that, partly due to the writings of Bruno Zevi, early Wright turned out to be a major reference for European architecture after World War II.
25   See Franz Schulze, *Philip Johnson: Life and Work* (Chicago: University of Chicago Press, 1994), 197.

26   On the house in Upper Lawn, England, by Alison and Peter Smithson, see Bruno Krucker, *Komplexe Gewöhnlichkeit: Der Upper Lawn Pavilion von Alison and Peter Smithson* (Zurich: GTA Verlag, 2002). For the photos of Robert Venturi and Denise Scott Brown, see Martino Stierli and Hilar Stadler, eds., *Las Vegas Studio: Images from the Archives of Robert Venturi and Denise Scott Brown* (Kriens/Frankfurt/Zürich: Museum im Bellpark/Deutsches Architekturmuseum/Scheidegger & Spiess, 2009), 139ff.

Le Corbusier, Chandigarh Capitol Complex, India, 1955.
View of the High Court building from the Secretariat. Photo: Ernst Scheidegger.

Saint-Dié after the clean up of the ruins, c.1947.

a landscape—never mind how much of it was in fact still there: "It would be criminal to allow a lazy and formulaic urbanism to bury this landscape again at the bottom of courtyards or behind the walls of corridor streets."[28]

By the end of 1947, the authorities had decided otherwise, probably to the relief of the majority of the inhabitants. As happened in most comparable cases throughout France and elsewhere, reconstruction followed a generically contextual master plan that imitated preexisting street patterns. Though nothing of it was built, Le Corbusier's plan for Saint-Dié (often discussed alongside his plans for Chandigarh) subsequently became a kind of gold standard for reconstruction following the canon of the Charte d'Athènes—primarily due to the vastly overscaled civic center. Indeed, success or failure of the proposed solution was difficult to measure. While in the United States, the earlier Corbusian models of total reconstruction were about to be emulated in New York's urban renewal (Stuyvesant Town was planned long before Saint-Dié became known in the United States[29]), France, and Europe altogether, was far from being able to go ahead with comparably radical projects.[30]

Yet is the metaphor of the phoenix rising from the ashes of war in Le Corbusier's oeuvre as unambiguous as the nature of Ville Radieuse would suggest? At least the nervous gesture of the late Saint-Dié renderings evokes a rather broken version of the "new." In an encrypted way, these drawings seem to speak of dark materiality, of violence even, as if involuntarily reflecting the somber experience the country had just gone through.[31] In the background, one notices the seventeenth-century towers of the cathedral and the ruined gothic nave covered by some sort of emergency roof. The glass envelope was thought to have inlays of stained glass. Was Le Corbusier aware of the earlier British efforts to maintain London's bombed-out churches in their ruined state?[32]

If Anthony Vidler is correct, architectural discourse in England during the postwar decades was characterized by "a culture of suppression and conscious self-deceit with respect to the psychological damages of war."[33] Reconstruction was synonymous with a radical beginning from scratch, and the postwar city could not be imagined as anything but a sparkling novelty. Yet the cleanup was not total. Early on, Kenneth Clark rationalized the ubiquitous effects of war by stating simply that "war damage in itself is picturesque."[34] Many of Christopher Wren's bombed-out churches now survive as ruins, and thus as war memorials in the form of picturesque urban amenities, thanks to Clark's initiative. The ruin of Coventry Cathedral has become a symbol of Britain's rebirth after the war, as has, mutatis mutandis, the badly

"I am wandering around among the ruins of Milan," the painter Alberto Savinio wrote in 1944: "Why this excitement? I'm supposed to be sad, but instead I almost explode out of joy. I should have musings about death, but instead ideas about life are striking my forehead, like the breeze of the purest and most radiating of all mornings. Why? Because I feel that new life will emerge from these ruins. I feel that a stronger, richer, more beautiful city will emerge from these ruins."[27] Three years later, Le Corbusier visited the city of Saint-Dié, in northeastern France. He had been commissioned by the government to develop a master plan for its reconstruction. Expecting the Allies' arrival in November 1944, the city was savagely plundered and set on fire by its German occupants. After the clearing up, all that was left was a patchwork of rectangular beds of rubble. On arrival to the site, Le Corbusier's reaction was similar to that of Savinio: he raved about the way the cleaned-up territory made the city readable again as

Saint-Dié after the departure of the German forces, 1944.

27 Alberto Savinio, *Ascolto il Tuo Cuore, Città* (Milano: Bompiani, 1944); quoted after Maria Virginia Cardi, "Für eine Ethik der Ruine," in *Die zerstörte Stadt: Mediale Repräsentationen urbaner Räume von Troja bis SimCity*, ed. Andreas Böhn and Christine Mielke (Bielefeld, Germany: Transcript Verlag, 2007), 83–99.
28 Mary McLeod, "Saint-Dié: 'A Modern Space Conception' for Postwar Reconstruction," in *Le Corbusier: An Atlas of Modern Landscapes*, ed. Jean-Louis Cohen (New York, Museum of Modern Art, 2013), 193–9; here 195.

29 The Saint-Dié project was shown at the Rockefeller Center, in New York, in 1945 and subsequently traveled throughout the United States; see McLeod, "Saint-Dié," 199. On the East River Houses in New York, built in 1941 (the New York City Housing Authority's "first true tower-in-the-park-project"), see Samuel Zipp, *Manhattan Projects: The Rise and Fall of Urban Renewal in Cold War New York* (New York: Oxford University Press, 2010), in particular 14–17; 258–60.
30 The demise of Marcel Lods's reconstruction plan for Mainz is symptomatic in this context; see Hartmut Frank, "Trümmer: Traditionelle und Moderne Architekturen im Nachkriegsdeutschland," in *Grauzonen, Farbwelten: Kunst und Zeitbilder, 1945–1955*, ed. Bernhard Schulz (Berlin: NGBK / Medusa, 1983), 43–83, in particular 50–52.

31 Le Corbusier, *Les Constructions Murondins* (Paris and Clermont Ferrand, France: Etienne Chiron, 1942).
32 On the chronology of the cathedral restoration project see Thomas Kesseler, "La pensée créatrice de Le Corbusier illustrée par le Poème de l'Angle Droit et l'évolution du plan de Sant-Dié," in *Le Corbusier et St. Dié*, ed. Daniel Grandidier (Saint-Dié, France: Musée Municipal, 1987), 89–111; Giuliano Gresleri, "Un Restauro Impossibile: La Cattedrale di St. Dié," in ibid.; and Glauco Gresleri, *Le Corbusier: Il Progetto Liturgico* (Bologna: Editrice Compositori, 2001), 70–73.

33 Anthony Vidler, "Air War and Architecture," in *Ruins of Modernity*, ed. Julia Hell and Andreas Schönle (Durham, North Carolina: Duke University Press, 2010), 29–40.
34 S. Christopher Woodward, *In Ruins* (London: Vintage, 2002), 212; and Marc Treib, "Remembering Ruins, Ruins Remembering," in *Spatial Recall: Memory in Architecture and Landscape*, ed. Marc Treib (New York and London: Routledge, 2009), 194–217, 216. T. S. Eliot and John M. Keynes were among the signers of the petition. A forgotten drawing by Louis Kahn basically makes the same point when it suggests that Europeans should use their bombed churches as war memorials (also 1944). The drawing must have been prepared (but not used) as an illustration to Kahn's "Monumentality," in *New Architecture and City Planning*, ed. Paul Zucker (New York: Philosophical Library, 1944), 577–88.

damaged Kaiser Wilhelm-Gedächtniskirche, in Berlin (completed 1958–62). Though not by coincidence, the Gedächtniskirche is also the latecomer in this series. In London, ruins represent a pain inflicted upon the country from abroad, a fatality. In Berlin, where the war originated, ruins apparently were more difficult to live with. By the force of circumstance, they carry the stigma of collective guilt.[35]

By 1948, once it became clear that the master plan for Saint-Dié would be shelved, the idea of the ruin as war memorial resurfaced on the agenda. Memories of World War I may have had a share in this renewed interest in the monumentality of the ruin. In the early months of World War I, in 1915, German artillery had attacked Reims Cathedral, a trauma that caused uproar far beyond France. This event more than anything else made Swiss architect Charles-Edouard Jeanneret identify quite viscerally with the French cause. Le Corbusier's proposal for the *cathédrale du témoignage* in Saint-Dié was charged with thoughts of martyrdom and resurrection that resonated with his Protestant upbringing. It appears as a belated acknowledgment of the historic trauma that had triggered the abstract program of the master plan to begin with. The architecture thus incorporates both the horror of war *and* the triumph of resurrection ("*horreur et résurrection*," as is noted on the drawing). Should the project's rough materiality and tragic aura be seen as a first step toward Brutalism?[36] The idea never reached the project stage; the cathedral's nave and the adjacent cloisters now survive in the form of a reconstruction à l'identique.[37]

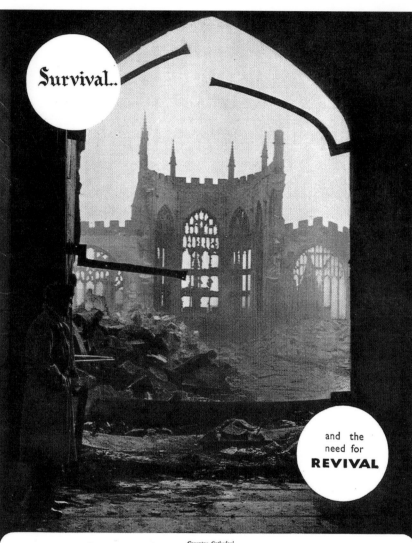

"Survival—Revival," advertisement in *The Architectural Review* (no. 354, 1941).

35 On the lingering controversy regarding the fate of the ruin, see Vera Frowein Ziroff, *Die Kaiser-Wilhelm-Gedächtniskirche: Entwicklung und Bedeutung* (Berlin: Gebrüder Mann, 1982, in particular 333–40 ("Vom Nationaldenkmal zum Wahrzeichen für West-Berlin") and Stephanie Warnke, *Stein gegen Stein: Architektur und Medien im geteilten Berlin 1950–1970* (Frankfurt/New York: Campus Verlag, 2009), 220–31.

36 Giuliano Gresleri and Glauco Gresleri, *Le Corbusier: Il Programma Liturgico* (Bologna: Editrice Compositori, 2001), 70.
37 In a text fragment dated April 4, 1946, Le Corbusier formulates his radical objection against reconstruction as a way of preserving monuments (Gresleri and Gresleri, *Le Corbusier*, 221–22).

4 Ronchamp: Dynamics of Mystification

The chapel Notre-Dame-du-Haut at Ronchamp was completed 1955, ten years after the end of World War II. Dominating the landscape from its lonely mountaintop in the Franche-Comté, it was built from the rubble of an earlier church that had been badly damaged in the last months of the war, when Allied bombing forced the Germans to retreat eastward. The first sketches of the site, made on May 20, 1950, on the train from Paris to Basel, show the outlines of the then extant walls and transept of the church. Many locals had voiced their preference for a simple consolidation and reconstruction of what was there. But preserving the neo-Gothic ruin made no sense to church officials, despite the fact that the last pilgrimage church had only been recently completed (in 1936) and was thus considered to be a stylistic fake (the preceding medieval church with eighteenth-century additions had been gutted by fire in 1913). A partial reconstruction in simplified forms didn't sound attractive either. Meanwhile proposals à la a "miniature bomb evoking Hiroshima and the celestial revenge" began to surface all over the archdiocese.[38]

Perhaps surprisingly, the issue of cost was key for contacting Le Corbusier. As concrete appeared to be a reasonable alternative to masonry (always considered far too expensive), the name that kept popping up in early discussions, albeit rather jokingly, was Le Corbusier's.[39] He turned out to have no problem with the brief stipulating that the new church rely on a combination of the rubble remaining from the old church and reinforced concrete poured on site. "I'll take some bags of cement and sand, and perhaps the stones left from the demolitions of the chapel with the broken roof; probably they […] will be good enough for filling, but not for carrying."[40] Subsequently, he decided to have the south wall built in concrete and the others with the stones of the old church arranged into curved shapes to keep them upright. From an engineering point of view, this must have sounded straightforward enough. The real challenge, in turn, was the double-shell structure of the roof, suspended from the edges of the walls and sagging toward the center point. Seen in retrospect, the project's mixture of primitivism and high tech placed it at the core of a vigorous debate about the ends of modern architecture. When Le Corbusier's first model was made public, the reactions were more than mixed, even among his more fervent supporters.[41]

With an extraordinary collection of contact sheets, Lucien Hervé allows us to participate in the building process and to retroactively experience Ronchamp in its genesis—as a "ruin in reverse."[42] In fact, those construction shots coincide in time with some drawings Le Corbusier made toward the transformation of a small barn in La Sainte-Baume, near

Le Corbusier, Sketch of the remains of the neo-gothic Ronchamp chapel (completed 1936), 1950.

38 Françoise Caussé, "Ronchamp et la Commission d'Art Sacré de Besançon," in *Ronchamp: L'éxigence d'une Rencontre* (Lyon: Fage Éditions, 2007), 61–83, here 69. See also Nicholas Fox Weber, *Le Corbusier: A Life* (New York: Knopf, 2008), 661–62.

39 The archbishop of Besançon, Mgr. Dubois, has been quoted as jokingly asking in one of the discussions of the diocese's "Commission d'art sacré": "But who is capable of doing noble concrete instead of vulgar concrete?" ("Qui est capable de faire du béton noble, et non pas vulgaire," in Françoise Caussé, *La Revue 'l'Art Sacré': Le D*ébat en France sur l'*Art et la Religion (1945–1954)* (Paris: Les Editions du Cerf, 2010), 397.

40 Caussé, *La Revue*, 402. Nicholas Fox Weber appears to take it for granted that the ruin was caused by German rather than Allied bombs (*Le Corbusier*, 654).
41 For details of the discussions preceding the commission, see Caussé, "Ronchamp et la Commission d'Art Sacré," 61–83, especially 69–71; *La Revue*, 395–411. By far the most accurate study on Ronchamp to date is Danièle Pauly, *Ronchamp: Lecture d'une Architecture* (Paris: Éditions Ophrys, 1979).

42 *Le Corbusier/Lucien Hervé: Contacts* (Paris: Éditions du Seuil, 2011), 88–92. Despite his aversion against having his buildings documented in an incomplete state, Le Corbusier included many of these shots in *Ronchamp (Les carnets de la recherche patuente*, vol. 2 (Zurich: Girsberger, 1957), 91–92, 97–99, 127; and Jean Petit, *Le Livre de Ronchamp* (Paris: Les Cahiers Force Vives/Editec, 1961), 136–37; 114; 141–42; 145)

L 3(7) 1 - (132 - 143)

E_1_163   134

E_1_108   135

E_1_37   138

E_1_16   139

FONDATION LE CORBUSIER

E_1_184   142

E_1_151   ↑ 143

Construction photographs of Le Corbusier's
Ronchamp chapel, c.1953–54. Photo: Lucien Hervé.

The model of the Ronchamp chapel in front of Le Corbusier's *La Menace*, c.1955.

Marseilles, as a "Chapel of the nativity and of Resurrection" (the "*bergerie*"). Here the idea was to preserve the simple building in its dilapidated form as a ruin.[43] Except for the small pyramid at the easternmost point of the site, nothing of the sort appears to have been intended in the chapel as such. (Made of rubble, the pyramid commemorates the soldiers who lost their lives under Allied artillery fire in 1944.) Radically subjected to the chastity of *espace indiscible* ("ineffable space"), the plastic expression of the chapel totally mystifies any notion of decay.

A carefully arranged photograph shows the model in front of a large painting whose date and subject matter bear no direct connection with the project, except for its Art Nouveau rhythm of sweeping outlines that reverberate with the model's curves.[44] Clearly, the picture of the model before the painting has been made illustrates the idea of the *synthèse des arts*; yet the painting itself, with its atmosphere of torment and mystery, is aiming beyond the purely formal. It resonates with Surrealism and its fascination with psychology, with the notion of the collective unconscious—as well as indirectly with the sensibilities of a growing bourgeois-bohemian public and its liability to the consolations of mystery and the mysticism of the sacred. Obviously Ronchamp is not

unrelated to those preoccupations. But can the pilgrimage chapel, with its whitewashed surfaces, be seen as a "cathedral of witness" like the proposed *cathédrale du témoignage* at Saint-Dié? Does the whiteness of the sanctuary not altogether disavow the rubble from which it is made? If Emmanuel Rubio is correct, at Ronchamp, architecture, "instead of turning its back on war [...] assumes war in its very form. By ways of incorporating war destruction, it helps ruin become one of the foundations of new life."[45] The comparison of the chapel's model with *La Menace* offers additional support to such a reading.[46] The painting is not of interest merely because of its formal makeup (though its correspondences with the chapel are obvious); nor does its iconography relate to a system of alchemical, astrological, or mythological concepts that can be seen as underlying Ronchamp's symbolism.[47] The subject is neither astrological nor alchemical. What is called upon is Greek mythology, albeit in the usual way.

The scene is martial. A tall nude woman stands by the side, barely identified by hip, leg, and navel. A much smaller man on the right side (a *maréchal ferrant*, or "farrier")[48] is holding a horse that clearly dominates the scene, its head and mane intersecting with the woman's face. The distressed expression of the "Amazon" and her brown face, turned to the right, is nearly drowned out by the grimace of the horse's head, above her. With its eyes and nostrils wide open, ears tense, and teeth bare, the horse dramatizes the pain and panic that is in the air—an allegory of despair. If animal form were not given in an almost cartoonlike way (reminiscent of a Disney animation movie), one might be reminded of Géricault's embattled horses depicted as allegories of human passions. A glance at Picasso's mural *Guernica*, shown at the 1937 Paris World's Fair, is enough to contextualize the painting within the universe of contemporary high art.[49]

A letter dated March 6, 1938, to Le Corbusier's mother, Charlotte-Amélie Jeanneret-Perret, casts further light on the painting. The architect refers to the "disquietudes of the times" that forced him to work on *La Menace* since early in the morning and deprived him of the "beautiful tranquility of the postwar years" (he is referring, of course, to the Platonic dreams of Purism after 1918). The "terrifying risks of a nameless war" are in the air, he says, not excluding, however, that "this terrible fever, this agony" may turn out to be "the end of the malady," bringing about "the delivery of a new civilization."[50] The Spanish Civil War appears to have played a key role in this "disquietude." In the year following the

43   Gresleri and Gresleri, *Le Corbusier*, 84–95.
44   *La Menace* ("*The Menace*," 1938, oil on canvas, 162 × 130 cm, private collection, Switzerland). A photomural made from the photograph was included in the 1952 Le Corbusier retrospective at the Musée d'Art Moderne in Paris (for an installation shot see *Le Corbusier ou la Synthèse des Arts* (Geneva: Musée d'Art et d'Histoire/Skira, 2006), 50. The picture was but rarely reproduced in subsequent years. On *La Menace* and its stylistic and iconographic antecedents, see Naima Jornod and Jean-Pierre Jornod, *Le Corbusier (Charles Edouard Jeanneret): Catalogue Raisonné de l'Oeuvre Peint* (Milano: Skira, 2005), 628–30.
45   Rubio, *Vers une Architecture Cathartique*, 37. In his slightly more optimistic reading of Ronchamp, Josep Quetglas sees the chapel as a demonstration that "ruin can be avoided"; see "Ronchamp: A Landscape of Visual Acoustics," in Cohen, ed., *Le Corbusier*, 212–16, here 215.

46   Note that already in 1980 Richard A. Moore, referring to the role of alchemy, astrology and Greek mythology as roots for Le Corbusier's poetic universe, described Ronchamp as "the most complete utilization of the fully developed symbolism of the Poème de l'angle droit," in "Alchemical and Mythical Themes in the Poem of the Right Angle 1947–1965," *Oppositions*, no. 19/20 (1980): 110–39. Moore's fundamental insights regarding the role of the "poème" as well as the 1948 mural in the Fondation Suisse for Le Corbusier's architecture have inspired many subsequent readings of Ronchamp, especially those by Mogens Krustrup and Josep Quetglas (Mogens Krustrup, "Det Uudsigelige Rum [The Ineffable Space]," *B. Arkitekturtidskrift/Architectural Magazine*, no. 50 (1993): 52–77; Josep Quetglas, "Ronchamp"). However, at least to my knowledge, *La Menace* has never been examined in this context.

47   As intriguing as the correspondences of certain formal devices of the chapel with themes in Le Corbusier's pictorial iconography may be (such as the formal kinship of the chapel's roof profile as seen from the south with Capricorn's single horn in the 1948 mural; see Moore, "Alchemical and Mythical Themes,"126–29), they remain internal to Le Corbusier's symbolic universe, whereas *La Menace* allows a glimpse beyond, into the immediate historic context.

48   See Jornod and Jornod, *Le Corbusier*, 596ff. Though it is with respect to another version of the painting that Le Corbusier gives these details, the analogies are sufficiently clear as to be transferred to *La Menace*.
49   Since World War I, Le Corbusier's painting has unfolded in an almost uninterrupted dialogue with Picasso, though the subject has hardly been discussed. *Guernica* in particular has been a major reference. We can take it for granted that Le Corbusier not only knew the mural as such but also Picasso's preparatory studies since many of them were published in 1937, in *Cahiers d'Art*. For some hints, see Stanislaus von Moos, "Le Corbusier as Painter," *Oppositions*, no. 18/19 (1980): 88–107; and von Moos, *Le Corbusier: Elements of a Synthesis* (Rotterdam: 010 Publishers, 2009), 274–77.
50   "Je viens de peindre comme un forcené depuis tôt ce matin. Les inquiétudes du temps agissent et me privent de la belle tranquillité d'après-guerre" (meaning, of course, the years after WWI). Then: "Risques effroyables de guerre sans nom. Derrière tout ça: rien! Des mots, des fantômes," in a letter to his mother dated March 6, 1938; quoted in Jornod and Jornod, *Le Corbusier*, 628.

painting of *La Menace*, Franco's brutal conquest of Barcelona, an event that forced many of Le Corbusier's republican friends to leave the country (José Luis Sert, among others), would be at the core of yet another series of allegorical paintings.[51] From Michel Leiris's *Miroir de la Tauromachie* (1937), France's intelligentsia learned to picture the civil war as an archaic ritual charged with obscure magic, ancestral religion, sexuality, suffering, and death—the ultimate corrida.[52] The myth of Spain's auto-destruction in the civil war, seen as the result of a savage fatality, was not without consequence in politics: if Juan José Lahuerta is correct, it offered legitimation for the official policy of nonintervention, which France shared with all democratic states in Europe. Note that Le Corbusier's own noninterventionism couldn't be more demonstrative: in 1938, he used the medium of a book cover to polemicize against France's efforts toward building up its military defense against Germany (*Des canons? Des munitions? Merci! Des logis, s.v.p....*). Later, by siding with the Vichy regime, he blurred the line between passive noninterventionism and active collaboration with the enemy even further—much to the dismay of many of his friends.[53]

While privately and not so privately committed to his ambivalent political ideas about democracy, fascism, war, and the Shoah, Le Corbusier liked to cast his political instincts in mysterious allegories. As an incarnation of archaic man nestling under the wings of ancient mythology and musing about the law of eternal return, he tended to experience war as a cosmic fatality, an inevitable purgatory rite at the service of man's (and architecture's) rebirth. In light of all this, the model in the photograph appears even more intrinsically bound to the "menace" represented in the painting. Le Corbusier himself compared the whitewashed walls of the church to "the Virgin carrying in her womb the martyrdom of her child."[54] In fact, in the photograph the chapel is presented next to the painting like a baby that has just been delivered from its mother's womb. The harmony of its outline appears like the counter-image to the agony and bloodshed that preceded its birth. In *Poème de l'Angle Droit* (1948–52), the cast of *La Menace* will reappear twice, in clarified form, explicitly linked to ideas of fights, battles, youthful Amazons, and soldiers—as if in anticipation of the dedication ceremony at Ronchamp, where the many decorated officers, music, flags, and veterans gave it, as one witness said, "a rather military accent."[55]

Pablo Picasso, *Guernica*, 1937.

51   In particular *La Chute de Barcelone* (1939, oil on canvas 70×103 cm private collection); see Jornod and Jornod, *Le Corbusier*, 664–65.
52   See Juan José Lahuerta, *Le Corbusier e la Spagna: Con la Riproduzione dei Carnets Barcelone e C10 di Le Corbusier* (Paris: Electa/Mondadori, 2006), in particular 63–65.
53   For some notes on Le Corbusier's collaboration with the Vichy regime, see Von Moos, *Le Corbusier: Elements of a Synthesis*, 210–12 and 343, note 93. The most authentic source for his political ideas are no doubt Le Corbusier's letters to family and friends, extensively quoted in Nicholas Fox Weber's biography.

54   von Moos, *Le Corbusier*, 43 (quoted after *Le Corbusier: Textes et Dessins pour Ronchamp* (Ronchamp, France: Association Oeuvres de N.-D. du Haut de Ronchamp, 1997).
55   Caussé, "Ronchamp et la Commission d'Art Sacré,"80. For the variations on the theme of *La Menace* in the "Poème," see *Poème de l'Angle Droit*, fols.122, 125.

5 Marseilles, War, and Myth

No Modernist building has been associated as persistently with ruin as the Unité d'Habitation, in Marseilles (1947–52). According to Reyner Banham, the traces of wooden coffering on the surfaces of the stairs, walls, chimneys, exhaust shafts, and elevator towers on the roof terrace make them look "like ruins." "The concrete work of Marseilles started as a magnificent ruin even before the building was completed," Banham writes.[56] With photographer Lucien Hervé's famous construction shots, the Unité became modern architecture's exemplary demonstration of the "non-finito," an ever-changing "ruin in reverse."[57] The *malfaçons* that resulted from the construction workers' lack of experience with on-site cast concrete, which was swiftly reclaimed by Le Corbusier as "noble rudeness" (since repairs would have been virtually impossible),

Le Corbusier, Unité d'habitation, Marseilles, 1952. "A striking example of badly executed reinforced concrete, considered as one of the constituent elements of a plastic symphony" [original caption from the *Oeuvre complète 1952–1956*].

are only part of the problem, though it is these technical defects that make the surfaces look "like the columns of the Doric temples eaten by time."[58] Vincent Scully saw the "sculptural drama" of Le Corbusier's late works (Unité, Ronchamp, and The High Court at Chandigarh) as being altogether linked to the Greek experience by virtue of their plastic power. For Scully, they are all "primitive Greek temples, sculptural bodies in whose gestures [we] feel a modern violence." As to the "muscular giant" of the Unité, he explicitly turned to maritime and military metaphors: "The Unité is a giant, a temple, an aircraft carrier," he writes. "Its pilotis are the legs of a colossus, a bomber's tires; the shapes of its roof are maritime, a medieval city, a dirigible's hangar. The roof is a mountaintop itself."[59] Le Corbusier was never secretive about the fact that for him, the Athenian connection had always been crucial.[60] It is via the "ruin" theme that the Unité ultimately connects with the architect's primary architectural interests.

All these implications of primitive violence do not make the Unité a war memorial, even though "Marseille was built on top of a battlefield," as the architect once wrote. In 1952, when the Unité was about to be completed, the Smithsons used photographs of London's bombed Golden Lane neighborhood to personalize their project site. The ruins were to become part of the reconstructed neighborhood, a testimony to the events London and its inhabitants had gone through during the war.[61] Though their project owes a lot to the Unité, the Smithsons knew very well that Le Corbusier had not envisioned anything of the sort.[62] What Le Corbusier had in mind when he referred to Marseilles as a "battlefield" was the battle against the unionized architects in France and their organizations, which were determined to stop the project.[63] However, without the battlefield of World War II, there would have been no Unité d'Habitation to begin with. Nor did Marseilles lack its share of bombing, ruin, and clearing up. In 1940, the Luftwaffe bombed the city, and under the German occupation, its core, the Vieux port, was razed and rebuilt entirely. Remember that French cities paid a heavy toll in the course of France's liberation by Allied Forces and reconquest of the territory under German control. Though less dramatically hit than Orléans, Caen, Royan, or Saint-Malo, Marseilles suffered 1,250 casualties during the Allied bombing in June 1944 alone.[64]

In 1947, in the American edition of *When the Cathedrals Were White* (a book dealing with New York that had been published first in 1937), Le Corbusier writes: "The American Army arrived in Europe, found its lands, its peoples, its cities,

56   Reyner Banham, *Brutalism in Architecture: Ethic or Aesthetic?* (London: The Architectural Press, 1970), 16; See also Banham, "The New Brutalism," *Architectural Review* (December 1955): 354–61.
57   It was these photographs that made Le Corbusier change his mind regarding the interest of architecture "in progress." See von Moos, "'Ruins in Reverse.'"
58   von Moos, "Ruins in Reverse." For Le Corbusier's own comments on the "malfaçons," see *Le Corbusier: Oeuvre Complète 1946–1942*, 189–91 and the captions on pp. 214 and 218.

59   Vincent Scully, "Le Corbusier 1922–1965," quoted after Neil Levine, ed., *Vincent Scully: Modern Architecture and Other Essays* (Princeton, New Jersey: Princeton University Press, 2003), 246.
60   "The immense construction is of Greek spirit; the roof, where the kids of the kindergarten play, is an acropolis." Le Corbusier, "Parisiana," 1954. See Stanislaus von Moos, "Le Corbusier's 'Hellas': Fünf Metamorphosen einer Konstruktion," in *Kunst + Architektur in der Schweiz* (1999), 20–30.

61   See Alison and Peter Smithson, "Human Associations," in *Ordinariness and Light* (London: Faber and Faber, 1970), 44–61; and Dirk van den Heuvel and Max Risselada, eds., *Alison and Peter Smithson: From the House of the Future to a House of Today* (Rotterdam: 010 Publishers, 2004), 61–78.

62   The Smithsons had visited the Unité's construction site before; see Alison and Peter Smithson, *Without Rhetoric: An Architectural Aesthetic* (London: Latimer New Dimensions, 1973), 4 et passim. For a recent discussion of the project, see Martino Stierli, "Taking on Mies: Mimicry and Parody of Modernism in the Architecture of Alison and Peter Smithson and Venturi/Scott Brown," in *Neo-avant-garde and Postmodern: Postwar Architecture in Britain and Beyond*, ed. Mark Crinson and Claire Zimmerman (New Haven, Connecticut: Yale University Press, 2010), 151–74.
63   See von Moos, *Le Corbusier: Elements of a Synthesis*, 156; Gérard Monnier, *Le Corbusier: Les Unités d'Habitation en France* (Paris: Belin-Herscher, 2002), 46–47, 60–62 et passim.
64   Wikipedia, *Bombardements de Marseille*, accessed March 1, 2015).

Construction photographs of Le Corbusier's Unité d'habitation, Marseilles, c.1950.
Photo: Lucien Hervé.

and its fields ravaged by four years of war, emptied and robbed, in ruins, covered with dirt and eaten with rust; found broken windows and nerves on edge, exhausted bodies, and tenacious morale." Following the trail of wartime Vichy rhetoric, he then goes to blame the Allies for much of the dirty job. "American aviators had bombed everything, blowing up bridges, stations, railroads, factories, ports."[65] It is no coincidence that, in a context where "functionalism" was about to reemerge in Europe under American auspices, he wanted the Unité to be seen as a manifesto of resistance against the clean, slick, and antiseptic modernism of "the others."

Nor should architecture illustrate history and biography—except in the language of allegory and metaphor, as chosen or even coined by the "genius." Architecture, one would assume, is no medium for autobiographical reflection: the shape of a ventilation shaft, an elevator engine casing, a gymnasium, or a child-care center should be determined by their functions. But the ventilation towers in the Unité emerge from box-shaped podiums like sculptures; and conical ventilator shafts look like tree trunks turned upside down, ending with a small slit from where one might ultimately get the panorama that the high parapet of the roof terrace forbids. It is Giorgio Morandi and Giorgio de Chirico turned into a grotesque Walpurgis Night. Granted Le Corbusier's own work in both architecture and sculpture, at times confirms and at others subverts the relevance of the suggested connections (and also perhaps suggests that the formal inventions might not have been exclusively his own). The obvious genealogical reference for the ventilator shafts is the periscope on the Beistegui roof terrace (all the more so since the high walls that cut away the foreground also refer to that project). As to the gymnasium, with its structurally unnecessary keel: is it an

65   Le Corbusier, *When the Cathedrals Were White* (New York: Reynal and Hitchcock, 1947; rev. ed. McGraw Hill, 1964), xl. The book was originally published as *Quand les Cathédrales Étaient Blanches* (Paris: Éditions Plon, 1937).

Nigel Henderson, View of the Golden Lane neighborhood after German bombing, c.1945. The photograph was later integrated by Alison and Peter Smithson into their Golden Lane housing project of 1952.

archaizing reference to the high-tech romanticism of the ocean liner, which is in many ways the conceptual key to the Unité; a memory of the fishermen's barges at Arcachon; or an allusion to the ship that carried Ulysses, Le Corbusier's alter ego, across the Aegean sea, cut in half and turned turtle?

Of course the Unité—"perhaps the most influential and controversial architectural image to emerge during the reconstruction period"[66]—was also, eminently so, an "art project." Many have written about the process by which concrete architecture in the twentieth century began to cannibalize the traditional arts, in particular sculpture (see Sigfried Giedion, James Hall, Alan Colquhoun or Rosalind Krauss). Detlef Mertins has done so more acutely than others:

> During the twentieth century, concrete was typically celebrated for enabling the realization of unique sculptural forms—expressionist, biomorphic fantasies of a postsymbolist, post–Art Nouveau, postfuturist world to come, which would supersede and correct mechanization. So strong was the desire for formal plasticity, complexity, and alterity in the cultural imagination—for the organic, libidinal, Dionysian, delirious, and dark— that concrete acquired a second material logic directly at odds with its rationalist Domino superego and the modernist ethos of honest construction.[67]

Mertins does not mention the roof of the Unité in this context. On the other hand, in the second edition of her seminal *Contemporary Sculpture* (1960; first edition, 1937), Carola Giedion-Welcker included a series of images of both sculptures by Le Corbusier, the Unité, and its roof terrace.[68] It is intriguing that while the building was under construction in 1950, Welcker would write a penetrating essay on De Chirico, who had already entered the pantheon of art history. Though her comments are on painting, not on architecture and much less on the Unité, they come irritatingly close to the magic of the roof terrace. Thus, they also reveal some of the more obscure reminiscences (or implied prophesies) invested in the building. "The entire world appears to survive as an abandoned theater whose stage set is made of historic and personal reminiscences," she writes. "We see bizarre concretions of human form emerging, born from a critical stance towards the present. Figurations evoking both Greek mythology and the mechanical present in Chirico's '*manichinos*' are looming over technical measuring instruments and architect's stencils like grotesque idols on fragile wooden podiums."[69]

In his book on Brutalism, Banham does not refer to De Chirico, but he has a sharp eye for "*béton brut*," that "messy soup of suspended dusts, grits, and slumpy aggregate" that evokes Art Brut, conjuring up architecture's "artistic turn" of the 1950s. As if referring to the first commandment of Brutalism's cult of technical imperfection—or indeed the "nonfinito"—he quotes Le Corbusier in French: "L'architecture, c'est, avec des matières brutes établir des rapports émouvants." For Banham, the Unité is the one building in which all the rhetorical consonances between modern technology and ancient architecture in *Vers une Architecture* most nearly come true.[70]

Breaking through the smoke screen of classicism that obstructs an authentic dialogue with antiquity was, for Le Corbusier, the only way toward bringing ancient architecture to life today. In that respect, the mysteries of his late art have more to do with the nineteenth-century heritage of Richard Wagner, Arnold Böcklin, Émile Jaques-Dalcroze, or indeed

66 David Crowley, "Europe Reconstructed, Europe Divided," in *Cold War Modern: Design 1945–1970*, ed. David Crowley and Jane Pavitt (London: V&A Publishing, 2008), 43–71, here 55.

67 Detlef Mertins, *Modernity Unbound* (London: Architectural Association, 2011), 180ff. Some of the ideas underlying the following lines have been developed in greater detail elsewhere; see "Die Welt als Skulptur: Zur Aktualität der 'Synthese der Künste'," in *Avantgarden im Fokus der Kunstkritik: Eine Hommage an Carola Giedion-Welcker (1893–1979)*, ed. Regula Krähenbühl (Zurich: SIK/ISEA, 2011), 17–32.

68 Carola Giedion-Welcker, *Contemporary Sculpture: An Evolution in Volume and Space* (New York: Wittenborn, 1960), 231–33.
69 Carola Giedion-Welcker, "Die magische Dingwelt der Pittura Metafisica," in *Carola Giedion-Welcker, Schriften 1926–1971: Stationen zu einem Weltbild*, ed. Reinhold Hohl (Cologne: DuMont Schauberg, 1973), 131–36. The essay was first presented as a lecture in 1950.

70 Reyner Banham, *Brutalism in Architecture*, 16.

Adolphe Appia than meets the eye: it is all about a maverick fin de siècle "Symbolism." In 1955, three years after the Unité was completed, Le Corbusier began a cycle of illustrations for the *Iliad*. The choice is interesting: mankind's archetypal war epic culminated in Troy's ruin and sent Ulysses on an odyssey that lasted twenty years. Le Corbusier's work began in an almost coincidental way—by taking a paperback edition of the epic poem with illustrations by John Flaxman as a point of departure. Subsequently, some of the drawings were erased or at least partly covered and made invisible by his representations of the events sung by Homer. "Not a single sign of life. Homer is assassinated," is all he has to say of Flaxman's drawings.[71] The first page depicts the muse who sings the anger of Achilles. In Flaxman's work, the muse sits politely, wrapped up in her peplos, across from the blind Homer, who is also playing the lyre. But Homer sits at the foot of a grave stele, designated by its helmet as that of Achilles. Le Corbusier shows the muse naked, her thighs open, crouching on a big rock and singing her lamentation with her head thrown back. The yellow stone on which she sits relates to self-portraits that depict Le Corbusier as a rock. Whereas here, he appears to identify with Achilles, elsewhere in the *Iliad*, he evokes Sarpedon, Zeus's son. Flaxman shows the dead hero being returned to his homeland above the clouds by Hypnos and Thanatos, the gods of Sleep and Death. Alluding to academic honors just received in New York, Le Corbusier notes, "1961, 30 April + return from N[ew] York, Gold Medal + Dr.H.C. 'Human letters.'" Thus, Homer is chosen as the platform for a reckoning with neoclassicism while also offering a self-indulgent perspective upon his own destiny as a hero of modern times.[72]

All this throws considerable light (or shadow?) on the Unité. "Born in furor,"[73] the project seems similarly imbued with archaic myths, restituted through the force of desire and destiny: a storm is in the air, as is the smell of blood and vengeance—not unlike many of Böcklin's paintings. Böcklin was a topical reference for the *pittura metafisica* and for Surrealism, as well as an occasionally cited name in Le Corbusier's early travel reports, but by 1950, he had obviously been forgotten. So are most of the formal tropes behind the biomorphic geometries of the roof terrace. Though they powerfully reverberate with ancient memories, there is obviously no simple key for deciphering them. Barge, column, stage, the organoid form of a tree trunk that embodies a memory of human form: like in Le Corbusier's painting, it is the layering of the fragments, their "automatic" interaction in time and space, "devoid of any visible link,"[74] that creates the crude and irritating mystery of the situation.

Giorgio De Chirico, *Two Sisters (the Jewish Angel)*, 1915.

71   Mogens Krustrup, ed., *Le Corbusier: L'Iliade* (Copenhagen: Borgen, 1986). Note on an unnumbered page in the 1954 pocket-book edition of Homer's *Iliad* used by Le Corbusier.
72   Ibid.
73   "Nées dans la fureur, elles sentent encore la poudre,"Gérard Monnier writes on Le Corbusier's Unités (*Le Corbusier: Les Unités d'Habitation en France*, 186).
74   "Mariant souvent sans lien apparent comme dans la vie / Les sons les gestes les couleurs les bruits / La musique la danse l'acrobatie la poésie la peinture / Les choeurs les actions les décors multiples" (Guillaume Apollinaire).

Unité d'habitation, Marseilles, 1952. The roof terrace during the inauguration ceremony.

```
M   M      A    TTTTTTT  TTTTTTT
MM MM     A A      T        T
MM MM    A   A     T        T
M M M   AAAAAAA    T        T
M   M   A     A    T        T

RRRRRR   OOOOO   M   M     A     NN   N
R    R  O     O  MM MM    A A    N N  N
RRRRRR  O     O  MM MM   A   A   N  N N
R   R   O     O  M M M  AAAAAAA  N   NN
R    R   OOOOO   M   M  A     A  N    NN
```

Collectors can be categorized both by what they collect and by how they regard the items in their collection in relation to one another. The first distinction is more obvious than the second. There are those who collect stuff—material things such as books, paintings, drawings, or houses—and those who collect data, in the form of digital files: PDFs, JPGs, MPGs, or DOCs. This may seem trivial: although metaphysically, there may appear to be little difference between material and digital things—they are all "things" after all—there is no question that a shift has occurred in the attitude toward the collection and storage of our analog and digital lives, beginning with the fact that the space needed to store such things is vastly different. Digital things are stored on hard drives or servers, which in turn are stored in abstract, often intentionally nondescript, data warehouses created by technology companies that value efficiency above all else. By contrast, when a material thing needs to be stored, having been plucked from obscurity or simply chosen to belong to a set of things worth keeping, that thing needs a space, a room, in which to be stored. And that thing's placement among all the other things in a collection has real physical consequences. The six square feet of space it occupies on a wall or the six square inches of space it occupies in a drawer affect the other things hanging beside it or placed on top of it; in other words the objects affect each other materially. A collector of material things recognizes and often exploits this condition.

The second distinction between types of collectors is more subtle, perhaps a matter of relative position more than an absolute, and certainly more paradigmatic than practical: one type of collector includes items in a collection because of their sameness, while another gathers them together according to their difference. While this distinction, too, may seem trivial at first glance, it has broad conceptual effects as collections today—or generically, sets of information—are viewed less as historical archives and more as pliable tools for creativity and invention. These distinctions are important to a discipline like architecture, whose artifacts (a sketch or a text, for example) often bear little resemblance to the anticipated product (strictly speaking, a physical structure). The easier it becomes to collect (and store) massive amounts of data, the more difficult—and imperative—it becomes to distinguish collectors of sameness from collectors of difference.

While Renaissance treatises by Leon Battista Alberti, Giorgio Vasari, and others were primarily personal and subjective reflections on society, painting, sculpture, and architecture, by the end of the eighteenth century, the imprint of scientific study, of seemingly "impartial" research, had grown in both possibility and significance. Rather than seeing the uncountable things around them as belonging to the unexplainable domain of an omniscient creator, the great archaeologists, collectors, and catalogers of the time hoped to document the world around them as a way to control their effect on that world, at least partially, and to substantiate the art and literature most closely tied to their own world views.

The desire to document the totality of the world or to create, through sheer volume, a simulation of such a totality—the ultimate, if unattainable, goal of the archivist/collector—masks a palpable fear of the unknown, of the unexplored. There is a certain satisfaction in being able to control one's surroundings, to organize and systematize the seeming chaos of the world around us. Architecture both reflects and embodies this illusion, the stasis of its finished product disguising the variability and dynamism of its process. The problem for Jean-Nicolas-Louis Durand, one of the first such archivist/collectors, was not necessarily the chaos itself, but rather the possibility that it all might end. So he measured and drew and recomposed and rebuilt on paper a world full of things that might never disappear. In one sense, Durand's project was more psychological than critical, perhaps driven by a desire, or a need, to produce in his world an unending stream of speculations and possibilities.

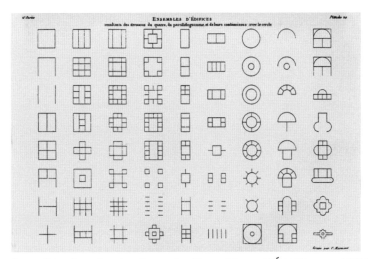

Jean-Nicolas-Louis Durand, *Ensembles d'Édifices*, 1805.

Although the ambition of Durand and his various disciples today (among them, Andrew Kovacs and others whose digital archives share a similar goal) to consolidate hundreds of volumes of objects into one master collection is commendable, the effort does not necessarily speak to rigor as much as the desire to simply make digestible a history full of things not so easily absorbed. The value of abridging thousands of years of architectural history is significant, but doing it so that others might "examine [it] without difficulty," as Durand instructs in his *Recueil*,[1] seems somehow misguided. To make history browsable is to render it mute. Durand established a set of guidelines for documenting building types to rationalize a burgeoning design sensibility of simple coincidental forms. But this act of rationality is oddly anti-historical because it erases the necessity, or even the possibility, of difference in favor of association.

Although this is an important discursive distinction, it is a difficult one to defend as it hinges on an attitude manifest in an architect's relationship (in drawing, writing, etc.) to precedent and contemporary work. An architect like Durand—who compiles and organizes things around him into categories, types, and standards—sees the world and evaluates progress by *association*, identifying sameness as grounds for reference and transformation. On the contrary, an architect who compiles and organizes while resisting sameness sees the world and evaluates progress through *difference*, putting into sharp contrast things that appear to have very little to do with one another but that become grounds for transformation through critical evaluation.

The difficulty for any collector, of course, is how to start collecting. The "collector by association" may follow a natural impulse to bring together things that are alike. Curating by type, this collector searches for basic similarities between objects—color, material, shape, size, and so on. This type of collecting is based on a generic, superficial assessment of similarity that establishes a fixed framework for understanding the relationship between the objects. The "collector of difference," on the other hand, searches for fundamental structural differences between objects, recognizing that the significance of their pairing lies not in how they are alike but in how they vary. The relationships between objects selected by the "collector of difference" are therefore more flexible and dynamic.

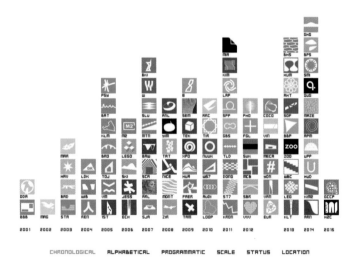

BIG home page, 2015.

The contrast between these two types of collectors can be seen in the "collections" of two contemporary architecture practices, BIG and Dogma, whose websites (which by now have taken the place of traditional physical archives) embody the divergent ideas of association and difference. Like those of many architecture firms today, BIG's home page comprises a matrix of sortable thumbnail ideograms

representing each of the firm's projects. The visitor has the option to browse by "chronological," "alphabetical," or "programmatic" classification and by "scale," "status," or "location."[2] Like the projects, the website is accessible through a series of graphic icons that correspond almost exactly to the shape of the actual buildings, as revealed in the multitude of renderings, models, and diagrams available in each project directory. BIG's work represents a project of association par excellence, and the framework of the firm's website succinctly summarizes a general attitude of its work: that by loose and coincidental association—drawing comparisons with easily accessible graphics, punchy colors, and cartoon-like diagrams—an architect can be both popular and profitable. Indeed BIG's work, as exemplified by its website, projects an image of difference (various shapes, sizes, materials, etc.), while ultimately recognizing the commercial possibilities of sameness and homogeneity.

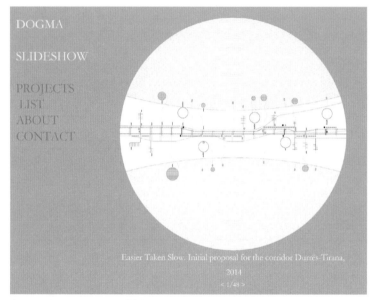

Dogma home page, 2015.

The website of Dogma, on the other hand, opens not with a series of projects but with the single word *DOGMA*.[3] The page leads in turn to the "Slideshow" directory, which presents a single image and caption navigable with small forward and backward buttons, rather than making browsable the thirty-four projects described in the "Projects List." As a strategy for presenting work, the Dogma site is like a book whose pages must be turned one by one. In stark contrast to BIG's website, Dogma's projects are presented as individual artifacts of a continuing study of drawing, representation, and scale, as well as the relationship between architectural and urban forms. It is a project of difference: by juxtaposing seemingly incongruous building types and contexts, along with drawing techniques and graphic media, the architects suggest through the collective medium of their website that an act of critical intervention might be possible only through the precise study of structural relationships, rather than the informal or incidental relationship of things, similar or not.

The differences between BIG and Dogma are apparent not only in the assessment of the various "archival" materials on their respective websites, but also in the productive materials; that is, the architectural projects themselves. If websites today represent the collective attitude of a body of work, they are also indicative of certain trends in the work as well. Framed conceptually here by an impulse toward either association or difference, the projects of BIG and Dogma can be seen as markedly different in terms of their investigation of architecture and the city. It is as if for BIG, parts of the city, like the icons on their website, are there to be synthesized into a legible whole, combined into aggregative form, generated by the ubiquitous plus sign ("+") and its tautologies, which amount to simple formal equations such as $A + B = (A + B)$. BIG's project for the West Side of Manhattan, W57, for example, combines two basic urban types, the tower and the courtyard building, into a hybrid tower-courtyard. There is little transformation of either type, other than that of shape, as the building morphs into a pyramidal form oriented naturally toward southern exposure. Although by all measures the firm has masterfully navigated both the political and economic waters to get the project built, there is seemingly little discursive depth in its relation to the city. By simple reduction and casual association, the project addresses little of the critical relationship between city and building, and the various forces impacting one from the other.

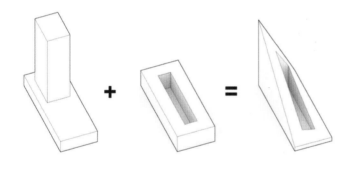

BIG, W57, generic diagram, 2012.

Conversely, Dogma's project might be represented by a minus sign ("−"), through which architecture is seen to resist, even negate, the forces of the city. In a master plan competition project for Neuchâtel, Switzerland, titled "Temenos" (deriving from the Greek *temno*, "to cut"), the form of the city is interrupted by a partial form of a building. Here the relationship between architecture and the city is crucial; neither can exist without the index of the other, and neither can be whole, in a sense, as long as the other exists. In the Dogma project, there is an intrinsic relationship between city and building based on the premise of difference rather than commonality.

Today, as some architects begin to reevaluate digital, practice and test the possibilities of a

Dogma, Temenos, competition drawing, 2012.

post-digital, critical project that turns back to history rather than away from it, the importance of assessing relationships through difference is all the more vital. To think only in terms of superficial association risks a return to architecture bound by stylistic homogeneity—or worse, a turn toward architecture stripped of its critical capacity. On the other hand, to think in terms of structural difference opens up real possibilities for discoveries beyond style, historical period, and parametric output. Today, there is little at stake in decisions about what to keep and what to throw out, what to remember and what to forget. Our digital culture loosens the significance of these decisions; it is just as easy to browse thousands of images as it is to erase them entirely. In a discipline like architecture, inevitably bound to the material world, how do we maintain critical function in a moment of immateriality? We are now collectors as much as we are makers, and whether we worship the book or the byte, our culture thrives on subtle differences of incredible significance.

===

1. Jean-Nicolas-Louis Durand, *Recueil et Parallèle des Édifices de Tout Genre, Anciens et Modernes [Collection and Parallels of Every Building Type, Ancient and Modern]* (Paris, 1801).

2. BIG, accessed April 7, 2015. http://www.big.dk.

3. Dogma, accessed April 7, 2015. http://www.dogma.name.

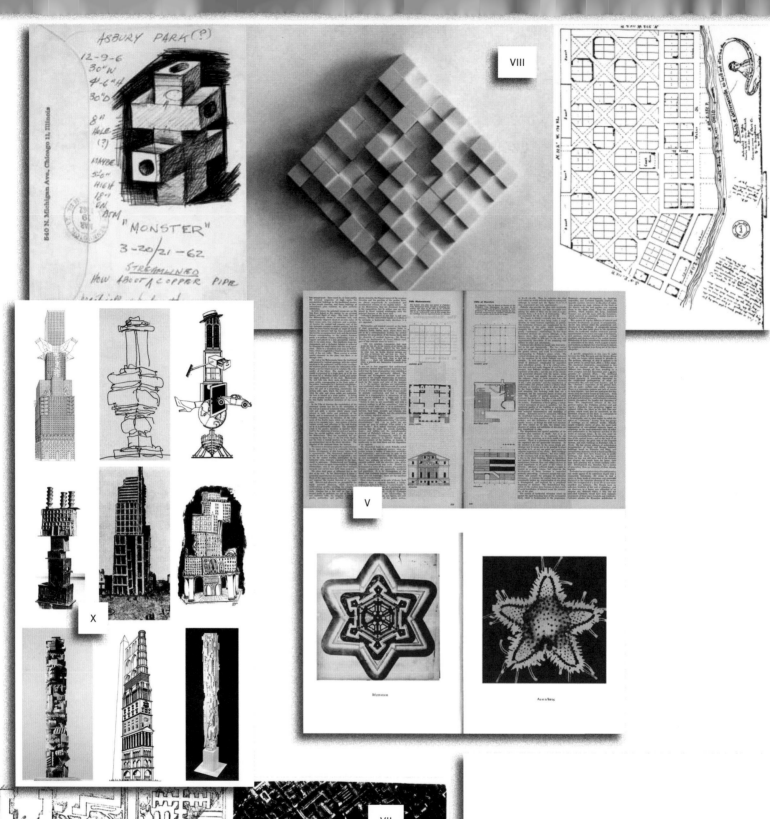

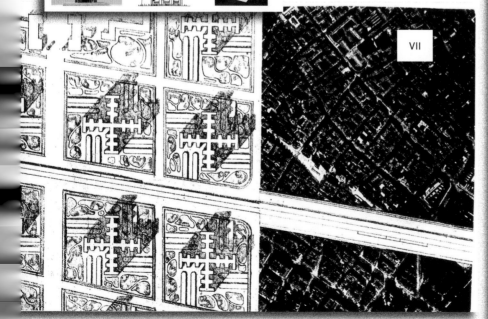

"You don't have to like something to learn from it." — Robert Venturi

IX. Sensibility Barometer

Archive of Affinities is not explicitly interested in history despite being historical. It is a sensibility barometer. At the beginning of the twenty-first century, architectural culture high and low is proliferated endlessly through Instagram, Twitter, Tumblr, Facebook, Pinterest, and countless architecture blogs. One is instantly able to collect and make images that project and define one's own tastes to the wider public. Through digitization, different media collapse into a single stream; the scale, the size, the context, and the time between images are all equalized. These new instant taste palettes are not so different from artwork such as Sol LeWitt's *Autobiography* and Gerhard Richter's *Atlas*. Quantity is integral to constructing and refining a sensibility. If practice makes perfect, then the refinement of sensibility is only amplified through the filtration of more images. One can only know what is better with the understanding of what is worse. The more inclusive and expansive *Archive of Affinities* can be, the more productive it becomes as a tool to think through the discipline of architecture and to refine its sensibilities, desires, and ambitions. More is never enough.

FIG. 9

UPPER LEFT: Gerhard Richter, Cities, 1968.
UPPER RIGHT: Fuck Yeah Brutalism, Archive Page Screen Shot.
LOWER LEFT: Autobiography Sol LeWitt, 1980.
LOWER RIGHT: @welcomeprojects Instagram Screen Shot, Laurel Consuelo Broughton.

II. The Year Architecture Broke

The late 1970s was an exciting time for architecture. *Collage City* was published, as was *Delirious New York*. Pamphlet architecture was launched. Thom Mayne turned his home in Venice into the "Architecture Gallery" for one-week shows by eleven architects. Arthur Drexler curated *Transformations in Modern Architecture* at the Museum of Modern Art, offering a glimpse at what late Modernism might constitute. Drexler proffered a host of architectural categories—sculptural form, structure, hybrids, elements, vernacular, and so on—providing the public with a point of entry into the discipline of architecture. At the same time, Charles Jencks published *The Language of Post-Modern Architecture*. If the death of Modern architecture occurred at 3 p.m. on March 16, 1972, with the demolition of the Pruitt-Igoe housing project, then by the end of the decade, architecture had been reborn with a new energy. Philip Johnson captured it on the January 8, 1979, cover of *Time* magazine, proudly showing off a new style of architecture with the AT&T Building as its trophy. The past became of such great importance to the present that the first Venice Biennale of Architecture, in 1980, was aptly named the "Presence of the Past" by its director, Paolo Portoghesi. The interior of the Strada Novissima, the main exhibition venue, with its competing visions for architecture built as stage-set facades, blatantly pitted one ideological vision against another. This Potemkin-like corridor offered a platter of sensibilities and intentions, evidencing a new and refreshing openness in architecture. *Archive of Affinities* reappropriates such energy and excitement for architecture by blowing the dust off forgotten and ignored architectural projects and placing them in deliberate contrast to one another in the public realm.

FIG. 2

TOP: *Demolition of Pruitt-Igoe housing complex on March 16, 1972*.
MIDDLE (FROM LEFT TO RIGHT): Cover, *Collage City*; Cover, *Delirious New York*;
Cover, *Pamphlet Architecture 1*; Thom Mayne's 1979 temporary "Architecture Gallery"; Cover, *Transformations of Modern Architecture*; Cover, *Time Magazine with Philip* Johnson; Cover, The Language of Post-Modern Architecture;
Cover, "The Presence of the Past" exhibition catalog.
BOTTOM: Facades of "Strada Novissima", 1981.

IV. The Architectural B-Side

Archive of Affinities has a propensity for architectural oddities, anomalies, accidents, misfits, mishaps, mistakes, failures, outtakes, follies, jokes, one-liners, caricatures, copies, duplicates, forgeries, fantasies, dreams, delusions, monsters, additions, subtractions, alterations, interventions, discards, aberrations, unorthodoxies, rarities, deviations, irregularities, peculiarities, abnormalities, discrepancies, disagreements, mismatches, alterities, rejects, scraps, junk, heaps, piles, mounds, mountains, and castoffs—or the architectural B-side. It exists on the periphery of the discipline of architecture. It allows the limits of the discipline to be tested and ultimately to contract or expand. *Archive of Affinities* brings together this selection of architectural no-nos and disciplinary castoffs. What is normally prohibited within the canon of architecture is acceptable within the *Archive of Affinities*.

FIG. 4

TOP LEFT: Constant Nieuwenhuys, *New Babylon, Concert hall for electronic music,* 1958–1961.
TOP RIGHT: Pascal Hausermann, Bruno Camoletti, and Eric Hoechel, *Egg-shaped house at Pougny*, Ain, France, 1962.
BOTTOM LEFT: Jean Arp, *The Rose Easter*, 1963.
BOTTOM RIGHT: Sanford Hohauser, Project for a Beach House, 1956.

I. Three-card Monte

The discipline of architecture is a shell game. One is constantly shifting perspectives from center to periphery—reconciling new technologies with established modes of thinking—simultaneously moving backward and forward into something new. Similarly, the small-time con game Three-card Monte provides a methodology for observing, creating, and thinking about architecture. Within its formal structure we can examine the discipline and history of architecture, as well as architecture itself. And as with gambling, there is always a loser, and it is the winners who write history. In Three-card Monte, the player's attention is intentionally misled through sleight of hand. The website *Archive of Affinities* aims to perform such deceptive shuffling to collapse the distance between center and periphery, architect and non-architect, high and low, banality and extravagance, intentionality and chance, useful and useless. *Archive of Affinities* seeks out the architectural and looks for the coincidental in the arbitrary.

FIG. 1

TOP LEFT: Mario Botta with Luigi Snozzi, *Competition for the New Administrative Center*, Perugia, Italy, 1971.
TOP RIGHT: B. Lavrov, *Linear City*, 1927.
BOTTOM LEFT: Ivan Leonidov, *Project for a Film Studio*, 1928.
BOTTOM RIGHT: Nikolai Suetin, *Suprematism*, 1931.

VI. Organized Mess

The overwhelming majority of images in *Archive of Affinities* are scanned from books, journals, magazines, and pamphlets, in other words, mediums of the past. As a website, its curatorial methodology is nimble, fluid, and pliable, a form of speed curating in real time. When viewed up-close, the selection of *Archive of Affinities* may seem like a mess that is difficult to decipher. Yet it can also be organized retroactively by criteria such as date, architect, location, and even superficial visual similarities that can be recognized by the computer, like shapes and values from color to lightness and darkness. The arbitrary imposition of such an ordering procedure results in a new and different set of readings between images. Adjacent images obtain new affinities not through the resemblance of an idea or content but merely through data. The importance of the content is momentarily suspended in favor of a totality that privileges the whole. In theory, if every architectural image could be collected and digitized, it would be possible to organize the entire discipline of architecture by such arbitrary values.

FIG. 6

TOP LEFT: Nils Ole Lund, *The Tower of Babel After 1970*.
TOP RIGHT: Kurt Schwitters, *Merz column*, 1923.
BOTTOM LEFT: Post card, *Unidentified tower of crates*, 1925.
BOTTOM RIGHT: Stephen Sykes, 65 foot tall tower called "Incuriosity," Aberdeen, Mississippi.

VIII. Disciplinary Slot Machine

As a website, *Archive of Affinities* can be understood as a real-time stream of consciousness of missed connections waiting to be resolved—ideas that are far from being fully formed, precedents without a project, references waiting to be mobilized, thoughts looking for a thesis, inklings without an agenda, and hypotheses without an experiment. As *Archive of Affinities* grows, the images produce new affinities and reveal serendipitous scenarios. For example, from a group of three images that were acquired together by chance—Tony Smith's sketch for *Monster*, on the back of an envelope from 1962; Mary Martin's *White Diamond*, from 1963; and the Plan of Jeffersonville, Indiana, from 1802—one can postulate Smith's as a series of aggregated towers forming a block that in aerial view might become Martin's *White Diamond*, further transforming into a portion of the Jeffersonville plan. By stripping each image from its historical context and juxtaposing it with seemingly disconnected images, a sort of Three-card Monte of architectural affinities generates a conceptual framework for an entirely new project. As such, *Archive of Affinities* is a disciplinary slot machine where emphasis is placed on visual relationships and affinities rather than historical contexts.

FIG. 8

LEFT: Tony Smith, *Monster*, 1962.
MIDDLE: Mary Martin, *White Diamond*, 1963.
RIGHT: *Plan of Jeffersonville, Indiana*, 1802.

V. Comparison, Comparison

In his 1947 essay "The Mathematics of the Ideal Villa," Colin Rowe juxtaposed two seemingly unconnected things—Palladio's Villa Foscari (La Malcontenta) and Le Corbusier's Villa Stein, at Garches—to demonstrate their unexpected similarities and articulate their differences in a rigorous, in-depth analysis. In *City Metaphors* (1982), O. M. Ungers offered a mass of comparisons between urban plans and both metaphorical and analogous images. In contrast to Rowe's exhaustive formal text, Ungers relied on visual contrasts and affinities between things. In the introduction he notes, "In the course of the twentieth century, it has become recognized that analogy taken in the most general sense plays a far more important role in architectural design than that of simply following functional requirements or solving pure technical problems." Comparison in the discipline of architecture—whether to demonstrate scale or metaphorical similarity, make a formal analysis or an architectural proposal against a context—is a way to collapse the distance between two seemingly disconnected elements and generate new connections and readings. The apparent simplicity and stupidity of placing one thing next to another creates a new context for both elements in which each can be read in relation to the other.

FIG. 5

TOP: Colin Rowe, *Mathematics of the Ideal Villa*, p 102–103.
BOTTOM: O.M. Ungers, *City Metaphors*, p 28–29.

X. Selections versus Collections

Collecting is dead and selecting is alive. *Archive of Affinities* has grown beyond a stock of images that offers up architectural inspiration. It aims to grasp the discipline of architecture through deliberately shuffling together competing agendas, time periods, and tastes to discover new connections and relationships. Effectively, this goal is to flip architectural liabilities into assets by placing them side by side. In the future, the discipline of architecture will be inclusive and accessible. Only when architecture is willing to throw away the past will it be able to find what really matters.

FIG. 10

LEFT TO RIGHT: Franco Purini, Barbaric skyscraper, 1985 / Frank O. Gehry, Hypotheses about the form of other presumably postmodernist entries, Chicago Tribune Tower Competition, Late entries, 1980 / Franklin Rosemont, Buster Keaton Collage.
Eduardo Paolozzi, Tyrannical tower, 1961 / V. Krinskii, Skyscraper project, 1923 / Bela Kadar, Architecture fantasy, 1925.
Gaetano Pesce, Project for a residential building, Sao Paulo, Brazil, 1987 / John Corkill Jr., Architectural caricature of Washington D.C. / Louise Nevelson, White column from Dawn's Wedding Feast, 1959.

III. Affinity

Affinity is a nice word. On one level, it may mean either a personal preference or an inclination toward someone or something. Alternatively it can point to a resemblance, an inherent relationship, or a similar characteristic among things. *Archive of Affinities* exploits this double meaning. It is a personal archive that presents a world unto itself, one that is not strictly an alternative to the canon of architecture but that runs parallel to it. While the traditional canon is lethargically limited, *Archive of Affinities* is briskly expansive. Its purview includes lesser-known works by well-known architects, works of people trained as architects that did not practice architecture, works of non-architects that have made architectural work, works of artists whose subject matter is architectural, alternate representations of canonical projects, and the architecture of the everyday. In short, *Archive of Affinities* is a selection of architectural B-sides.

FIG. 3

Scanned image of hand-written dedication by Robert Venturi found in *Complexity and Contradiction*, 1st edition.

VII. Compound Whole

In 1925, Le Corbusier placed his Plan Voisin next to the existing built fabric of Paris. While this was a powerful rhetorical image in both its claim and its representation, it can also be read as a comparison: Le Corbusier's image collapses the distance between the two images such that the proposal willingly pits new with old, clean with messy, drawing with photograph, open with contained, tall with flat, bigness with smallness, order with disorder, and singular with many. Collaged together, the two seemingly unconnected parts emerge, simply through the logic of contiguity, as a new whole. This totality is amplified by the extension of the highway from Le Corbusier's proposal, which insolently cuts through the built fabric of Paris. The alliance between these individual parts suggests a coherence that, despite being dependent on each individual part, is greater as a compound whole. Thus, Le Corbusier needs the existing fabric of Paris to demonstrate that his proposal is radically new and visionary, while the built city needs Le Corbusier to assert its own importance and need for preservation. The two parts work collectively to make a new totality; when one is without the other, the equation falls apart. *Archive of Affinities* purposefully takes up this logic of comparison, contiguity, and compounding where adjacencies produce new totalities.

FIG. 7

Le Corbusier, Plan Voisin de Paris, 1925.

THE THREE TO FIVE POINTS OF ARCHITECTURAL PHOTOGRAPHY

Gary Leggett

Center for Land Use Interpretation, *Morgan Cowles Archive, Image #clui_MCA_269_19adj*, [date unknown].

I grew up in a damp place. My father used to store his camera equipment in a deep drawer with a light bulb permanently switched on inside to keep things dry. I developed the habit of opening the drawer several times a day to check that the light was still working. Sometimes I would leaf through my father's old photographs. I once asked him what it felt like growing up without color, since all the photographs in the drawer were black and white. He seemed concerned by the question. I suppose he thought I was a bit too literal, maybe even slow for my age.

This memory captures something about photography that still haunts me today: can a photograph capture reality in any significant way? Or is it like the bulb in the drawer, containing a truth claim (the light inside the closed drawer is on) that is immediately voided the moment you try to answer it? And how literal, how slow, should we be when looking at a photograph?

Writing about photography in a way requires that you flip the script on the old adage about pictures and words: *you need at least a thousand words to look at a picture.* Obviously, you don't. But the exercise seems worthwhile precisely because it forces you to look descriptively at things that for the most part do not need to be described.

The following, then, is a series of observations about architectural photography. I call them points because architects are fond of points, particularly in sets of three or five, but I doubt that any of it amounts to a guide, a method, or even a discourse. Nonetheless, in a moment when new media has dramatically increased the dominance of the photograph as a means of disseminating architecture—almost to the exclusion of all other modes—some consideration of the two mediums' relationship seems exigent.

The collection of images presented here might seem arbitrary at first. I sifted through thousands of images in digital archives and chose ones that, in their oddity, might offer a backchannel or an alternate entry into the relationship between architecture and photography. The format seemed promising: a heavily captioned photo essay about architectural photography. Things could be said laterally; shouted from the sidelines. Captions could grow beyond their corresponding images.

The photographs would still do most of the talking.

Opposite: Julius Shulman, *Bailey Residence, Case Study House #21*, 1958.

We're looking at a glass house some thirty feet away. A man sits at his study smiling at a woman who is standing at the door holding an envelope. The camera is positioned alongside a shallow pool beneath the edge of a steel structure that juts out from the house. The light of the study bounces off the pool as if it were being stretched, not reflected, and the water runs off into the lower right corner of the photograph. Perspective is marked by a line of black columns leading the eye towards the left of the picture, through the kitchen, and out to the other side of the house, where we see a cabin perched on a distant hill. The woman stands at the center of the image behind a glass pane. Her dress is a few shades darker than the color of the sky. It might be early in the morning or late in the afternoon. From the upper right corner of the image, a hill descends towards the house. The house looks provisional next to it; foldable, portable, like a view camera. A yellow chaise lounge sits outside the man's studio, wedged between the right edge of the photograph and the last column of the covered patio on the foreground. The hill grows behind it like a tuft of unkempt hair.

compelling. We are left with an image of glamorous defeat, a forensic coolness that is not concerned with evidence or consequence, only style. The formless appears as something to be composed, not reckoned with. Did he use artificial lighting? Did he move stones around? One possible conclusion: If Atget could make Paris look like a crime scene, Shulman could probably make a crime scene look like Paris.[2]

These landslide photographs also reveal Shulman's insistence on a vision of postwar Los Angeles that was blissfully sanitized. Shulman deployed people as props and pieces of furniture, making his photographs feel more like

On March 15, 1952, Julius Shulman was wheeled out of his house by paramedics. A landslide had crushed the back of his Hollywood home during a rainstorm.[1] He had broken his leg trying to shore up the door with a wooden bench. The photographs of the aftermath, taken by Shulman himself, show the earth plowing through the window like a giant geological tongue. The interior shot starkly frames the dirt between two wooden volumes but it is unclear which is out of place, the earth or the house. The composition of the exterior shot evokes that of the Case Study House described above except that now the hill is swallowing the house and the vanishing point is absent. One senses that Shulman insisted on making the landslide look "architectural." He failed at this, of course, but the failure is

Julius Shulman, *Landslide on the exterior of the Shulman (Julius) House (Los Angeles, Calif.)*, 1951.

Julius Shulman, *Landslide entering the living room of the Shulman (Julius) House (Los Angeles, Calif.)*, 1951.

architectural tableaus than domestic scenes. Nonetheless, reality sometimes managed to leak in (when it did not come crashing through the door). Leslie Dick tells the story of a woman living in a Neutra-designed apartment in Los Angeles who had a good chunk of her bottom sliced off after being bitten by a brown recluse spider. "Nature entered with a vengeance, rupturing the surface of her body, leaving a gaping wound, an opening to the outside." It was only after losing part of her body that she could understand Los Angeles: "under the surface it was malevolent desert and terrifying earthquakes, it was lethal."[3] Shulman of course saw it differently. His photographs of the same apartment building from 1939 cast it as the modern heir to the Mediterranean villa—a beautiful object surrounded by a domesticated landscape.

Tall, skinny, cheap, and shadeless—the palm tree seems designed for the camera and the highway. It is easy to transport, it does not block the sun, it never cracks pipes, and it stands straight up like a telephone pole. Once a biblical symbol (*the righteous shall flourish like the palm tree*), it is now infrastructural staccato.

In preparation for the 1932 Olympic Games, Los Angeles's City Hall announced a Depression-relief program to plant some 40,000 Mexican fan palms along major boulevards, effectively three-dimensionalizing the city's road system.[4] Since then, a boulevard can not be photographed at street-level without it looking contrived. The repetition of verticals loudly emphasized a cinematic perspective. First paradox: photographing Los Angeles from above gives us a better understanding of what the city might look like at eye-level than photographing it at eye-level. Recall Ed Ruscha's photographs of parking lots. As a series, they capture an ethos, a substance that could only be expressed by abstracting what was already abstract to begin with. Second paradox: sometimes parts are a better representation of the whole than the whole itself. Doug Muir's photograph of the Sheraton Hotel's landscaping in the early 1980s shows us a city, pants down, in the process of being assembled. Los Angeles's constitutive elements—highways, glass, and palm trees—are strewn across the desert floor, not adding up to anything. One gets the impression that the street has somehow disappeared, or that it never existed in the first place.

1   John Crosse, "Julius Shulman Chronicles: May 15, 1952," posted on *Southern California Architectural History,* June 22, 2010, http://socalarchhistory.blogspot.com/2010/06/julius-shulman-chronicles-march-15-1952.html.

2   Walter Benjamin, *Illuminations: Essays and Reflections* (New York: Schocken Books, 1988): 226.

3   Leslie Dick, "Nature Near" *ANY* 18, (May 1997): 21.

4   Nathan Masters, "A Brief History of Palm Trees in Southern California," posted on *KCET,* December 7, 2011, http://www.kcet.org/updaily/socal_focus/history/la-as-subject/a-brief-history-of-palm-trees-in-southern-california.html.

Palm trees in front of the Longstreet Residence on Palm Avenue (Adams Street), Los Angeles, c.1920.

Doug Muir, *Landscaping at the Sheraton Grande Hotel in Los Angeles*, 1983.

POINT 2: SPACE

"It is my greatest pride," wrote Adolf Loos, "that the interiors which I have created are totally ineffective in photographs. I have to forgo the honor of being published in the various architectural magazines."[5] He did not, of course, forgo the honor but the point is taken: magazines tend to flatten things. You lose depth, volume, and resonance going from three to two dimensions. You lose space! But if architecture is concerned with what is not visible—space, as opposed to surfaces—then photography can never truly reproduce it. The camera can only point to it, suggest it, give us enough information to reconstruct it *as something else*.[6] The Müller House, for instance, is impossible to photograph "effectively" if the intention is to show it all. Are we to assume, however, that Loos thought his interiors could be fully captured even in person? If anything, photography, in its capacity for metonymy, is the perfect medium to represent a design concept—the *Raumplan*—which relies precisely on the impossibility of apprehending the whole, where each part behaves autonomously and yet requires the suggestion of the whole to assert its autonomy.

Alois Riegl had already observed that it is "only by drawing on previous tactile experiences [that] we mentally flesh out in 3-dimensional form the 2-dimensional surface that our eyes perceive."[7] This seems a far more accurate description of how we perceive space than Ezra Stoller's claim that, despite the limitations of the medium, "there seems to be no substitute for photography in aiding the perception of what is essentially a visual experience."[8] The oddity of this thought becomes clear if its equivalent terms are reshuffled to yield the tautology, "there seems to be no substitute for photography in aiding the perception of what is *essentially a perception aided by photography*." Modern architecture thrived on this circularity. Its image was essentially photographic. Despite an effort to transcend the body, release architecture from the facade, and produce objects that could be perceived from multiple angles, architectural photography reinstated the earlier role of the facade by embodying a single vantage point (allowed by context, popularized through magazines) from which to apprehend a building.[9] Even a faceless wedge like the Flatiron Building could be given a "front" by insisting on a typical view—an angle that purportedly captured its "wedgyness." Interiors were similarly "exteriorized," emptied out, released from their content and context in order to become pure inhabitable surfaces. What Allan Sekula writes about the photo archive—that it functions as a kind of "clearing house" of meaning—can also be said about architectural photography. It liberates architecture from the contingencies of use and reality;[10] it liberates space from the problem of being *truthfully*—as opposed to accurately—represented.

5   Adolf Loos as quoted in Andrew Higgott and Timothy Wray, eds., *Camera Constructs: Photography, Architecture and the Modern City* (Surrey: Ashgate Publishing Limited, 2012), 9.

6   "The photograph might not represent, but it might approximate. It might exaggerate certain properties (in the photograph) in an attempt to relay different but related qualities of architecture, since those were beyond reach in a two-dimensional image. It might compensate the viewer for one sort of deficiency by enhancing and intensifying visual experience itself." Claire Zimmerman, *Photographic Architecture in the Twentieth Century* (Minneapolis, MN: The University of Minnesota Press, 2014), 134.

7   Alois Riegl, *Historical Grammar of the Visual Arts* (New York: Zone Books, 2004), 361.

8   Ezra Stoller, "Photography and the Language of Architecture," *Perspecta* 8 (1963): 43.

9   Filip Mattes, "The Aesthetics of Space: Modern Architecture and Photography," *The Journal of Aesthetics and Art Criticism* 69, No. 1, (Winter 2011): 109.

10   Allan Sekula, "Reading an Archive: Photography Between Labour and Capital," in *The Photography Reader*, ed. Liz Wells (New York and London: Routledge, 2002), 444.

POINT 3: TIME

The debate over whether architectural photography should be "about" buildings or "about" uses was in a sense inscribed in the medium from the beginning. Exposure times were too long to capture movement. Buildings were relatively static. You could not photograph a work of architecture in use without at once erasing its uses. The image as an instant in time, a freeze-frame of a particular moment, had not yet emerged.

Buildings were objects to be *reproduced*, not *captured*. Even photographers who had not received formal training as fine artists, such as William Henry Fox Talbot, insisted on the painterly and objective qualities of early photography: "I made [...] a great number of representations of my house in the country [...] And this building I believe to be the first that was ever yet known *to have drawn its own picture*."[11] Louis Daguerre described his invention in similar terms, "not merely [as] an instrument which serves to draw Nature [but one that gave] her the power to reproduce herself."[12] The photographer could not be considered an author, a creator, or an artist if reality could effectively draw itself. Photography's claim to objectivity, after all, relied on the elimination of agency and human error from the picture.

This perception began to change as soon as photographs were commoditized. Consider the landmark 1884 Supreme Court case *Burrow-Giles Lithographic Co. v. Sarony*.[13] Burrow-Giles had reproduced and intended to sell some 85,000 copies of a photograph of Oscar Wilde taken by one of the country's most celebrated portrait photographers, Napoleon Sarony. Sarony naturally demanded compensation. Burrow-Giles argued that a photograph was only a compilation of facts—a reproduction of existing objects—and that there was neither creativity nor authorship involved in the process of transferring a slice of reality (i.e. something belonging to the public domain) onto a photographic plate. The company therefore owed nothing to Sarony. The Supreme Court's opinion in the case, however, sidestepped the issue of reality altogether. Justice Samuel Freeman Miller noted that the First United States Congress had already granted copyrights to authors of other fact-recording mediums such as maps, charts, and books. He then argued that "the only

Louis-Émile Durandelle, *Pillar in the crypt, with figures added in ink by Hubert-Jean-Baptiste Rohault de Fleury, Basilica of Sacré-Coeur, Paris*, 1882. Albumen silver print and ink.

reason why photographs were not included in the extended list in the act of 1802 is, probably, that they did not exist."[14] In other words, the court's opinion was not a defense of artistic worth—which is a slippery thing—but artistic labor. If one could prove that a photograph carried the mark of an author's work—that it showed any signs of creative labor—one could defend its copyright in most cases. Content was only relevant inasmuch as it said something about the process of its making. In the case of Sarony, the captured scene would not have existed without him. So rather than elevating types of photographs to the status of art works, the Supreme Court's decision leveled the field for all mediums of expression thereafter: a camera was no different than a piano or a paintbrush.

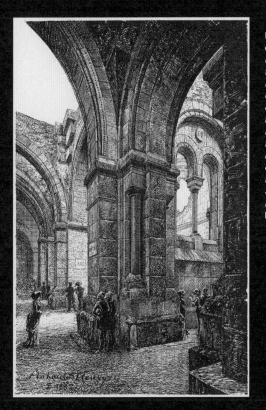

Hubert Rohault de Fleury, *Pillar in the crypt with figures added by Hubert Rohault de Fleury based on a photograph by Louis-Émile Durandelle from an album recording the construction of the Basilica of Sacré-Coeur, Paris*, 1882. Line block print.

something precious and factual but as something to be constructed, manipulated, and exaggerated.

A blind belief in photography's objectivity also tended to gloss over the incredibly rich and fluid relationship established early on between photography and drawing. The photograph shown here was taken by Louis-Émile Durandelle in 1877. The etching next to it was made by Hubert Rohault de Fleury. Presumably they were made in the same year. But which came first: the drawing or the photo? If the photograph came first, which it did, it nonetheless also *followed* the drawing, as it reproduced certain conventions historically associated with drawing. This was relatively common at the time. Many architectural photographs replicated popular drawing tropes such as view point, choice of details, or perspective.[17] It was less common for photographs to be drawn over, embellished, and "entouraged." Interestingly, the etching not only reproduces Durandelle's photograph, it also tries to "fix" it. The left-most pillar in the foreground is omitted, opening up a view straight down the transept and making the space appear considerably larger. As technology improved during the following decades, it became increasingly easier to "fix" architecture through photographic means—a tendency that demonstrates a perverse operating assumption: that architecture can sometimes interfere with its own image and that photography is the safest way to prevent this from happening.

Accepting photography as a fact-recording medium, however, also ignored the extent to which reality, precisely because it could now be "accurately" represented, had lost some of its inviolability. Édouard Baldus, for instance, was erasing buildings in Paris long before Le Corbusier was airbrushing his own. "If another building encroached too closely and reduced the sense of grandeur or otherwise obstructed the view, Baldus carefully removed it by painting it out on the paper negative."[15] He called this technique *dégagement* (clearing), echoing Haussmann's demolition strategies for Paris. Charles Marville was also commissioned to photograph the city during the "boulevardization" campaign. His photographic style and technique are telling: he chose to depict old streets vertically using anachronistically long exposures.[16] The resulting images are petrified and unpeopled, as if the city had already been abandoned by the time the boulevards came rolling in. Even in the early days of the medium, then, photographers treated reality not as

11 James S. Ackerman, "On the Origins of Architectural Photography," in *Origins, Imitations, Conventions: Representation in the Visual Arts* (Cambridge, MA: The MIT Press, 2002), 97.

12 Susan Sontag, *On Photography* (New York: Farar, Straus and Giroux, 1977), 188.

13 Justin Hughes, "The Photographer's Copyright: Photograph as Art, Photograph as Database," *Harvard Journal of Law and Technology* 25, No. 2, (Spring 2012): 340–346.

14 Hughes, "The Photographer's Copyright," 343. My emphasis.

15 Higgott and Wray, *Camera Constructs*, 126.

16 Shelley Rice, *Parisian Views* (Cambridge, MA: The MIT Press, 2000), 86.

17 Ackerman, "On the Origins of Architectural Photography," 98.

POINTS 4 AND 5: ARCHITECTURE

A photograph does not *describe* anything;
it only documents itself. Any discussion
of what a photograph is "about"
necessarily implies an assumption about
the photograph's purpose. "It is my
conviction," wrote Ezra Stoller, "that
there is only one kind of architectural
photograph, and that is the one which
conveys the architect's idea."[18] But are
all architectural photographs necessarily
photographs of architecture? Are all
photographs of architecture necessarily
architectural? No. When László Moholy-Nagy
photographed the facade of Notre Dame,
he was using architecture as a means
for something other than a photographic
depiction of Notre Dame. He used the
building as a referent from which to hurl
the viewer skyward—a revolt against the
"straightness" of perspective, against
the fixity of the eye. Conversely, when
Bernd and Hilla Becher photographed a
coal mine tipple in Pennsylvania, they
were projecting an architectural idea
onto an otherwise formless accretion of
lines. The caption, in this case, is
hardly innocent—learning that it's a coal
mine tipple makes all the difference. The
fact that the Bechers photographed other
tipples and that this tipple is part of
a typological exploration of tipples,
strips away time from the object being
represented. The photograph thus acquires
a certain universality or instrumentality
that transforms the anecdotal (a clutter

Bernd and Hilla Becher, *View of a coal mine tipple of S&T Coal Co., Bear Valley,*
Pottsville, Pennsylvania, 1974.

László Moholy-Nagy, *Notre-Dame, Paris*, 1925.

Today We Collect Everything

Sylvia Lavin

Over the course of 2012–13, a team of graduate students and I investigated the interaction between architecture and other visual arts in Los Angeles during the 1970s as we prepared the exhibition and catalog Everything Loose Will Land. *Despite a weak historiography on the subject, the commonly accepted view was that the architecture of LA during that period was artlike and we thus expected to find all kinds of traces of links between the fields. We conducted extensive explorations of many long-standing and well-organized archives, sifted through the miscellany of personal collections, and recorded lengthy oral histories.*

Every passion borders on the chaotic, but the collector's passion borders on the chaos of memories. More than that: the chance, the fate, that suffuse the past before my eyes are conspicuously present in the accustomed confusion of these books. For what else is this collection but a disorder to which habit has accommodated itself to such an extent that it can appear as order? *Walter Benjamin, "Unpacking My Library: A Talk about Book Collecting," in* Illuminations, *ed., Hannah Arendt (New York: Schocken Books, 1969), 60.*

It is no small irony that the history of modernism is the history of forgetting. The modern movement famously forged its future in the conflagration of forgetting: Marinetti imagined a fiery crash that would burn away all remnants of the past at the same moment that photographs of American grain silos were being stripped of their historical forms, a rite of purification necessary to cleanse modernity not only of ornament but of even the memory of ornament.[1] These well-known acts of erasure were preceded by less-known but just as structurally transformative efforts to induce forgetting. In 1803, at the height of the Enlightenment, at the very moment, in other words, that the modern science of history was being established—Quatremère de Quincy, the most formidable neoclassicist of that era, deliberately excluded data about ancient architecture developed during the Napoleonic expedition to Egypt from his "history" of the origins of architecture. The information was novel, highly publicized, and "scientifically" gathered, and for these very reasons Quatremère preferred not to contest it. Instead, he simply excluded any mention of it from his account.[2] Even earlier, when Claude Perrault instructed architects to side with the Moderns in the famous seventeenth-century quarrel, it was not just the mythologizing of the classical orders and their proportions that he hoped to evacuate from the nascent discipline, but the continuous history of interpretation and dispute about the orders that many now would consider the very DNA of the discipline.[3] Today no such erasures, exclusions, or omissions are possible because culture operates on the premise that nothing can be forgotten or should be considered merely forgettable. The prevailing ethos, disseminated by a more and more pervasive technological infrastructure, maintains that we can, and more importantly should, remember everything. Architecture increasingly equates its historiography with disciplinarity, and historians have replaced architects as the protagonists

Everything in your closet should have an expiration date on it the way milk and bread and magazines and newspapers do, and once something passes its expiration date, you should throw it out. Andy Warhol, *The Philosophy of Andy Warhol (From A to B and Back Again)*, (San Diego, New York, London: Harcourt publishes Ltd, 1975), 144.

Gropius wrote a book on grain silos, Le Corbusier one on aeroplanes, And Charlotte Periand brought a new object to the office every morning, But today we collect ads. Alison and Peter Smithson, "But Today We Collect Ads," *Ark* no. 18, (November 1956).

NOTES ON CONCEPTUAL ARCHITECTURE:
Towards a Definition

Peter D. Eisenman

.1

.2

.3

.4

.5

1. For an example of the use of the term architecture or 'environment' as an over-simplified metaphor, see Benedikt, Michael, "Sculpture as Architecture: New York Letter, 1966-67," ed. by Battcock, Gregory, **Minimal Art: A Critical Anthology,** E. P. Dutton and Co., Inc., New York, 1968.

2. For an example of such a text, see Panofsky, Erwin, **Idea, A Concept in Art Theory,** University of South Carolina Press, Columbia, S.C., 1968.

3. For example, it is debatable in terms of a conceptual art whether there has been much change in the last fifty years, if one were to, say, compare the work of Mondrian with, say, a Sol Lewitt.

4. See Karshan, Donald, "The Seventies: Post-Object Art," insert in catalogue, **Conceptual Art and Conceptual Aspects,** Karshan, Donald, The New York Cultural Center, New York, 1970.

5. Lippard, Lucy R. and Chandler, John, "Thus the difficulty of abstract conceptual art lies not in the idea but in finding the means of expressing that idea so that it is immediately apparent to the spectator . . . ." can be considered similar in intention. "The Dematerialization of Art," **Art International,** Volume XII, No. 2, February, 1968.

EISENMAN 1

of recent histories of architecture.[4] The field, in fact, is in the midst of a strongly historicist moment that is transforming not only the history of architecture but architecture more broadly as well. Paradoxically, the mandate to remember facts written out of the grand narrative of high modernist architecture was first issued by someone not thought of as a historian a generation ago, and certainly not thought of as enamored with the impact of historicism on architecture: Reyner Banham, at least in a casual sense, was most widely read in his own time as a critic of architects' overattachment to historical lore.[5] However, his first intellectual stake took the form of a reminder—and here lies the irony mentioned above—to include Marinetti himself and the Futurism for which he stood within the logic of modernism. Banham issued this call in his doctoral thesis, written under Nikolaus Pevsner at the Courtauld Institute of Art and published in 1960 as *Theory and Design in the First Machine Age*, where he argued that the neglect of Futurism in accounts of the formation of the modern movement left architecture vulnerable to empty formalism and to what he called a mere "machine aesthetic." Marinetti, who wanted to forget as much as possible himself, could not be forgotten.

Banham's emphasis on the importance of remembering more (which might have begun in relation to Futurism but ultimately led to his insistence on the importance of radically expanding what might be considered relevant to the architectural record) has exacted its own revenge: today Banham is being increasingly recast as a historian rather than a critic. Manfredo Tafuri, on the other hand, structured his own legacy so that there could be no such flexibility in its effects. He explicitly took up history's siren call, using history to arm architecture against the contemporary encroaches of capitalism and making it the dominant mode of discursive engagement with design, even if through a manifestly negative dialectic.[6] Tafuri turned history as a corrective into architecture's master discipline. The historicist bent of postmodernism during the 1980s needs no rehearsing here; and while the theoretical turn of the 1990s at first appeared as counter-historical, one principal impact of the reception in the field of Jacques Derrida, who almost always wrote about historical philosophical texts, was precisely the emphasis on historiography that accounts for much current writing on architecture.[7]

If, as Walter Benjamin argued, history is written by the victors, history is now itself the victor.[8] The effects of this regime change are numerous and remarkably palpable in the institutional structures that constitute the technical support for the manufacture of contemporary history. The profession of historian, for example, is being radically restructured, or rather professionalized, in a new way. Well into the 1950s, no specialized degree was required to profess the

Surprisingly these efforts yielded little material documenting explicitly shared concerns and few moments of direct interpersonal contact or other traditional forms of evidence used to understand interaction between agents or to calibrate flows of influence and interest. Although initially frustrating, the emptiness of the historical record ultimately became less a lack or merely a symptom and more a cornucopia of opportunities and provocations to develop alternative forms of argumentation.

The key to this potentiality was the instability and pliancy of what turned out to be a hypothetical archive in formation. It was not just that the record was emptier than anticipated but that the nature of evidence—of the constitution of facts that might produce a record—was fantastically unstable. Archival work is always a matter of tension between the fiction of evidence and the obdurateness of memory, a struggle between seeking proof for an idea that already appears to be a fact, on the one hand, and seeking facts for what might prove to be ideas, on the other. As such, it is never a straightforward process but rather a pleasure inextricably linked to the unexpected. The emergent archive—unindexed, dispersed, and without limit—increases the potential for the uncontrollable. The 1970s, the subject of our exhibition, is for now the historical period that is passing from memory into history, a transition that is further adding to the convulsive shifts in the nature of "the facts" and their documentation inherent to an archive. For example, since no "evidence" of historical relation between the craftiness of Mike Kelley's work and the aesthetic of the everyday promoted by firms like Morphosis and others was found, a curatorial strategy to provoke a retroactive dialog developed. These plans were thwarted by Kelley's sudden suicide, which plunged the works that until that moment belonged to him into probate court, where they were caught in a limbo between the studio and the archive, and hence between different kinds of claims to their memory. His death also triggered a massive worldwide appetite for his work, including interest from

The production of papers is acknowledged by participants as the main objective of their activity. The realization of this objective necessitates a chain of writing operations from a result first scribbled on a sheet of paper and enthusiastically communicated to colleagues, to the final registering of published literature in the laboratory archives. The many intermediary stages (such as talks with slides, circulation of preprints, and so on) all concern literary production of one kind or another. It is thus necessary carefully to study the various processes of literary production which lead to the output of papers. Bruno Latour and Steve Woolgar, "Documents and Facts," in Laboratory Life: The Construction of Scientific Facts (Princeton: Princeton University Press, 1986), 71.

history of architecture. When during the 1960s American universities increasingly required a PhD of anyone involved in conferring a PhD, a professional degree in the practice of architecture was often used as a substitute. At least one by-product of this history was a form of institutional intimacy between history and design, since often the same person taught both subjects in schools or departments of architecture.[9] Today, in contrast, PhDs in architectural history are much less casually given. Not only is it increasingly necessary to hold a

GUESTBOOK, TAPERECORDER & PRESS (stop)...
Do you have an Austrian sense of humor? Visit the museum and find out. NEW YORK DAILY NEWS (stop)...So informal. No more 'sacred cows' in art. MARIA VIUZINIA (stop)...A great way to loose the NYC inhibitions. Love BETH (stop)...Three young Austrians have found their solution to pollution and life in the 20th Century. Just pop into a plastic balloon and get away from it all. NEWARK STAR LEDGER (stop)...It could only happen in America. BETSY ROSS (stop)...Your worst exhibit yet. JP (stop)...Send one to Nixon. It might bring him to his senses JOAN REID (stop)...A 5-foot thick..vinyl mattress turned a reception for delegates to a museum's convention into a massive bounce-in..and the dusty image of their institutions may never be the same again. ASSOCIATED PRESS (stop)...Haus-Rucker-Co, I love you. CATHY G. (stop)...As a young architect I found your exhibit O.K. T. BROWN MCMAHON (stop)... It's interesting, but I don't understand any of what I feel--what the message is--but I guess that's the message. J. MAHONY (stop)...The trio must be doing something right. UNITED PRESS INTERNATIONAL (stop) ...Put a wasp's nest or one of your mattresses in Hollein's Feigen Gallery, because all of its visitors are yawning. GORDON CHESY (stop)... American Art Museumland. Manhattan. 53rd Street. Freaking out the Museum of Modern Art next door. A bunch of crazy kid architects making themselves and everybody else an art work. Plastic sexies--sexy plastics. JIM BURNS (stop)...Top of the week was the entertainment in West 53rd Street, where the Museum of Contemporary Crafts deployed a gigantic air mattress that filled the street from curb to curb..The hushed world of museums was clearly shook up. TIME MAGAZINE (stop)...I will come back with the entire staff of the Austrian Counsulate to bounce-in. HEINRICH GLEISSNER, AUSTRIAN GENERAL COUNSUL (stop)...Everyone is beautiful. PATROLMAN LEONARD KIRSHNER (stop)... This mattress should be in St. Stephens Cathedral in Vienna. MISS AUSTRIA, 1951 (stop)... Publicity seekers. Humpf. A WOMAN JOURNALIST (stop)...The best thing about this exhibit wasn't a thing--it was a she--namely Kirsten, my girl/women/everything. KENNETH E. WARE (stop)...If Shoupenhauer could be here to see all of this, what would he say? SIGNED DAVID SPIRA, VIET NAM VETERAN, LONER OF LIFE, PEACE & HOPE (stop)...Exhibit's better exercise than the gym. NEW YORK TIMES (stop)......................

EXHIBITION HAUS-RUCKER-CO: LIVE. MUSEUM OF CONTEMPORARY CRAFTS, NEW YORK, MAY 15 - JUNE 7, 1970. GIANT BILLARD STREET EVENT, 53RD STREET, JUNE 2, 9 P.M. TO MIDNIGHT.

30

3

PhD to confer one, it is now increasingly necessary to hold a PhD to teach the history of architecture even to those, like architects, who are not going to be professional historians. Furthermore, a growing percentage of the most sought-after applicants to architectural history programs in recent years have not held professional degrees in architecture but rather are trained in the humanities. These increasingly distant academic formations and professional specializations point to a future in which architectural historians and architects will have the same kind of institutional relationship as art historians have with artists—which is to say, no relation at all. For the most part, practicing artists do not teach the history of art at the university level (where art is generally taught in art schools and art history in the humanities), and it has long been commonplace for art historians to consider the artist/historian with contempt.

The architectural historian, like the art historian, is now fully bonded, licensed, and insured. Meanwhile an inverse series of transformations are restructuring the habits of museums and collecting institutions. On the one hand, the culture of collecting in architecture that was spurred by the development of a market for architectural drawings in the 1990s continues unabated. Architects are increasingly self-conscious about preserving their materials and of establishing ways of construing what they have in their offices and studios as "archives," just as institutions, often in competition with one another, work hard to procure these collections. On the other hand, more important than the simple appetite for archives is the fact that they are no longer considered a naturally occurring or organically coherent body of material, isomorphic with the shape of a life, be it human or institutional (eg., the Mies Archive, the CIAM Papers). The "completeness" required by this notion of coherence implies a substantial amount of material, which means that a traditionally conceived "total archive" requires significant storage and other infrastructural support that most institutions can no longer afford. More important than this financial constraint, however, is the fact that institutions prefer not to accommodate or serve the interests of naturally occurring archives.[10] With a much more activated sense of ambition and agency, institutions now sift and sort material while it is in limbo between the living memory of the architect's studio and traditional archives conceived of as repositories of knowledge to be used by historians. The emergent archive is a structure that is designed in this liminal zone that belongs neither to present nor past and is the natural purview of neither historian nor architect.

Nothing is less reliable, nothing is less clear today than the word "archive." [...] With the irreplaceable singularity of a document to interpret, to repeat, to reproduce, but each time in its original uniqueness, an archive ought to be idiomatic, and thus at once offered and unavailable for translation, open to and shielded from technical iteration and reproduction. Nothing is thus more troubled and more troubling today than the concept archived in this word 'archive.' Jacques Derrida and Eric Prenowitc, "Archive Fever: A Freudian Impression," *Diacritics*, vol. 25, no. 2 (Summer, 1995): 57.

architects who had previously been utterly disinterested and who now, without anyone to contradict them, claimed natural allegiance with the artist. What had begun as fact and then turned into fiction, ended up as a false memory, a myth that was much more interesting than the truth.

Many similar although less tragic versions of this quixotic turn of events took place over the course of our research. Exponentially oversized frames were made for Archigram collages because a glitch in data transmission confused centimeters for feet. Rather than a simple mathematical error, however, this misunderstanding of scale was made plausible by the media-ready images themselves: the objects were meticulously handcrafted precisely to produce images that could migrate from medium to medium and scale to scale without loss of fidelity. As a result, it was possible to both know and not know the images at the same time. Attributions had to be manufactured because women previously minimized in the record, like Denise Scott Brown, had to be more fully acknowledged, even if adding their names contradicted the documents. We had to field complaints from certain artists, such as Maria Nordman, who were displeased by our selection of works to be used as exhibition material. However, the particular objects selected belonged to archives and no longer to the artists who had produced them, and hence were legally unencumbered by artistic intention. Conversely a drawing by Andrew Holmes,

an architect who produces photo-realistic renderings that circulate through the art market, could not be shown because the drawing in question had been sold and resold until no one, not even Andrew, could locate the original.

These peregrinations, that together anticipate structural changes in the way historical material will be accessed in the future, reached their most convoluted state in the search for the one piece of evidence that should have been able to bear witness to a direct and active intersection between the art world and architecture: sometime in 1979 a conversation took place in the then recently completed Frank Gehry House between Gehry, Michael Asher, Benjamin Buchloh, and Daniel Buren, triggered by the

"The archive" is a new category of architectural object, and its contours, modes of manufacture, and value can be analyzed with the same techniques used to consider a more conventional architectural object such as a building, drawing, or book.[11] No longer found, the archive is produced by the act of information extraction that transforms a collection of things into a momentary coherence. The active and visible design of the archive lays bare its once feigned neutrality: just as there is no natural ground for buildings to innocently sit upon but rather always a process preceding building that transforms the

[T]hese pictures no longer simulate vertical fields but opaque flatbed horizontals. They no more depend on a head-to-toe correspondence with human posture than a newspaper does. The flatbed picture plan makes its symbolic allusion to hard surfaces such as tabletops, studio floors, charts, bulletin boards—any receptor surface on which objects are scattered, on which data is entered, on which information may be received, printed, impressed—whether coherently or in confusion. The pictures of the last fifteen to twenty years insist on a radically new orientation, in which the painted surface is no longer the analogue of a visual experience of nature but of operational processes.

Leo Steinberg, "The Flat Bed Picture Company," in *Other Criteria: Confrontations with Twentieth Century Art* (Chicago: University of Chicago Press, 2007), 55–92.

ground into a site, there never was a naturally occurring foundation for a body of material within an archive. The new archive is not concerned with unities or wholeness; it is not isomorphic with a single author, a complete opus, or often not even with an entire work or project. Instead it is often organized around partial objects, archaeologies of themes and concepts, and events: categories that do not lend themselves to wholeness. This fragmentation—often reinforced by the collective means of archive production—succeeds in warding off the traditional archive's tendency to substantiate hagiography while permitting other forms of authorship to emerge.[12]

The archive can also be ground zero for new forms of mythologizing, particularly those that celebrate crowdsourcing, data mining, and other contemporary means of naturalizing everything from gossip and rumor to trivia and epistemological flotsam and jetsam as fact. Without constraints, the architectural archive risks becoming an eBay of information through which everyone drifts like armchair data tourists. Unlike the avant-garde flea market, which the Surrealists argued permitted unlimited new objects to emerge since discovery was conceived as an act of projection generated by the beholder

5

rather than an attribute of the object itself, on eBay every object has already been discovered and classified. Instead of renewable projections, eBay focuses on the assignment of monetary value.[13] The reduction of all things to their place in the market is productive in some regards—unconcerned with the difference between real and fake, for example, the logic of eBay both permits the collection of real fakes on an unimaginable scale and expands the centripetal force outside of the architectural discipline, generated by what Mel Bochner once called working drawings and other things not normally considered "architecture," toward an infinite flicker stream of images, those visual databases of ephemera that are the digital analog of the marginalia of previous eras.[14] However, through this virtualization additional values infiltrate the logic of the archive: not just the spectacle culture associated with the visual orientation of postmodernity in general but searchability, popularity, and other criteria invented by the accession protocols of contemporary search engines and other related technologies.

establishment of MOCA and the design for what would be called the Temporary Contemporary. Getting a taste of this incongruous concoction of institutional critiquers and institution architects, moving in on the ground floor of a structure that imagined itself to be an anti-institution, became an intoxicating desire. Who would not want to know what was said? Each conversant acknowledged that the conversation did in fact take place and each claimed that a tape recording had been made of the conversation, in other words, that at the time, the conversation was already imagined to be worth remembering. A couple of the participants were quite confident that Buren ended up with the tape. No tape was ever found. I decided to stage a redo—to hold the conversation again, to see what provoking four different memories of this conversation would produce in the present. I sent an invitation via e-mail on October 14, 2012. Asher died while the email was in transit, leaving the conversation unclaimed by the false certainty of memory and the certain falsehoods of history, loose and available for future imaginings.[†]

This is not a book of history. The selection found here was guided by nothing more substantial than my state, my pleasure, an emotion, laughter, surprise, a certain dread, or some other feeling whose intensity I might have trouble justifying, now that the first moment of discovery has passed. [...] And then it had to be just this document, among so many others scattered and lost, which came down to us and be rediscovered and read. So that between these people of no importance and us who have no more importance than they, there is no necessary connection. Nothing made it likely for them to emerge from the shadows [...] The commonplace ceased to belong to silence, to the passing rumor the fleeting confession. All those ingredients of the ordinary, the unimportant detail, obscurity, unexceptional days, community life, could and must be told—better still, written down. They became describable and transcribable, precisely insofar as they were traversed by the mechanisms of a political power. Michel Foucault, "Lives of Infamous Men," in The Essential Foucault: 1954–1984, edited by Paul Rabinow (New York: The New Press, 1994), 157–175.

"But today we collect ads," wrote the Smithsons in 1956.[15] In today's today we collect everything, and are increasingly surrounded by archival piles and wallpapers. Like most hoarders, we have a propensity to collect certain things, and the focus of contemporary archive appetites is material from the late 1960s and '70s. On the one hand, the figures at work during that period are nearing death, an expected eventuality that is unexpectedly generating feverish interest in keeping their memories alive. A more important if less articulated reason for the attraction, however, is the fact that much work from that period was already reflecting on the implications of the archive as a work product. As is well known in the history of art, Bochner, Asher, and Harald Szeemann, to name just a few examples close to architecture, established conceptual approaches to understanding the archive's administration in specifically aesthetic terms.[16] Although today's emergent archive is more vast, pliable, and volatile than they could have imagined, their work signals the importance of giving aesthetic specificity to the contemporary archive. Further, it argues that this specificity transforms the way beholders engage with information and insists on the decisive issue of how means of access and organizational systems are designed. It is essential to exploit the productive design potential of the archive as an architectural object in order to resist its too rapid conversion into a new normal system of evidence. This is to say that the remembered thing is a thing in stasis, trapped in the subjective privilege of whoever remembers it and always at risk of being reduced to mere facts. Objects, agents, and events require passage through a period of infantile amnesia, a moment without memory or belonging: their most transformative work takes place in that interval between escaping the clutches of personal memory and being subsumed into history.

Notes

1   See the opening lines of F.T. Marinetti, "The Founding and Manifesto of Futurism," *Le Figaro*, February 20, 1909. Le Corbusier's long unnoticed manipulation of the photographs in Walter Gropius's *Juhrbuch de Deutschen Werkbundes* is by now a well-known episode in the history of Modernism. For one of the earliest accounts, see Paul Venable Turner, *The Education of Le Corbusier* (New York: Garland Publishing, 1977).

2   See Sylvia Lavin, *Quatremère de Quincy and the Invention of a Modern Language of Architecture* (Cambridge, Massachusetts: MIT Press, 1992).

3   There is by now a significant literature on architecture's entry into the *querelle*. Two distinct points of view can be found in Alberto Perez-Gomez's introduction to *Ordonnance for the Five Kinds of Columns after the Method of the Ancients*, by Claude Perrault, trans. Indra Kagiz-McEwen (Santa Monica, California: Getty Center, 1993); and Lucia Allais, "Ordering the Orders: Claude Perrault's Ordonnance and the Eastern Colonnade of the Louvre," *Future Anterior* 2, no. 2 (2005): 52–74.

4   One only needs to look at the list of recent titles from architectural publishers such as MIT Press, Princeton Architectural Press, or Yale University Press to notice that the majority of authors are professional historians rather than practicing architects.

5   According to Peter Hall, in his foreword to Reyner Banham's *A Critic Writes*, "Paul Barker [the editor of *New Society*] gave [Banham] virtual carte blanche in his monthly column, 'Society and Design.' Most of his best writing, outside the big books, certainly the most perceptive, appeared there between 1965 and his death in 1988." See *A Critic Writes: Selected Essays by Reyner Banham*, ed. Mary Banham, Sutherland Lyall, Cedric Price, and Peter Hall (Berkeley: University of California Press, 1999), xiii.

6   Key texts by Tafuri on the role of history include "Introduction: The Historical Project," in *The Sphere and the Labyrinth*, trans. Pellegrino d'Acierno and Robert Connolly (Cambridge, Massachusetts: MIT Press, 1987); and *Theories and History of Architecture*, trans. Giorgio Verrecchia (New York: Harper & Row, 1980). See also Gevork Hartoonian, "Beyond Historicism: Manfredo Tafuri's Flight," *Art Criticism* 17, no. 2 (2002): 28–40; Andrew Leach, *Manfredo Tafuri: Choosing History* (Ghent, Belgium: A&S University of Ghent, 2007); Anthony Vidler, "Renaissance Modernism: Manfredo Tafuri" in *Histories of the Immediate Present: Inventing Architectural Modernism* (Cambridge, Massachusetts: MIT Press, 2008), 156–189; James S. Ackermann, "The Historical Project of Manfredo Tafuri," *Casabella* 619–20 (1995): 165–7.

7   See Jacques Derrida, "Declarations of Independence," *New Political Science* 15 (Summer, 1986): 7–15; and Jacques Derrida, "Preface" and "Writing Before the Letter," in *Of Grammatology*, trans. Gayatri Chakravorty Spivak (Baltimore: Johns Hopkins University Press, 1976), lxxxix–93.

8   See Thesis VII in Walter Benjamin, "Theses on the Philosophy of History," in *Illuminations: Essays and Reflections*, ed. Hannah Arendt (New York: Schocken, 1969).

9   For some recent views on architecture in the academy, see Zeynep Celik Alexander, "Neo-Naturalism," *Log* 31 (2014): 23–30; and John Harwood, "How Useful? The Stakes of Architecture History, Theory, and Criticism at MIT, 1945–1976," in *A Second Modernism, MIT, Architecture, and the "Techno-Social" Moment*, ed. Arindam Dutta (Cambridge, Massachusetts: SA+P Press with MIT Press, 2013), 106–43.

10   A history of recent transformations in the collecting practices of those institutions that significantly shape the field by determining the shape of architectural archives—notably the Canadian Centre for Architecture, the Getty Research Institute, the Avery Library, MoMA, and the RBI—has yet to be written.

11   Contemporary exhibition practices have been significantly transformed by the archival turn, just as the exhibition as platform has been an essential instrument in the efforts to disseminate "the archive." The research exhibition that presents documents, arguments, and data rather than objects—or rather, that designs the presentation of documents, arguments, and data using all the design tools available today—is a growing presence in museums and curatorial work. Recent examples include Diller Scofidio + Renfro and Matthew Monteith's *The Look* (2013), for the DESTE Foundation's "capsule collection"; and the Canadian Centre for Architecture's *Journeys: How Traveling Fruit, Ideas, and Buildings Rearrange Our Environment* (2010), which examines physical changes triggered by exchanges across environmental, architectural, and geopolitical parameters. The largest-scale example is "Fundamentals," the Venice Architecture Biennale 2014, focused on displays of research in twentieth-century architecture.

12   The research that undergirds the archival turn often begins in university settings, where design and architectural history students increasingly work in more collectivized as well as hierarchical ways, closely resembling the mode in the sciences, where faculty set topics and students produce research. Potentially this structure will simultaneously limit the kinds of things that get researched as topics are defined by fewer and fewer agents as well as broadly promote an interest in using research as an architectural medium.

13   EBay assigns value at a speed and precision far beyond the already impressive systems of value produced in essays such as Alois Riegl's "Cult of Monuments" or in Emilio Ambasz's almost Borgesian system for domestic objects. See Alois Riegl, "The Modern Cult of Monuments: Its Character and Origin," trans. K. W. Forster and D. Ghirardo, *Oppositions* 25 (1982), 20–51; and Emilio Ambasz's exhibition *Italy: The New Domestic Landscape*, Museum of Modern Art, 1972.

14   EBay, Flickr, and other digital platforms that conflate things, their distribution, and social formations constitute a radical transformation to the flows of mass-produced consumer goods and kitsch items, as described in John McHale, "The Plastic Parthenon" [1967], in *Kitsch: The World of Bad Taste*, ed. Gillo Dorfles (New York: Universe Books, 1969).

15   See Alison and Peter Smithson, "But Today We Collect Ads," *Ark* 18 (1956).

16   The essential essay here remains Benjamin Buchloh, "Conceptual Art 1962–69: From the Aesthetic of Administration to the Critique of Institutions," *October* 55 (1990): 105–43. On Harald Szeemann, see the catalog of Germano Celant's recreation of his 1969 show *Live in Your Head: When Attitudes Become Form*, Germano Celant, *When Attitudes Become Form: Bern 1969/Venice* (Milan: Fondazione Prada, 2013).

17   As Gilles Deleuze protested when asked to give a more thorough autobiographical account of his work, "Arguments from one's own privileged experience are bad and reactionary arguments." See Gilles Deleuze, *Negotiations*, trans. Martin Joughin (New York: Columbia University Press, 1997), 11–12.

Notes

†   *See Sylvia Lavin*, Everything Loose Will Land: Art and Architecture in Los Angeles in the 1970s *(Nürnberg: Moderne Kunst Nürnberg, 2013).*

Images

1   Andy Warhol, *Time Capsule 44*, Components, photograph.

2   Peter Eisenman, "Notes on Conceptual Architecture: Towards a Definition," image of the original text, 1970.

3   Haus-Rucker-Co, Info Sheet from *Giant Billiard*, 1970.

4   Rem Koolhaas and OMA/AMO, *Display of Displays*, Exhibition in Manège Hall and Shuvalov Passage of the Hermitage Museum, 2014. Concept collage for the exhibition.

5   MOS Architects, *Rainbow Vomit*, model of the installation at the Creators Project Network, 2010.

6   Tacita Dean, *The Russian Ending*, 2001. One from a set of 20 etchings.

62ⁿᵈ **Shikinen Sengu**

My study [of history] has led me to the conclusion that tradition cannot continue to live of its own force, and that it cannot be considered in itself a creative energy. To be transformed into something creative, tradition must be denied and, in a sense, destroyed. Instead of being apotheosized, it must be desecrated. (Kenzō Tange, "An Approach to Tradition," *Japan Architect*, Jan.–Feb. 1959: 55.)

The ability to add new rooms without upsetting the order of the whole meant, conversely, that rooms could be removed at will. The design, one might say, had its own *metabolism*, which allowed it to keep pace with the cycles of life in Nature and society. To paste new paper on the shoji, which set the basic tone of the Japanese room, was enough to create a startling effect of freshness and light. In the same way, to have the tatami re-covered was to fill the room with the faint, clean smell of rice straw. By such a means, the Japanese house was able to create an air of freshness however old the building itself was, and it was a Japanese custom to redecorate the house in just such an atmosphere. The custom might even be described as an echo of the regular rebuilding of the Ise Shrine. (Noboru Kawazoe, "The Ise Shrine and Its Cultural Context," in Kenzō Tange, Noboru Kawazoe, and Yoshio Watanabe, *Ise: Prototype of Japanese Architecture*, Cambridge, MA: The MIT Press, 1965, 166.)

Even if the Parthenon had not been blown to ruins, it would today still be only a monument of ancient times, as life is missing from it. How very different are the shrines of Ise! Not only are the religious rites and the everlasting stream of worshippers a living presence, the shrines have yet another vital quality, which is entirely original in its effect, intention, and perception. This is the fact that the shrines are always new. (Bruno Taut, *Houses and People of Japan*. Tokyo: Sanseido, 1937, 139.)

Here is a hint of the mindset haunting modernity and its conflation with genealogy: discovery of origin is all that is needed to perform an evaluation. [...] Ise is a mechanism whose origin itself must be somehow fabricated, for there is no origin as such. What is seen deep in the cedar forest is a swindle—of sorts. [...] The ambiguity of mythological narrative also obscures the fact of its own fabrication. What we have to pay attention to is the rhetoric of veiling employed in this fabrication of origin—the only real 'truth' at Ise. (Arata Isozaki, *Japan-ness in Architecture.* The MIT Press, Cambridge, Mass, 2011, 130–131.)

The shrine is 1,200 years old, it's true, but it's reconstructed every 20 years. Do you understand? Everything we see is impermanent. Whole cities can vanish in a day of warfare. It's this idea that the Japanese believe in, not the outward form. It's the philosophy. Kawazoe talked about the concept of Ise because of the simplicity it shares with the modern style. Hitler was obsessed by neo-classical style and tried to copy Karl Friedrich Schinkel. That is the difference. It's scandalous that Tange proposed a Shinto shrine-style project for the Greater East Asia Co-Prosperity Sphere Monument competition during the war. (Kisho Kurokawa, *Project Japan: Metabolism Talks*.... London: Taschen, 2011, 385.)

New Holland Island   :   Strategies of the Void

Amale Andraos

Even in its heyday, New Holland Island was a void in the city of St. Petersburg. The canal-bound triangular island was always there, yet always inaccessible: monumental in its architectural scale, yet absent from the lives of ordinary Petersburgians. Peter the Great carved the island out from the city in the early eighteenth century and built a small palace from which he could show visiting dignitaries Russia's growing fleet. Catherine the Great lined the island with massive warehouses designed to dry timber for shipbuilding and outfitted them with neoclassical exteriors. For nearly two centuries afterward and under the control of the Russian navy, New Holland Island led the charge of Russia's technological innovation. Its central lagoon doubled as a testing basin, an experimental water tank facilitated early submarine research, and its buildings hosted Russia's first radio station and earliest rehabilitative prison. As the twentieth century progressed, however, its importance waned. No longer a locus of research and development, the island fell into disuse and later to ruin. Abandoned, overgrown, and more mysterious than ever, it became a site of romantic projection for artists and writers alike.

WORKac, New Holland Island, St. Petersberg, 2011. Entrance to the island & Contemporary Art Museum.

LEFT   Radio equipment, New Holland Island, 1916. Period photograph.

RIGHT   De la Mothe Arch, New Holland Island. Photo: Evgeny Gerashchenko.

In 1977, architect Veniamin Fabritsky suggested converting the island into a cultural center. In 2005, a competition was launched to restore the site and transform it into a cultural destination. Foster + Partners was awarded the project with a seemingly earnest strategy to restore the island to its never fully realized self, proposing to build a "missing" warehouse—an originally proposed fourth structure—to complete the island as an "ensemble." With this earnestness, though, came a subversive flattening of history best embodied by the competition entry's renderings, which purposefully blurred all difference between the existing warehouses and the architect's interpretation of them. The new so neatly complemented the old that Foster's design implied a retroactive *parti* for New Holland Island: an object with a uniform

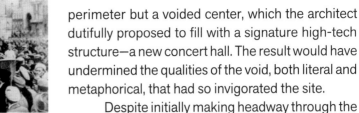

perimeter but a voided center, which the architect dutifully proposed to fill with a signature high-tech structure—a new concert hall. The result would have undermined the qualities of the void, both literal and metaphorical, that had so invigorated the site.

Despite initially making headway through the city's approval process, Foster's scheme was eventually rebuffed and later abandoned as a result of the economic downturn. Yet the island had already been irreversibly changed. In the name of restoring the eighteenth-century grandeur, much of everything else was demolished: the testing pool where nineteenth-century ice-breaking technology reached its zenith, the laboratory where Dmitri Mendeleev devised the periodic table of elements, and the radio station where Lenin made a historic announcement to the fleets that the revolutionaries had seized control of the navy. Where a panoply of buildings once bore witness to disparate episodes of Russian history, an act of erasure now threatened to leave only a single moment, irrevocably locked in the eighteenth century. In addition, new foundation work had begun on one of the warehouses but was never completed: a precarious situation for the monumental structures that had survived for centuries.

In 2010, WORKac was invited to partake in a second invited competition to reimagine the site. Well aware of this recent history, we approached the design with only the most surgical ambitions and a series of challenges for ourselves: *How could we intervene in the most minimal ways? How could we do more with less? What strategic operations—insertions, combinations, and consolidations—would open up the most possibilities? How could we entangle architecture and infrastructure in irreversible ways? What would an architecture of subtraction be like? Finally, how could we preserve the island's mystery and aura as an object of public imagination while providing public access for the first time?*

To answer these questions, our competition entry adopted a stance of "strategic amnesia." Faced with so much history and so little time to unravel it, we felt that the less we knew, the smaller risk we took of making value judgments as to what did or did not merit preservation. We evaluated each option as part of a strategy of minimal impact, as if excavating an archeological site just enough, leaving something for future generations to uncover and interpret in new ways. Rather than attempting to discover and then reveal the island's lesser known histories, or recover its now destroyed pasts, we worked with the island's extant material conditions to address its most obvious needs.

WORKac, New Holland Island.
Aerial view of the project and urban context.

Strategies of the Void

Inspired by the island's combination of monumental presence and mysterious, inaccessible "absence," we started to understand New Holland Island as a series of nested voids: the void of the lagoon at the center of the island and the void of the island in the heart of the city. Adopting the void as the main strategy by which to surgically adapt and transform the island's existing buildings, we found inspiration in staging a critical dialogue between two other kinds of voids: OMA's Très Grande Bibliothèque and Gordon Matta-Clark's *Conical Intersect*.

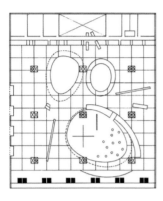
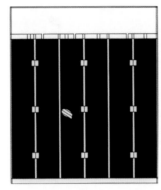
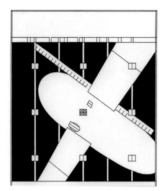
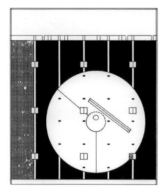
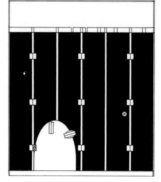
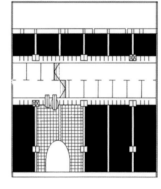

Rem Koolhaas & OMA, Très Grande Bibliothèque competition entry, Paris, 1989. Conceptual building sections.

In his seminal competition entry for the Très Grande Bibliothèque (1989), in Paris, Rem Koolhaas proposed the void as the promise of freedom, the place of "potential," and a moment of programmatic and formal disruption carved out of the dense mass of books. The void of Très Grande Bibliothèque builds on the long history of the void as a space of exception within the city—of continuous public experience and unexpected collective encounter—from Nolli's map of Rome to Candilis-Josic-Woods's courtyards at the Free Berlin University. And yet, while inspired by the void of the city, the void of the Très Grande Bibliothèque is no longer that of the city but rather deeply embedded within an endless and hermetic interior.

Through strategic subtraction and precision torquing, *Canonical Intersect* adopts a similar diagram of carving away mass to produce new forms. However, by extending his carved voids to the edge of the host building, Matta-Clark erodes the boundary between inside and outside, thereby rendering the personal, as embodied by the Parisian domestic spaces, as an integral part of the public experience of the city. *Conical Intersect* thus recasts the relationship between inside and outside, charging both with equal importance in the making of the city.

Gordon Matta-Clark, *Conical Intersect*, 1975.

An interior bay of Building 17.
New Holland Island.

We enlisted Koolhaas's void to introduce programmatic otherness into the density produced by the warehouse walls—creating larger public gathering spaces and gardens to interrupt the relentless series of overstructured and tightly spaced brick walls that formed the isolated wood-drying chambers. At the same time, our voids turned to the formal and operative strategies of *Canonical Intersect* to undermine the buildings' hermetic interiority, opening them up to the sky. In this way *Conical Intersect* offered guidance for an architecture that undermined traditional approaches to preservation, which typically focus on exterior facades while disregarding a building's interiority.

In the case of New Holland Island, the city's preservation guidelines had emphasized exteriority over the warehouses' interiors, regardless of the fact that their lofty *interior* bays specifically contributed to the island's history as a center of technological innovation. In addition, this single operation of cutting through the dense layers of the warehouses and exposing them to the sky eroded the illusion of solid mass, which the city's preservation guidelines were designed to create. This operation reframed them as a series of complex and textured surfaces. Given the intimate relationship between the interior functions, the architecture of the warehouses, and the land formed around them, it seemed opportune that the unique monumentality of the warehouses' interior walls and bays be revealed as an integral part of the public experience of the island.

With the single literal assertion of the "island-as-void," the accepted preservationist hierarchies between *exterior* and *interior*, and *mass* and *surface* were undermined. Indeed with the metaphorical embrace of the void, the island's status as a site of mystery, projection, and fantasy became the most critical aspect to preserve over its mere material presence.

Existing exterior conditions,
New Holland Island. Photo: Serj Nickel.

Existing exterior conditions,
New Holland Island.

Operations

Following our embrace of a "strategic amnesia" that favored tactics of subtraction, strategic interventions, and minimal impact, we devised a series of operations that would be sequenced and layered to both preserve and recreate the "island-as-void" in and for the city.

Operation: Nature

WORKac, Building 16, New Holland Island. Interior promenade and courtyard.

Despite St. Petersburg's extreme climate, one of the most intriguing characteristics of the island was the presence of trees and "nature" throughout its history. The warehouses were originally built to store and dry tree trunks that we leaned vertically against the thick interior walls. The wood was then fashioned into ships, which were tested in the central lagoon. After the island was abandoned, trees and tall grasses once again occupied its buildings, this time as overgrown live "nature" among the ruins. By maintaining the current density of green while introducing new kinds of landscapes, gardens, and trees, we could at once enlist the island's historical past, preserve its present aura of mystery, and point to new possibilities for its future use. Like the scene from the movie *WALL-E* in which the slightest hint of nature is taken as a prophecy of future natural redemption, the moment in which nature reasserts its perseverance can be a powerful catalyst for projection—a critical aspect to the island's preservation as an object of collective imagination.

With the island's grounds now conceived of as a park—partly preserved as it was, partly restored as historical gardens, and partly designed as a newly constructed landscape—nature was reintroduced inside the warehouses. Within the voids punctuating the roofline of the buildings, we introduced patches of forest to interrupt the regular, dense rhythm of the interior bays and recreate the hybrid of city and nature that the ruin had become. Articulated as courtyards, the new gardens and tall trees brought the park into the buildings and cemented the roof space as an integral part of the public experience of the island.

Operation: Inside/Outside

Despite the fortresslike quality of the warehouses, the relationship between inside and outside had always been one of continuity. The buildings originally had open facades to maximize airflow for drying wood, and the interiors were constructed with a seamless connection between inside and outside at ground level, corresponding to that between the interior of the island and the exterior embankments. The newly created openings at the roof level further connected the interior of the warehouses to the city, with new vistas both from within the buildings looking out and from the city looking back at the island. Through this subtraction of mass, the warehouse interiors' unique density and structural rhythm was made tangible even from a distance. With increased exteriority, the warehouse interiors became important to a contemporary interpretation of the island's history.

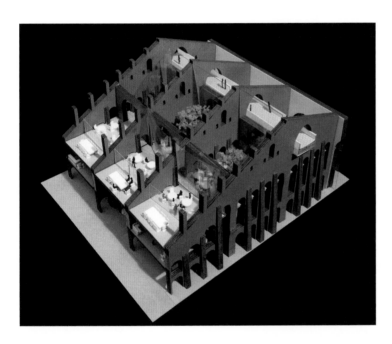

WORKac, Model of Building 16, New Holland Island. View of interior gardens, courtyard and restaurants.

Operation: Infrastructural Promenade

The insertion of exterior courtyards within the interior roof zone not only echoed the historical continuity between inside and outside, but also created the possibility for a continuous public experience from the ground up to roof level, and back down. The result was a diagram in section that sandwiched all private programs—residential and commercial—between two public zones at the ground and roof levels. To connect these spaces to the continuous public experience, we created a three-meter-wide promenade that wound its way through the attics of the warehouses. This had the effect of maintaining public access through the long winter months, echoing the winter gardens found throughout the palaces of St. Petersburg

The promenade also embodied another logic of our preservation approach—that of entangling architectural interventions and infrastructure to maximize opportunity while minimizing impact. Weaving its way through newly cut arches, the elevated promenade carried not only the public but also many of the systems designed to feed the warehouses—power, water, data, and ducts—minimizing any underground perforation that would have threatened the warehouses' brick foundations and timber piles.

While the promenade reinforced surface continuity and extended the park into the interiors, tying the grounds and buildings together in a single gesture, it also reinforced the island's architectural character as an "ensemble" (one of its most important qualities according to the preservation guidelines) in new and unexpected ways. The promenade strategically bridged buildings, creating a strong architectural statement, embodying a counterpart to Vallin de la Mothe's arch, and offering a new entrance gate for the contemporary cultural complex.

Operation: Infrastructural Landscape

Our consolidation of architecture, landscape, and infrastructure continued with the rest of the island. The only new structure, the contemporary art museum, was designed to hold both the art pieces and the largest programs as well as the island's new infrastructure—a central plant, loading dock, and server. Shaped like a multi-faceted wedge, the museum building acted as a hinge between the interior of the island and the surrounding city. On the island side, the building sloped gently to meet and extend the park, raised just enough to make room for the required mechanical spaces underneath. On the side facing the city, the building's height and roof form echoed those of the existing warehouses, completing the island as an "ensemble" and occupying the space of the fourth, unbuilt warehouse. Part building, part land-form, the structure comprised stepping and slopes that allowed seating from which to experience the island's interior void.

This hybrid condition of landform and building also became a connection through time: half of the structure registered the historical warehouses and the other half continued the newly designed park. Negotiating the two halves of the building was another, long rectangular cut, which exposed the museum's interior to the outside and connected its two sides. Designed to occupy the former foot-print of Mendeleev's testing pool (demolished during the early days of the Foster plan), the cut registered the void left by the missing pool and manifested the era of the island's history dismissed by the preservation guideline's reductive focus on the nineteenth century.

To further the idea of creating new perspectives of the island and allowing for different understandings and experiences to emerge, we proposed a large bal-loon—a temporary vertical interruption to contrast the endless horizontality of the city. From above the public could reflect on St. Petersburg's urban fabric and New Holland Island's place in it, producing a counterpoint to the perspective of the island as romantic, monumental, and mysterious.

Operation: Intangible Heritage

Upon winning the competition, we invited artist and preservation architect Jorge Otero-Pailos to collaborate with us in exploring nontraditional modes of preserva-tion. In particular, his interest in revealing New Holland Island's intangible heritage offered new insight for experiencing its multilayered, complex past. From his previ-ous work with dust at the 2009 Venice Biennale to his *Olfactory Reconstruction of Philip Johnson's Glass House* (2008), Otero-Pailos's design research was a perfect complement to our approach of surgical interventions.

Otero-Pailos's intent was three-fold: first, to layer the idea of multiple narra-tives by identifying a series of markers, each of which would tell one of the many stories of the island and its transformation across time. This strategy found expres-sion in the promenade already weaving its way through the warehouse building, now conceived as a continuous narrative loop. Second, to propose a careful restoration of all of the warehouses' surfaces, inside and out, while preserving the sense of aging, unevenness, and overall texture that centuries of St. Petersburg's climate had lay-ered on top. Finally, Otero-Pailos's long-standing interest in the power of scent to trigger memory was enlisted to create a series of surprising and varied experiences. Along the promenade, the island's history as a center of nautical innovation was reg-istered not only through the gardens and trees but also through a small number of "preserved bays," where the smell of eighteenth-century wood drying was reconstituted. After extensive research into the types of pitch and species of wood used, and other olfactory elements, Otero-Pailos staged a sensory experience that layered carefully reconstructed historical information with more personal memories, thereby reenforcing the project's questioning of traditional modes of preservation in favor of new means that reveal complex histories.

Conclusion

As the project developed, we realized that underlying all of the strategies and operations was an unconscious desire to discover something other than the expected and official narratives for the island. While the cuts along the roofline of the warehouses explored the possibilities of an architecture of subtraction and questioned the hierarchies codified in the city's preservation guidelines, they also helped tell the manifold history of the island we "discovered" in searching for past moments that resonated with our present disruptions.

Mendeleev flying the aerostat Henri Giffard Balloon, Paris, 1878. Period photograph.

The balloon and the wedge building acted in much the same way. By projecting a balloon for the future, we found one in history. While researching old archives to construct Otero-Pailos's interpretative path, we found a photograph of Mendeleev in Paris in one of the very earliest balloons. Similarly, as the wedge took form under the encouragement of local preservation officials, it grew from its understated competition silhouette to registering the forms of the adjacent warehouses and thus completing the proposed historic ensemble. The wedge and the balloon provided not only new experiences of the site but also a new framing of the island, and therefore a new approach to understanding its history.

Finally, the coupling of infrastructure and promenade created a new kind of public space for St. Petersburg that enabled a reinterpretation of history along a narrative loop connecting the warehouses to the grounds. This also served to preserve the sense of the island and its history as belonging both to the public and as an object of imagination and collective memory.

WORKac, New Holland Island. View of the park in springtime.

Stephan Petermann   &   OMA/AMO

Gütersloh
Ice
Core
Drilling

Blessed are the forgetful:
for they get the better even of their blunders.
—Friedrich Nietzsche

A pausenzone at the Buch und Ton offices, Gütersloh, Germany, c.1965.

GÜTERSLOH
ICE CORE DRILLING

One of the most notable omissions from current thinking on the future of our workplace is history. For some reason—probably the difficulty of fitting it into the requirements of the market economy—the topic plays an almost negligible role in most brochures-cum-studies by major parties of the consulting world. One or two contain an obligatory mention of iconic office projects by Frank Lloyd Wright, Louis Sullivan, and the like.[1] Most others relegate history to a "siloed legacy" that should be overcome technocratically. Collectively their narratives, drenched in management speak, read like social-realist poetry: we used to be slaves, we became laborers, we are now networkers, and soon we will be free-floating endless collaborators. And since every concrete answer means less business for consultants, these studies are littered with self-interested clichés and vague announcements of an uncertain future.

HOMEOPATHIC

Most consultant reports are at best homeopathic by design. The quantifiable data they so eagerly present comes almost exclusively from small surveys or self-referencing sources—the reliability of the data is never disclosed. The narrowing of the temporal horizon—at most these surveys amount to an endless series of weather reports—creates a continuous tabula rasa to the benefit of the weatherman. This would be justifiable if the research were part of an innovative or evolving enterprise. However, typological considerations of our workplace have remained highly stagnant over the last sixty years. Design strategies have oscillated between obvious poles: from single-cell to open-plan offices, from flexible workstations to permanent desks, or, understood more broadly, from control to relative freedom. The only constant in this oscillation is a desire to shrink capital expenditures while raising productivity. As understandable as it is unsettling, this situation mimics the supposed brain of the CEO—thinking only of the next quarter's revenue. The result is a blind spot for the sort of long-term climatic forecasting needed to achieve progress. Yet to move forward our thinking about the workplace must first evolve, jettisoning its obvious agendas and inherent biases in favor of collaborative and systematic methods.

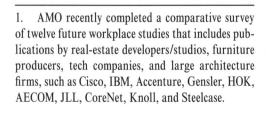

1.   AMO recently completed a comparative survey of twelve future workplace studies that includes publications by real-estate developers/studios, furniture producers, tech companies, and large architecture firms, such as Cisco, IBM, Accenture, Gensler, HOK, AECOM, JLL, CoreNet, Knoll, and Steelcase.

3 – 8 – 10

Two particular aspects of generic consultant research do consider time, though paradoxically they are disconnected. One of the most suggestive "statistics" found in multiple studies deals with the rate of change in office organizations, configurations, and transformations. On average offices are reorganized every three years, have a staff turnover of eight years, and renovate every ten years.[2] The other common temporal consideration is the complete opposite, namely the case study. As a moment frozen in time, the case study appears in most reports, typically just after renovation. In almost every one, likeable people seemingly performing at the top of their potential fill a clean and shining office. The juxtaposition of the two suggests—like a "best before" sticker seen too late—that such research is by definition instantly out of date. Taken together, the implications lobotomize the design process and eschew any notion of permanence. Earlier this year, AMO started looking into the one of the turning points of office development, which arguably triggered the tyranny of the open plan: the *Bürolandschaft*, or office landscape, a veritable safari of a workplace tried out in the 1960s, most notably by the German office consultancy Quickborner Team. Given the unheralded importance of this experiment, we decided to reconstruct exactly what happened to the Bürolandschaft after its initiators had left the scene.

GÜTERSLOH, 1961

This floor plan is a perennial, known by anyone who has ever opened a book about modern office design.[3] It is the floor plan that arguably launched the casual "collaborative" open floor plans that dominate offices today. In textbooks, the famous drawing is usually flanked by one or more photos showing a woman at a typewriter, surrounded by plants, with a jungle of seemingly randomly placed desks in the background. It is the plan of the first realized Bürolandschaft in Gütersloh, Germany. This particular floor is on top of the first super-high storage facility in Europe. The space houses the sales and distribution department of Buch und Ton, a mail-order division of the Bertelsmann Media Group for books and records.

Not uncharacteristically among postwar West German businessmen, Bertelsmann's then CEO Reinhard Mohn had been to the United States in the 1950s and was inspired by the American way of working. Upon his return, he hired architect Walter Henn, a professor at Technische Universität Braunschweig, to design a new experimental office based on the deep open-plan offices he visited.[4] For the interior planning Mohn commissioned the Hamburg-based Quickborner Team, a recently established office-consultancy firm linked to TU Braunschweig and founded by Eberhard and Wolfgang Schnelle. The Schnelle brothers were inspired by the United States, specifically by Frederick Taylor's theories of scientific management. Accordingly Quickborner used mathematical models to extend Taylor's theories and create what might have appeared as a haphazard jumble of desks but was in fact a rationally designed office environment.

---

3.   There are many books that mention the *Bürolandschaft*, most notably those of Frank Duffy and Caruso St. John Architects. For a description of the history of the *Bürolandschaft*, see chapter 6 in Nikil Saval, *Cubed: A Secret History of the Workplace* (New York: Doubleday, 2014) and Andreas Rumpfhuber, *Architektur Immaterieller Arbeit, Kollektive Gestalten*, vol. 1 (Vienna: Turia und Kant, 2013).

4.   Please see the Bertelsmann company archive.

2.   Knoll, "Shaping the Dynamic Workplace" (2013), http://www.knoll.com/knollnewsdetail/shaping-the-dynamic-workplace.

FOLLOW THE LETTER

With the assistance of Bertelsmann's management, the Schnelles spent ten days sifting through the minutest details of the company's internal workings. They followed every letter that came into the office, tracking which hands it passed through, what departments and decision makers received it, and how it was ultimately filed.[5] Their research was synthesized into impressively complicated flow charts and subsequently connected to tables with standardized basic units for physical requirements. This was finally translated into office planning. The result was a highly defined floor plan based on a rationalized proximity between relevant teams and roles, sight lines, and other practical considerations.

Absent easy access to light and air, the Schnelle brothers also designed the employees' personal environments. They determined the most optimal synthetic replacements: 1,900 light tubes to introduce three different light conditions; 50,000 m^3 of artificially purified air pumped in per hour; a modicum of acoustic dampening delivered via cognac-colored velour carpet; an acoustical ceiling; small movable partitions; and high-quality modern furniture made specifically for the space. The colors used for the few walls were based on a physiological analysis of workforce behavior.

AN APPARENT NOVELTY

The plan in Gütersloh is about half the size of a soccer pitch and offers space for 250 employees. Four external cores containing elevators and stairs, one internal elevator, and a regular column grid anchor the space. Visitors arrive in the southeast corner, where there is a small reception. Originally a diagonal axis defined by loosely positioned plants created the main circulation artery. From the artery, a small number of stubs enclosed smaller workgroups. Management sat behind the reception and to the right was human resources; behind and to the left were two fields of typists and distribution employees. The far corners contained an apparent novelty on the work floor: a small pantry and some lounge chairs providing access to hot and cold beverages throughout the day.

A typical work space at Buch und Ton, c. 1965.

SHOWCASE

In November 1961, Bertelsmann's internal newspaper ran a glowing review of the project that highlighted the technical advances made in the new space.[6] This article was followed two months later by another report, which spoke highly of the initial results of the experimental office layouts: "The move of the sales departments of the commission house into the transformed sixth floor was the most important achievement of 1961. Six months after completion, you could say that the experiment is a success and has brought significant improvements to workflow." There were no complaints at all, it suggestively reported.[7] Echoing a similar sentiment, a substantial article in *Baumeister* by architect Walter Henn discussed the design in Gütersloh and several other offices, giving detailed explanations of how they improved on the American precedents.[8]

In March 1962, the first jokes about the space started to appear. The Bertelsmann internal newspaper published the ironic review "How to behave in the open-plan." Most notably, it discussed the difficulty of giving people directions to reach your desk, the physical shortcomings of the space, and the new *pausenzones*—informal break areas.[9]

5. Andreas Rumpfhuber, "Space of Information Flow," in *Experiments: Architektur zwischen Wissenschaft und Kunst* (Berlin: Ákos Morávanszky and Albert Kirchengast [publishers], 2011), 200–225.

What in retrospect must have been the most significant visit occurred in 1963. Frank Duffy, then a student at the AA, paid Buch und Ton a visit. Having heard about the Quickborner Team, he was intent on seeing some of their built work. Subsequently he wrote an article for *The Architectural Review* that would, as he says, determine his career.[10] Duffy signaled some technical and organizational problems but was convinced of the Bürolandschaft's potential. He concluded, "In general the impact of this development lies more in its broad human implications than in its detailed technical achievements."

In November 1964, Mohn sent a five-page report of a fourteen-day working experience in the Buch und Ton office to Bertelsmann management. In it he systematically reviewed a variety of issues with the new office space, signaling technical shortcomings in acoustics, lighting, and climate, and concluding that due to issues regarding secrecy the environment was not suitable for management. In the end, however, he—like Duffy—remained convinced of the space's principles and encouraged management to do more research: "The criticism against the open plan was made by people with only superficial knowledge of the workplace conditions. It would be great if, through your personal experience, our discussions could be further developed into a more deeply founded knowledge so we can determine what the true problems are."[11] It is not clear whether management accepted his offer.

In 1966 Ottomar Gottschalk reviewed the Quickborner Team's work, mentioning that earlier in the year the office environment at Buch und Ton had been upgraded. "Despite significant oversights in construction (climate, blinds, power supply) [the space is] in good shape. Excellent acoustical conditions. The space has [...] facilitated many organizational improvements."[12] In the meantime business was going well for Quickborner. Since its debut in 1961, it had started consulting to major industrial firms like Goodyear, Ford, and Osram. In 1967, Quickborner opened a branch office in the United States and, not long afterward, another in Caracas.[13] In his 1964 report, Mohn also mentioned the significant number of visitors coming to the space in Gütersloh.

EXPANSION

In the 1960s Bertelsmann was also doing well. The recently introduced Bertelsmann book clubs had quickly exceeded one million subscribers. In 1968, the company decided to build a new headquarters a few hundred meters down the newly named Carl Bertelsmann Straße. While developing the new design, management remained convinced of the Bürolandschaft principle, though the internal courtyards reveal a stronger concern for access to daylight. By the time of its completion in 1972, however, Bertelsmann's management had altered its opinion and did not implement the Bürolandschaft. Instead they chose a middle road between the old plan and traditional celled offices—a cubicle-based configuration.

A 1974 aerial photo of the Buch und Ton Bürolandschaft building shows little exterior change. Stories confirmed by former employees suggest, however, that workers were making modifications to the original design by adding partitions and creating smaller confined spaces. A survey at Bertelsmann in 1977 indicated that support for the Bürolandschaft was dwindling. More than thirty percent described themselves as unhappy with their working conditions.[14] In 1981, Mohn retired from his position as CEO. In 1982, another survey by Quickborner showed that the spaces had become unacceptable to the majority of the staff. A smaller annex added to the main building returned to single-cell offices. In 1983, a report in the internal newspaper asked employees to refrain from making changes to the partitions.[15] In 1985, a competition was launched to refurbish the headquarters. Although the brief spoke respectfully of the Bürolandschaft experiments, it recognized its failure.[16] The Quickborner Team was not involved in the competition; four German architects participated instead and most of the plans featured larger partitioned spaces. Within this discussion, faith in the Buch und Ton building and the revolution it began remains unclear.

6. "Großraum im Kommissionshaus," *Bertelsmann Illustrierte*, November 1961, 8.

7. The original German: "Der Umzug der kaufmännischen Abteilungen des Kommissionshauses in die zum Büro umgebaute Ebene 6 dürfte wohl das wichtigste Ereignis im Jahre 1961 gewesen sein. Ein halbes Jahr nach Inbetriebnahme kann man sagen, das Experiment ist gelungen und hat in der gesamten Arbeitsabwicklung erhebliche Vorteile gebracht." *Bertelsmann Illustrierte*, January 1962, 10.

8. Walter Henn, "Bürogrossraum und Architekt," *Baumeister*, July 1962, 655–66.

9. "Sein Arbeitstag im Großraum," *Bertelsmann Illustrierte*, March 1962, 15.

10. Francis Duffy, "Skill: Bürolandschaft" in *The Architectural Review* 135, no. 804 (1964): 148–54. Duffy notes the importance of this visit in the preface to his book *The Changing Workplace* (London: Phaidon Press, 1997).

11. From the Bertelsmann company archive, accession number Akte 0041_76_Erfahrungsbericht Grossraum: "Bisher ist es häufig so gewesen, daß Argumente gegen den Großraum vorgebracht wurden von Personen, die sich nur oberflächlich oder überhaupt nicht mit den Arbeitsverhältnissen vertraut gemacht hatten. Entsprechend würde ich es begrüßen, wenn durch eine persönliche Erfahrung unsere Diskussionen versachlicht werden könnten, bzw. wir durch fundierteres Wissen schneller zu den eigentlichen Problemen gelangen könnten."

12. Ottomar Gottschalk, *Flexible Verwaltungsbauten: Richtwerte, Lösungen, Kosten* (Hamburg: [publisher unknown], 1968), 212.

13. Rumpfhuber, "Space of Information Flow."

14. "Umbau der Hauptverwaltung der Bertelsmann AG," *Deutsche Bauzeitung*, October 1990, 220.

15. The following quote illustrates the situation nicely: "The management would like to stress again that due to your personal safety no one is allowed to move partitions by him/herself, as it could damage the stability of the partitions. A phone call suffices that the required change will be processed and done." In "Don't hit your head through the wall," *Bertelsmann Illustrierte*, January 1983.

16. "Tendenz heute: Vom Großraum zum Individualraum," *Baumeister*, October 1985, 17–27.

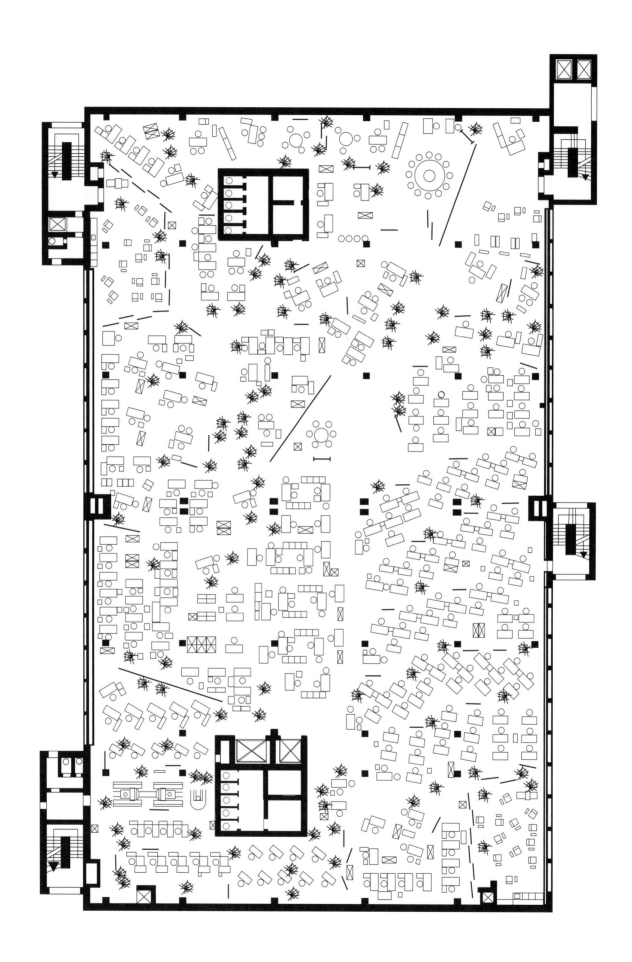

Historic floor plan of the Buch und Ton division of the Bertelsmann Media Group, Gütersloh, Germany, 1961.

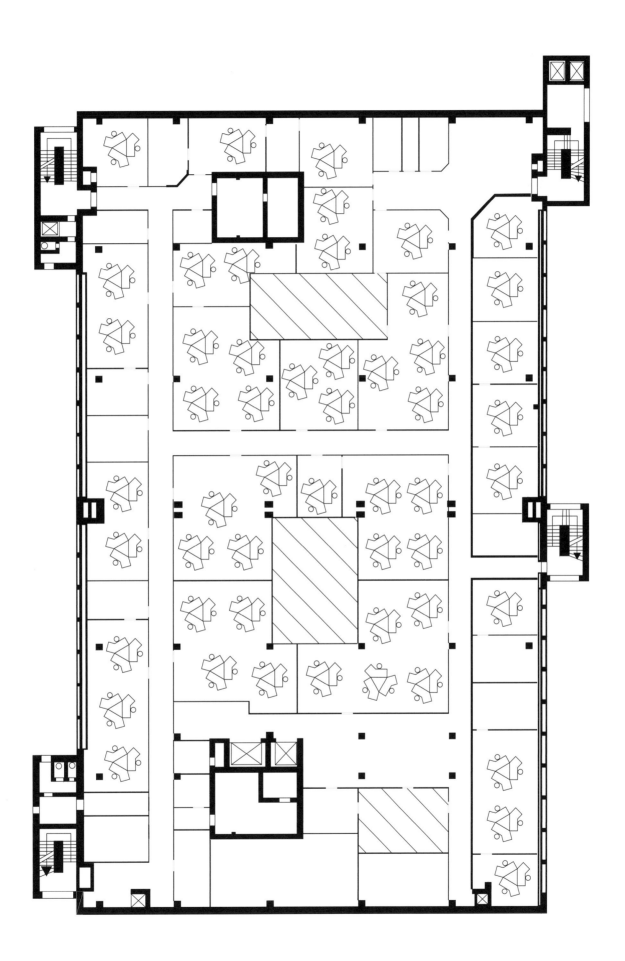

Current floor plan of the Buch und Ton division of the Bertelsmann Media Group, Gütersloh, Germany, 2014.

GÜTERSLOH, 2014

Our request to visit the space was initially greeted with skepticism. At first it was somewhat unclear which section we were actually referring to, and the staff was uncertain whether there was anything left for us to see. Both the chief facilities manager and one of the company archivists, who have both worked at Bertelsmann for decades, found the images we showed them highly unfamiliar.

Past the entrance gate, we walked to the northwest corner of the enormous campus, mostly occupied by huge production plants. Lorries were coming in and out of the transport bays on the ground floor. A small, modernized and well-maintained entrance led us to the elevator. From the fifth floor we walked up a small staircase to what used to be the entrance. Within seconds the facilities manager's doubts were clear: we were confronted by sheetrock panels—lots of them. Behind an abandoned reception desk we faced two angular corridors, one short and another long. We walked into the long corridor, where an egress plan explained that the entire space has a new infill of small and large rooms and, toward the center, two new patios.

The majority of spaces we saw were recently abandoned and awaiting new occupants—although, the facilities manager informed us, additional refurbishment due to new fire regulations and the replacement of various parts of the plumbing will be necessary. A standard dropped ceiling system hides an equally standard plethora of mechanical systems. Everything is generic. The eighty-centimeter-wide office partitions have light plastic seams. Small sockets in the forty-by-forty-centimeter raised floor tiles provide power and network access. New operable facade windows add to a forced-air cooling system with small radiators. The only original parts we found were the concrete column grid and the internal elevator. Although we were not able to determine the exact date of the massive transformation, by appearances it seems that the changes likely occurred somewhere in the early 1980s, around the time of other refurbishments, perhaps shortly after Mohn's departure as CEO.

The current Bertelsmann staff is not aware of any contact with the Quickborner Team, which still has an active practice, though now mostly in Germany. The firm's website offers only a marginal description of their current work, and nothing suggests that it still employs the Bürolandschaft approach.

The mood in the occupied rooms is bureaucratic but good. It's quiet on the floors, and the temperature is nice. A middle-aged team with a large amount of personal space, occupied by prism-shaped desks most probably from a mail-order catalog, is designing birthday calendars. One of the patios has a

A contemporary pausenzone at the remodelled Buch und Ton offices, 2014.

large table that is used in the summer for meetings and lunchtime. Almost everything seems to be done without specific interest in a conceptual understanding of workplace consultancy, yet it all seems to be functioning quite well. There is a lounge area with a small coffee bar, a couch, and some comfortable chairs in bright colors—the only trace of the revolutionary past? Visiting the spaces makes you think about the undeniable prospect of a tidal wave of creative, entrepreneurial, and motivational efforts washing over them, changing everything yet again according to the latest fashion. There is only one certainty: the concrete will remain solid until it is demolished or left behind to decay.

A summer-time patio at Buch und Ton, 2014.

An unused office at Buch und Ton, 2014.

In
Conversation:

Hans Ulrich Obrist

Hans Ulrich Obrist in his Berlin archive/apartment, 2009. Photo: Wolfgang Tillmans.

Perspecta 48: One of our primary interests in this journal is technology's role in mediating the relationship between memory and history. If we can say that the digital seemed for a time to promise a more perfect and transparent view of memory, one where information could be accessed and cross-referenced in increasingly powerful ways, we have come to realize that this is hardly the case. Instead the digital seems to present only another lens through which the past is distorted.

In this vein, we're interested in an odd story that often circulates about you: we've heard of a mythic apartment in Berlin where books arrive every day and are stacked in monumental heaps, leaving space for nothing else. The story conjures images of Borges's *Library of Babel*. How did this manic obsession to collect develop?

Hans Ulrich Obrist: I suppose it started right at the beginning, when I was a teenager. I was interested in art, and many of the artists I met were working on books. For them the book was a primary medium—a sort of extended exhibition space. The material qualities of books also had a hold over me from the outset, although their physicality can be quite a burden! My Berlin apartment is a clear result of the stubborn materiality of books.

I wouldn't call myself a book collector, though. My collection is not an end in itself; rather, I have always needed a lot of books around in order to make books. When I am editing or writing, I am more focused on the production of reality than the production of a book per se. In fact, my archive began almost by accident. When I started to get all of these catalogs, publications, and correspondences, I put them into cardboard file boxes. It has always been a chaotic situation because I have never wanted to spend the extra time to archive. Sometimes these piles of boxes collapse, creating an entropic architecture in the apartment.

The reciprocal relationship you describe between your archive and your activities as an author brings to mind the similarity between the words *inventory* and *invent*. So much of your work is to record, catalog, and address often ephemeral aspects of art and architecture—the interviews project and the marathons, for instance. This begs the question of how you see archives more broadly. Would you agree with the idea that the archive will be the most significant cultural institution of the twenty-first century?

I think archives are certainly more relevant now than they have ever been. Many artists are thinking, "How can I activate the archive?" In 1994, I met the great American artist Joseph Grigely, who became deaf at the age of eleven. Even then, he was making conversation pieces using the little scraps of paper he would exchange to communicate with people, but at the same time he was also very interested in the archive as a medium. Joseph knew that ordinarily a curator would archive an artist, but he thought it would be interesting to turn the tables, to have an artist archive a curator.

Did you let him?

Well, I've always been hesitant to look back. I am always focused on the next project or preparing for the next exhibition, so I find that it can be kind of suffocating to archive one's own work. Not surprisingly, I have completely neglected the idea of making a more systematic archive. I am very glad that Joseph came up with this idea—ever since, I have had a Grigely Box in my office. Every publication, invitation, catalog, group show, artist book, press release—every single document I receive—I just throw into this cardboard box. When the box is full, it goes to Joseph in Chicago. He has what I don't have: the full material scope of my work. With the collaboration of a group of students at the University of Chicago, Joseph and his team have produced both a full bibliography of my work and a systematic archive of all my activities. He plans to do an exhibition of these that will be similar to his work last year at the Whitney Biennial, where he explored the archive of critic and curator Gregory Battcock.

So while most of your work ends up in books and boxes, it usually starts as either an exhibition or an interview. How do your activities as a curator relate to your interviews? Does one precede the other, or do they coexist in a more reciprocal relationship?

There is definitely an interdependence between the interviews and my curatorial work. Rem Koolhaas said that the commitment to the interview is a reaction against the stranglehold of curating. The interviewer is extremely promiscuous, and as Etel Adnan has also pointed out, amidst the present din my conversations are an important act of listening. On the other hand, the curator is very selective and more reserved. Maybe these two sides coexist in a reciprocal fashion. I suppose my interest in the interview as a format came out of Giorgio Vasari's attempt to record the lives of the great artists of his time. The fact that he did not separate artists and architects is critical for me. Having photographed so many of the great artists of twentieth century, from Martine Franck to Matisse and Picasso, Henri Cartier-Bresson once told me that he spent hours and hours in conversation with each one. I don't think it's by any means unusual that a curator or a photographer would have conversations with the protagonists of the subjects he or she studies. I didn't document any of these conversations at the beginning. Like Cartier-Bresson, I didn't immediately see the curatorial or archival value in such casual conversations. This changed as I became more aware of Jonas Mekas's work. His movies served as the inspiration for my impulse to record these conversations. There are also Warholian overtones to this idea of recording everything: to have your camera in a café, or wherever you are, throw it on a table, and film very poorly. By making these interactions concrete and traceable, my ambition was to protect an ephemeral but vast category of information from being lost.

Archive boxes in the Swiss Pavilion at the 2014 Venice Architecture Biennale, 2014. Photo: Francesco Totaro.

Archival materials on display in the Swiss Pavilion, 2014. Photo: Ivo Pisanti.

As you mentioned earlier, you rarely have the time or patience
to revisit your immense intellectual production. If this is the case,
why do you bother recording anything? Do you see the value
of documenting these interactions as a type of fodder for future
artists and architects?

Obviously there is a fear of forgetting. It could very well be
that amnesia is at the core of the digital age. I want to preserve
traces of twentieth-century intelligence, especially that of
the very old people who are not on the grid. But even more than
the fear of forgetting, I feel very lucky to speak with such
amazing people and I want to share the experience with the world.
As a teenager, I was obsessed with the Jesuit priest Athanasius
Kircher, with his theories of the world and his desire to know
everything. He was the last person who could actually claim to
know everything—today this is obviously not possible. His
work on the Orient, acoustics, archaeology, and religion is
extremely impressive. But even more amazing is his museum
in Rome, where he was able to synthesize all of these disparate
disciplines. Through the museum, he was able to make
his research accessible to others. I like to feel that my ambition
is not so dissimilar.

That's an astounding thought; it's inconceivable today that
anyone would claim to know everything or even aspire to.
On the one hand, it seems highly romantic, and on the other,
entirely alien. Still, even such a quintessentially Renaissance
ideal has an uncanny contemporary resonance, thanks to recent
technological developments. Perhaps the enterprise to
know everything has reemerged in the twenty-first century.

To an extent I agree. However, there is now also a need to
forget. As Viktor Mayer-Schönberger writes in his book *Delete*,
digital technology has made forgetting almost impossible,
and this produces the terror of an infinite memory. Memory can
be dangerous and can lead to a situation where forgetting
becomes important. It's an essential task of the present
to reconcile the need to remember and the need to forget.
In a way, it is more a question of *how* we remember. Very
often archives are dead—they are just boxes full of stuff that
go to the Getty or some other institute when a person
dies. It is interesting to consider how an archive can be alive,
how it can become a toolbox.

Like your Grigely Box?

Yes! When I gave everything to the University of Lüneburg,
Hans-Peter Feldmann began a project with a group of
PhD students that used my archive. He classified the books
according to color and to smell. He weighed the different boxes
and started to make towers out of the contents of each.
In a way, he designed the architecture of my archive and
explored new possibilities for its structure—a prelude to what
has been happening in my Berlin apartment. Then McKinsey

was hired by the University of Lüneburg to figure out how to
make things more efficient, and the analysts said it was
wasteful to use so much space for an artist's experiments with
the weights and colors of books—so they threw my archive
out overnight! Because of McKinsey efficiency!

That's stunning! It's incredible how European universities have
become much more businesslike since the Bologna Accords.

Indeed. We then had to find an apartment in Berlin since
London was too expensive to store books. But what
Feldmann had started was already in the DNA of the archive.
He continued his experiments with the books arriving in
Berlin, and it became another form of architecture. I learn
everything I know from artists!

It's very telling that you refer to your archive as a site for
experimentation; it seems to imply that your idea of an archive
is not so different from that of an exhibition. Against any
idea of the medium as fixed and retrospective, you insist that it is
pliable and dynamic—that it's a springboard for exploration.

Yes, very much so. When I curated the Swiss Pavilion at the Venice
Biennale in 2014, it was a great opportunity—especially
given Koolhaas's theme, "Absorbing Modernity." There were two
simultaneous ambitions. First off, I wanted to dive into history
and develop the archives of two of the most important figures of
twentieth-century architecture, the sociologist Lucius Burckhardt
and the architect Cedric Price. My co-curator, Lorenza Baroncelli,
and I thought it could be interesting to invent the future with
elements from the past by foregrounding the work of two
visionary figures, both of whom died in 2003. At the same time,
the project was a sort of laboratory in itself—an experiment
on how to activate an archive and reanimate a medium that's
so often inert. We approached this by inviting a group
of collaborators. Liam Gillick created a new sign for the Swiss
Pavilion, temporarily renaming it "Palazzo F" after Cedric's
Fun Palace and Dominique Gonzalez-Foerster did a Cedric and
Lucius neon display. Herzog & de Meuron were the lead
designers. They came up with the idea that the display features
should be trollies—this was extremely clever in my mind
because it both drew inspiration from Lilly Reich, whose seminal
work on exhibition design is too often forgotten, and at the same
time implicitly responded to Marcel Duchamp's famous quip
that "we mainly remember exhibitions which also develop a new
display feature." Putting everything on wheels was also very
much in the spirit of Cedric—everything he did was mobile
in some manner. Then Tino Sehgal choreographed the entire way
in which the viewer interacted with the archival material.

The pavilion would begin the day empty, according to Tino's
script. As soon as someone entered, a trolley would be pushed

towards the visitor and a pair of architecture students would engage them in conversation. This way, the viewer would discover the contents of the archive through a dialogue about Lucius and Cedric. As more people came, more trollies would come out. Then, all of sudden, the gallery would start to become dark as the twenty-seven blinds that Philippe Parreno created for the space drew shut. Later, we would show a movie about Cedric or Lucius. On the roof of the pavilion, Atelier Bow-Wow created an homage to Cedric's aviary. Taken together, the exhibition was a highly collaborative environment in which the whole was greater than the sum of its parts.

It seems that you are not alone in reevaluating the manner in which the artist and the viewer interact. What are the intellectual foundations of this idea?

The main gallery of the Swiss Pavilion, 2014. Photo: Pro Helvetia.

Seating in the garden gallery of the Swiss Pavilion, 2014. Photo: Francesco Totaro.

Eugène Ionesco was one of the first artists to influence my approach to curatorial practice. I met him on the street in Switzerland when he was very old and I was very young. Even then, his writing had already enraptured me. We had a coffee. At the time, *La Cantatrice Chauve* had been performed in Paris for about twenty-five years in a row—by now it must be fifty or sixty. One could imagine doing the same thing with an archive. Instead of buying a painting that will vanish into an off-site storage facility, an institution could have an endowment that would allow artists to activate an existing archive. Like our exhibition in Venice, the archive could reinvent itself every day, and this could go on for decades or even be permanent. It's critical that we begin to think about how archives can function in the future.

Your curatorial intentions in Venice are very clear; the subject matter is a little harder to grasp. Lucius and Cedric were not close collaborators. Why did you select them?

In the '90s, I was working on an exhibition called *Cities on the Move* with Hou Hanru, which explored emerging trends in Asian architecture and urbanism. While I was preparing the exhibition, I happened to visit Rita Donagh and Richard Hamilton for another project I was working on. At one point in our conversation, we were casually discussing *Cities on the Move* and Rita said,

"If you're doing an exhibition on Asian art and architecture you have to meet Cedric Price!" They immediately got their address book out and gave me Cedric's number. The very next day, I was in Cedric's studio, in the famous white room, and this quickly evolved into a friendship from 1999 to his death in 2003. During these four years, I saw him almost weekly. It was a very productive relationship. He was famously antagonistic to the architecture world—he did not want to participate in biennales or exhibitions. I was from the art world, however, and he felt comfortable accepting my invitations to collaborate because they weren't coming from this hostile environment. In just four years so much happened: we did a show of his drawings at the Musée d'Art Moderne, an exhibition at the Institute for International Visual Art in London, we also published a set of interviews with Rem Koolhaas, and organized a book—*Re: CP*—that had an expiration date after which it couldn't be sold which, of course, drove the publisher nuts. Lucius is another story. When I was a teenager, Beatrice Curiger, the great Swiss curator, took me to meet Jacques Herzog and Pierre de Meuron. They were the first architects I ever met. I knew nothing about architects at the time, and I asked them, "who were your teachers?" They told me about this sociologist, Lucius Burckhardt, who had been a very important figure in their education, and soon after they introduced us. So, the genesis of this Venice project was very personal. Both Cedric and Lucius were close friends of mine, and when I began to formulate my response to Rem's call for the biennale to dig deep into history, I didn't pick these two figures because they were fashionable subjects but because of a long, long personal history. What I think is incredible, though, is that through this exhibition Cedric and Lucius became collaborators despite the fact that they are no longer here. We put so much energy into revisiting these highly influential figures, activating their archives, and choreographing the viewer's interaction with the documents and artifacts, that I think what we created is a new model for how to exhibit architecture in the twenty-first century.

There is certainly a shift in the architecture of museums toward an interactive approach. From Herzog & de Meuron's Schaulager to Diller Scofidio's Broad Museum, the visitor is engaged as an active participant rather than a passive spectator. This issue of an active versus passive audience seems to have a relationship to your work on relational aesthetics, in addition to the work of Price and Burckhardt.

No, I don't think the Swiss Pavilion should be understood in terms of relational aesthetics, I think it is a much more complex web. Although I had done many time-based exhibitions before, they usually lasted a week or a month; this was unique because it lasted six months. At the same time, The Living Theater founded by Julian Beck and Judith Malina is very relevant to this idea of the archive. Their staging of Cocteau and Brecht in the 1940s and '50s experimented with ways to remove the fourth wall between the actors and the spectators. Tino Sehgal often says that from the nineteenth century to the 1960s our history is mostly a narrative of objects. It's not that there are no objects any more—artists still make objects—however, there is a whole other art history of non-objects and quasi-objects. This is an art history that is still very much neglected, and I think it's time that museums and exhibitions explore these forms.

Do you see your work at the Serpentine Gallery as part of this agenda? You've frequently used the term laboratory; to what extent do you consider the summer pavilions as laboratory experiments?

I think of the pavilions very much as laboratories. Julia Peyton-Jones invented the program in 2000 when she invited Zaha Hadid to do the first pavilion. It was initially built for a fundraising event and was meant to last only for an evening. It was quickly decided, however, that it could stay up a bit longer. I joined the gallery six years later and have since co-commissioned the pavilions. It was interesting for me because I have always worked with architects in the context of exhibitions, but I had never really worked with an architect as a client. It was a very exciting new experience—it's a very different thing to be a client! In 2006 we invited Rem Koolhaas along with Cecil Balmond. Rem felt that a pavilion without content would be nothing more than a meaningless shape, so he wanted to make the building a content machine. Yet as it turned out, it was not only the content that was an experiment but the form as well. This is often the case: many of architecture's most important inventions have come from temporary pavilions.

Like Bruno Taut's Glass Pavilion of 1914 and Alvar Aalto's Finnish Pavilion at the 1939 World's Fair.

Yes, or my favorite, the Le Corbusier and Iannis Xenakis Philips Pavilion of 1958. There is sort of an unwritten history of architecture through these extraordinary pavilions. Architects can experiment with them in free and daring ways that might not be possible with a building. In England, there was a resistance to engaging contemporary architecture. Now there is the possibility to challenge that tradition and bring in younger architects with new ideas. In this sense, the pavilion is a site for experimentation, which we test every Friday night by giving it over to a young musician or an emerging artist. They take over the entire pavilion and turn it into a Gesamtkunstwerk. In this way, we took the idea of the public experiment and extrapolated it into a nonstop experiment in the public realm. It was a move away from a symposium or lecture and toward something more like a group show where we would give artists time instead of space.

How does the Serpentine Pavilion affect the rest
of the park, or the rest of the city for that matter?

First, admission is free. There is a problem in cities where
most public spaces require you to consume. We wanted
to create a situation in which there would be free art and
architecture for all. At six in the morning, joggers and dogs
make up a very important constituency of our visitors.
Throughout the day you have people who read newspapers,
work on their laptops, or simply use the pavilion as a
meeting point. In the evenings, we rent it out for parties,
dinners, and book readings. And then there are Park
Nights, where literature, music, or art takes over. Everything
culminates in the Marathon, which happens in October.
And then it's gone. A few days later, it's just a small patch
of land next to the gallery.

You say that as if it were a good thing. Is this an instance
where you are in favor of ephemerality?

The pavilion's temporary nature means that every year we get
to build a new one. Institutions have the tendency to freeze—
this is why Picabia called the museum a cemetery. Every
twenty to thirty years an institution builds a new wing, and
by the time it's finished it's already outdated. By building a
new pavilion every year, we keep the institution flexible in the
belief that institutions need to be constantly questioned
and redefined.

We often think about architecture as the most durable of the
arts, however, these buildings have relatively short life spans.
Is there a value to an architecture that has a willingness
to be short-lived?

I suppose the pavilions are somewhat sustainable, and they
often have a second and even a third life. They go south or north
to distant climates and develop completely new lives. The
journey continues; they are nomadic structures, which goes back
to Cedric Price. It is a great tragedy that he died so early.
We would have loved to commission a pavilion from him, and
I suppose giving him the pavilion in Venice is a way of making up
for that big regret.

This thought of an unrealized project for Cedric Price brings
up another point: though his projects were rarely realized,
his architectural ideas have endured with hardly any physical
presence. Given that your work ranges from temporary pavilions
to archival interviews, how do you understand architectural
preservation, which aims to maintain the presence of a building
over its idea?

Well, if you think about the Barcelona Pavilion, it was rebuilt
from instructions, so it is not the original building.
The Serpentine Pavilions are somewhat ephemeral on their
sites as well; at the end of the season they must move
somewhere else!

A cluttered hallway in the Berlin archive/apartment, 2009. Photo: Wolfgang Tillmans.

We understand that in recent years many of the pavilions have
gone into private collections as a way to raise funds for the project.
Do you think that collecting architecture in the form of pavilions
differs from collecting models and drawings?

One of the many things Julia and I have in common is we believe that
one cannot experience architecture through models and drawings.
The other day, I had the chance to see an excellent retrospective
of Louis Kahn—an exhaustively researched and beautifully presented
exhibition. It was as good as a show of models and drawings could
be; however, you cannot compare it to the experience of the Kahn
business school I visited recently in Ahmedabad—its microclimate
and play of light and shadow are very physical things. It is only when
you are immersed in art or architecture that you really see the
work. Exhibiting architecture in terms of built reality is very important.
When Julia started the Serpentine Pavilion project, she said,
"Now we will show everyone world-class architecture at a one-to-one
scale." As a child growing up in Switzerland, I would have loved
it if my parents had taken me to a Le Corbusier pavilion. *Collecting* is
perhaps not the right word in this case: it is the idea of creating
a space, creating a situation, creating an occasion. I don't think
it is the object that matters; it is the occasion and the situation where
it is built, where it is installed, where it is alive. Ultimately the goal
is to create an immersive experience for the visitor—one that is likely
not possible through models and drawings.

You seem to be drawing a distinction between space and place.
From this perspective, you might say that there are a multitude
of spaces to exhibit architecture, but a dearth of good architecture
museums. How would you envision an architecture museum
for the twenty-first century?

You are correct, there is a lack of good architecture museums.
There are some, the CCA in Montréal, for instance. But compared
to art museums there are very few. What could an architecture
museum for the twenty-first century be? Well, I suppose it could be
a park full of pavilions. They would have to be continuously
changing pavilions, otherwise it would be a dead collection. Of
course, I think that it is very important that there are drawings and
models of architecture. I don't think that we should omit them.
The question is how to avoid the trope of framed drawings with wall
texts. If this dominates a show, why not just stay home and read
a book? I believe we can make the exhibition into more of an
experience through collaborations between artists and architects.
As with the Swiss Pavilion, there is a huge potential for architecture
museums in the future. Looking back to Vasari, we need to ask
ourselves if it makes any sense to split art and architecture into
separate museums. It may be interesting to reunite them,
particularly when we have so much crossover between the two
fields. But more interesting than a museum or a park of pavilions
would be a new *Weissenhofsiedlung*.

Yes, everyone is there: Le Corbusier, Mies, J.J.P. Oud, Taut.

It's fantastic.

Indeed, and you can experience them one-on-one. Each of them is an important work, and there is a social dimension to it. Every morning when I wake up, I ask myself: what could be a *Weissenhofsiedlung* for the twenty-first century? I really hope that one day I will find the necessary support to build it—otherwise it may be my own unrealized project! In this regard, though, I feel a little like an architect. Architects have so many unrealized projects—often famously so—few understand, though, that curators similarly have an abundance of unrealized projects.

This is a topic of general interest for me; one my recurrent questions to artists and architects is about unrealized work. There are many categories of the unrealized, of course. There are projects that are too big to be realized, or too small; there are lost competition entries, or utopic projects, or projects that can only be partially realized; and then as Doris Lessing points out, there are the unrealized projects we don't dare to do. I have an archive of about two thousand unrealized projects from various artists and architects that I would like to curate into an exhibition. Very fittingly, though, whenever I get close to realizing this project, it slips away!

Esra Akcan

Esra Akcan is an associate professor in the Department of Architecture at Cornell University. She is the author of *Architecture in Translation* (Duke University Press, 2012); *(Land)Fill Istanbul: Twelve Scenarios for a Global City* (124/3 Press, 2004); and co-author of *Turkey: Modern Architectures in History* (Reaktion/Chicago University Press, 2012) with Sibel Bozdogan.

Amale Andraos

Amale Andraos is Dean of the Columbia University Graduate School of Architecture, Planning and Preservation. Andraos has taught at numerous universities including the Princeton University School of Architecture, the Harvard Graduate School of Design, the University of Pennsylvania Design School and the American University in Beirut. Her recent design studios and seminars have focused on the Arab City, which has become the subject of a series of symposia entitled "Architecture and Representation" held at Studio-X Amman in 2013 and on campus in New York in the fall of 2014. Her publications include *49 Cities* (Inventory Press, 2015), a re-reading of 49 visionary plans through an ecological lens; *Above the Pavement, the Farm!* (Princeton Architectural Press, 2010); and the forthcoming *Architecture and Representation: the Arab City*.

Andraos is a co-founder of WORKac, a 25-person architecture firm based in New York that focuses on re-inventing the relationship between urban and natural environments. WORKac has achieved international recognition for projects such as the Edible Schoolyard at PS216 and PS7, the Centre de Conferences in Libreville, Gabon and the Beijing Horticultural Exposition Masterplan and Pavilions.

Andraos received her Master's Degree from the Graduate School of Design at Harvard University and her B.Arch. from McGill University in Montreal.

Iwan Baan

Iwan Baan's love for photography goes back to his twelfth birthday, when his grandmother gave him his first camera. After his studies in photography at the Royal Academy of Arts in The Hague, Baan followed his interest in documentary photography, before narrowing his focus to record the various ways in which individuals, communities, and societies create and interact within their built environment.

Baan is the inaugural recipient of the Julius Shulman award for photography, and was awarded the Golden Lion for Best Installation at the 2012 Venice Architecture Biennale for his images of the Torre David in Caracas. Alongside his architecture commissions, he has collaborated on several book projects such as *Insular Insight: Where Art and Architecture Conspire with Nature* (Lars Muller Publishers, 2011); *Torre David: Informal Vertical Communities* (Lars Muller Publishers, 2012); and *Brasilia & Chandigarh—Living With Modernity* (Lars Muller Publishers, 2010). Baan's work also appears on the pages of architecture, design, and lifestyle publications such as *The Wall Street Journal*, *The New York Times*, *Domus*, *Abitare*, and *Architectural Digest*.

Mario Carpo

Mario Carpo is the Reyner Banham Professor of Architectural Theory and History at the Bartlett School of Architecture, UCL London.

After studying architecture and history in Italy, Dr. Carpo was an Assistant Professor at the University of Geneva in Switzerland, and in 1993 received tenure in France, where he was first assigned to the École d'Architecture de Saint-Etienne, then to the École d'Architecture de Paris-La Villette. He was the head of the Study Center at the Canadian Centre for Architecture in Montréal from 2002 to 2006, and the Vincent Scully Visiting Professor of Architectural History at the Yale School of Architecture from 2010 to 2014.

Mr. Carpo's research and publications focus on the relationship among architectural theory, cultural history, and the history of media and information technology. His award-winning *Architecture in the Age of Printing* (MIT Press, 2001) has been translated into several languages. His most recent books are *The Alphabet and the Algorithm* (MIT Press, 2011); and *The Digital Turn in Architecture, 1992–2012* (Wiley, 2012). Mr. Carpo's recent essays and articles have been published in *Log*, *The Journal of the Society of Architectural Historians*, *Grey Room*, *L'Architecture d'aujourd'hui*, *Arquitectura Viva*, *AD/Architectural Design*, *Perspecta*, *Harvard Design Magazine*, *Cornell Journal of Architecture*, *Abitare*, *Lotus International*, *Domus*, *Artforum*, and *Arch+*.

David Chipperfield

David Chipperfield was a Professor of Architecture at the Staatliche Akademie der Bildenden Künste, Stuttgart from 1995 to 2001 and the Norman R. Foster Visiting Professor of Architectural Design at Yale University in 2011, and has taught and lectured worldwide at schools of architecture in Austria, Italy, Switzerland, the United Kingdom, and the United States. In 2012, David Chipperfield curated the 13th International Architecture Exhibition of the Venice Biennale. In 2014, he was appointed Artistic Director of the Italian furnishings firm Driade.

He is an honorary fellow of both the American Institute of Architects and the Bund Deutscher Architekten, and a past winner of the Heinrich Tessenow Gold Medal, the Wolf Foundation Prize in the Arts, and the Grand DAI (Verband Deutscher Architekten- und Ingenieurvereine) Award for Building Culture. David Chipperfield was appointed Commander of the Order of the British Empire in 2004, appointed a Royal Designer for Industry in 2006, and elected to the Royal Academy in 2008. In 2009, he was awarded the Order of Merit of the Federal Republic of Germany and in 2010, he was knighted for services to architecture in the UK and Germany. In 2011, he received the RIBA Royal Gold Medal for Architecture, and in 2013, the Praemium Imperiale from the Japan Art Association, both given in recognition of a lifetime's work.

T.J. Demos

T.J. Demos is a cultural critic and professor in the Department of the History of Art and Visual Culture, University of California, Santa Cruz, where he is also the director of the Center for Creative Ecologies. He writes on contemporary art and politics, and is the author, most recently, of *The Migrant Image: The Art and Politics of Documentary During Global Crisis* (Duke University Press, 2013); and *Return to the Postcolony: Spectres of Colonialism in Contemporary Art* (Sternberg, 2013). In 2013, he guest-edited a special issue of *Third Text* (no. 120) on the subject of "Contemporary Art and the Politics of Ecology." Demos co-curated the international group exhibition *Rights of Nature: Art and Ecology in the Americas*, opening at Nottingham Contemporary in January 2015, and *Specters: A Ciné-Politics of Haunting*, a screening series of artist films at the Reina Sofia Museum in Madrid in 2014. He is currently finishing a new book, entitled *Decolonizing Nature: Contemporary Art in the Age of Climate Change*, for Sternberg Press, due out in 2015.

Kyle Dugdale

Kyle Dugdale is an architect and a graduate of Corpus Christi College, Oxford, of Harvard's Graduate School of Design, and of the Yale School of Architecture, with a particular interest in architecture's claims to metaphysical significance. He recently received the Theron Rockwell Field Prize from Yale University for his doctoral dissertation, "Architecture After the Death of God: Uriel Birnbaum's *Der Kaiser und der Architekt*."

Edward Eigen

Edward Eigen is an Associate Professor of the History of Architecture and Landscape Architecture at the Harvard Graduate School of Design. He has written in a narrowly focused way on a wide variety of topics, severally addressing the theme of the difficulty of knowing.

Marco Frascari

Marco Frascari was born under the shadow of the dome of Alberti's Sant'Andrea in Mantua. He received a Dottore in Architettura at the Istituto Universitario di Architettura di Venezia in 1969. After practicing and teaching in Italy, he moved to the United States and earned an M.Sc. in Architecture at the University of Cincinnati and a Ph.D. at the University of Pennsylvania. He taught for several years at the University of Pennsylvania, and as a Visiting Professor at Columbia and Harvard. He then became a G. Truman Ward Professor of Architecture at Virginia Tech. In 2005, he was appointed Director of the Azrieli School of Architecture and Urbanism in Ottawa, Canada. He passed away in 2013, shortly after submitting his manuscript for publication in *Perspecta*.

Maria Shéhérazade Giudici

Maria Shéhérazade Giudici is an architect and writer whose work is centered on the project of the construction of modern subjectivity through the design of public space. Maria has been Studio Master of Diploma Unit 14 at the Architectural Association since 2011, after working on large-scale urban projects in Asia and Eastern Europe as well as teaching at the Berlage Institute and BIArch Barcelona. In 2014, Maria founded Black Square, a publishing and educational platform for architectural research (www.black-square.eu).

Karsten Harries

Karsten Harries is the Howard H. Newman Professor of Philosophy at Yale University. He is the author of more than 200 articles and reviews and the following books: *The Meaning of Modern Art* (Northwestern University Press, 1968); *The Bavarian Rococo Church: Between Faith and Aestheticism* (Yale University Press, 1983); *The Broken Frame* (The Catholic University of America Press, 1990); *The Ethical Function of Architecture* (MIT Press, 1997); *Infinity and Perspective* (MIT Press, 2001); *Art Matters: a Critical Commentary on Martin Heidegger's The Origin of the Work of Art* (Springer, 2009); *Die bayerische Rokokokirche: Das Irrationale und das Sakrale* (Hawel-Verlag, 2009); *Between Nihilism and Faith: A Commentary on Either/Or* (De Gruyter, 2010); *Wahrheit: Die Architektur der Welt* (Wilhelm Fink, 2012).

Sam Jacob

Sam Jacob is a Professor of Architecture at the University of Illinois at Chicago, a Visiting Professor at the Yale School of Architecture, and Director of Night School at the Architectural Association. He is the principal of Sam Jacob Studio for architecture and design and was one of the co-founding directors of FAT Architecture. He has been responsible for a range of internationally acclaimed and award winning projects ranging from the large scale—such as the master plan and design of the Heerlijkheid park and cultural center in Rotterdam—to the cultural, including co-curating the British Pavilion at the 2014 Venice Biennale. He is currently working on projects that include a master plan for 250 homes, the reinvention of a business park, and a mixed use development in London's Shoreditch.

Jacob is also a writer and critic, acting as contributing editor for Icon magazine and columnist for both *Art Review* and *Dezeen*. He is the author of *Make It Real: Architecture as Enactment* (Strelka Press, 2014).

Andrew Kovacs

Andrew Kovacs was born in Chicago, Illinois. He is a Visiting Assistant Professor at UCLA Architecture & Urban Design in

Los Angeles. Kovacs studied architecture at Syracuse University (B.Arch.), The Architecture Association in London, and Princeton University (M.Arch.). His written work on architecture and urbanism has been published in *Pidgin*, *Project*, *Clog*, *Domus*, and *Fulcrum*. Additionally, Kovacs is the creator and curator of Archive of Affinities—a website dedicated to the architectural B-side.

Sylvia Lavin

Sylvia Lavin is a critic, historian, and curator whose work explores the limits of architecture across a wide spectrum of historical periods. She received her Ph.D. from the Department of Art and Archaeology at Columbia University and published her first books, *Quatremère de Quincy and the Invention of a Modern Language of Architecture* (MIT Press, 1992); and *Form Follows Libido: Architecture and Richard Neutra in a Psychoanalytic Culture* (MIT Press, 2007). Recent books include *Flash in the Pan* (Architectural Association, 2014); *Kissing Architecture* (Princeton University Press, 2011); and *Everything Loose Will Land* (Moderne Kunst Nürnberg, 2013), the catalog accompanying an exhibition focusing on art and architecture in Los Angeles during the 1970s. Her next exhibition, *The New Creativity*, explores the relationship between architecture and the radical redefinitions of creativity that have taken place since the advent of computing. She is a frequent contributor to journals such as *Artforum* and *Log* and serves as a member of the board for the Canadian Center for Architecture. Currently the Director of Critical Studies in Architecture at UCLA, Lavin has taught at Princeton, Harvard, Columbia, and numerous other institutions and has been recognized by many grants and awards, most recently from the American Academy of Arts and Letters, the Getty Research Institute, and the Graham Foundation.

Gary Leggett

Gary Leggett takes photographs. He lives in Lima, Peru.

Richard Mosse

Richard Mosse was born in 1980 in Ireland. He earned an M.F.A. in Photography from Yale University in 2008, a PG Dip in Fine Art from Goldsmiths, London, in 2004, an MRes in Cultural Studies from the London Consortium in 2003, and a first class honors B.A. in English Literature and Language from King's College London, 2001. Mosse represented Ireland at the 55th Venice Biennale with *The Enclave*. Pulitzer Center on Crisis Reporting co-published his first monograph, *Infra* (Aperture, 2012). Other monographs include *The Enclave* (Aperture, 2013); *Better The Devil You Know* (Centro Atlantico Arte Moderna, 2014); and *A Supplement to the Enclave* (Broken Dimanche Press, 2014). Mosse has exhibited internationally at museums which include the Louisiana Museum of Contemporary Art, the Irish Museum of Modern Art, the Kemper Museum, the Bass Museum, Palazzo Strozzi, Palais

de Tokyo, Kunsthalle Munich, Barbican Art Gallery, Akademie der Kuenste Berlin, Portland Art Museum, and others. Mosse is a recipient of the Deutsche Boerse Photography Prize (2014), Yale's Poynter Fellowship in Journalism (2014), the B3 Award at the Frankfurt Biennale (2013), an ECAS Commission (2013), Visual Arts Bursary from the Irish Arts Council (2012), Kuenstlerhaus Bethanien Residency (2012), the Guggenheim Fellowship (2011), and a Leonore Annenberg Fellowship (2008–2010). He lives in New York City.

Hans Ulrich Obrist

Hans Ulrich Obrist is Co-Director of the Serpentine Galleries, London. Prior to this, he was the Curator of the Musée d'Art Moderne de la Ville de Paris. Since his first show *"World Soup" (The Kitchen Show)* in 1991, he has curated more than 250 shows. Last year, for the Swiss Pavilion at the 14th International Architecture Biennale in Venice, Obrist presented *Lucius Burckhardt and Cedric Price—A stroll through a fun palace;* the building was designed by architects Herzog & de Meuron, and the program was developed with artists Liam Gillick, Philippe Parreno, Tino Sehgal, and Dominique Gonzalez-Foerster, with scientific director Lorenza Baroncelli, and a collaboration between Pro Helvetia and the LUMA Foundation. Obrist's *Art of Handwriting* project is taking place on Instagram and protests against the disappearance of handwriting in the digital age.

In 2011, Obrist received the CCS Bard Award for Curatorial Excellence, and in 2009, he was made Honorary Fellow of the Royal Institute of British Architects (RIBA). Obrist has lectured internationally at academic and art institutions, and is contributing editor to several magazines and journals. Obrist's recent publications include *Lives of the Artists, Lives of the Architects* (Allen Lane, 2015); *Ways of Curating* (Faber & Faber); *A Brief History of New Music* (JRP|Ringier, 2014); and *The Age of Earthquakes: A Guide to the Extreme Present* (Blue Rider Press, 2015) with Douglas Coupland and Shumon Basar.

Stephan Petermann

Stephan Petermann holds a Master's degree in History of Architecture and the Theory of Building Preservation at the University of Utrecht and studied architecture at the Technical University of Eindhoven. He worked for *VOLUME* before joining OMA in 2006, working with Rem Koolhaas on lectures, texts, and research. Petermann assisted Rem Koolhaas at the EU Reflection Group, a "wise men council" of prominent Europeans advising on the future of the European Union, and he collaborated with the OMA Asia office on the cultural masterplan for WKCD in Hong Kong. Petermann curated the exhibition *OMA Book Machine* at the AA Gallery in London and worked on research for the *Cronocaos* exhibition about the current state of preservation at the Venice Biennale 2010 and at the New Museum in NY. In 2012, he was a teacher at Strelka Institute in Moscow looking at the Russian hinterland. He was one of the project leaders for the Venice Biennale 2014.

Matt Roman

Matt Roman is an architect and teacher. He is currently an architectural designer at RAMSA in New York and an adjunct instructor in design at The Cooper Union. Previously, he was a project architect at Eisenman Architects in New York and an adjunct instructor in design and theory at the New Jersey Institute of Technology School of Architecture. From 2010 to 2013, he co-taught graduate studios and seminars with Peter Eisenman at the Yale School of Architecture, from which he received an M.Arch. in 2009. Matt graduated *summa cum laude* in Architecture from Princeton University in 2003 and received an M.Phil. in Architecture and the Moving Image from Cambridge University in 2004. He worked previously for Ziger/Snead Architects in Baltimore, LTL Architects in New York, and Joeb Moore + Partners in Greenwich, Connecticut. He is the co-editor, with Tal Schori, of *The Real Perspecta 42* (MIT Press, 2010) and writes for various architecture journals.

Saskia Sassen

Saskia Sassen is the Robert S. Lynd Professor of Sociology and Co-Chair of The Committee on Global Thought at Columbia University. She is the author of several books, including the recent release *Expulsions: Brutality and Complexity in the Global Economy* (Harvard University Press, 2014). She has received diverse awards, from multiple doctor honoris causa to being chosen as one of the Top 100 Global Thinkers by Foreign Policy, Top 100 Thought Leaders by GDI-MIT, Top 50 Global Thinkers by Prospect Magazine 2014, and she received the 2013 Principe de Asturias Prize for the Social Sciences.

Russell Thomsen

Russell Thomsen is an architect in Los Angeles. He co-founded IDEA office with Eric Kahn in 1988, and has explored questions of architecture and culture within a wide spectrum of scales and contexts. In addition to the work of their office, they are both senior design studio faculty at the Southern California Institute of Architecture (SCI-Arc). Kahn passed away in May of 2014.

Anthony Vidler

Anthony Vidler, Ph.D., Dipl. Arch., is a Professor and former Dean of the Irwin S. Chanin School of Architecture at the Cooper Union in New York, and the Vincent Scully Visiting Professor of Architectural History at the Yale University School of Architecture. A historian and critic of modern and contemporary architecture and urbanism, he previously taught at Princeton University (1965–1993) and UCLA (1993–2001). His publications include *The Writing of the Walls: Theory and Design in the Late Enlightenment* (Princeton Architectural Press, 1987); *Claude-Nicolas Ledoux. Architecture and Society in the Ancien Regime* (MIT Press, 1989); *The Architectural Uncanny: Essays in the Modern Unhomely* (MIT Press, 1992); *Warped Space: Art, Architecture, and Anxiety in Modern Culture* (MIT Press, 2000); *Histories of the Immediate Present* (MIT Press, 2008); and *Scenes of the Street* (The Monacelli Press, 2011). He received the Architecture Award from the American Society of Arts and Letters in 2011 and the ACSA Centennial Award for Contributions to Architectural Education in 2012. He is a Fellow of the National Academy of Arts and Sciences.

Stanislaus von Moos

Stanislaus von Moos is an Art Historian based in Lucerne, Switzerland. His books include *Le Corbusier: Elements of a Synthesis* (MIT Press, 1979); *Turm und Bollwerk* (Atlantis, 1975); *Venturi, Scott Brown & Associates: Buildings and Projects* (Rizzoli, 1987); and *Industrieästhetik* (Ars Helvetica, 1992). More recently, his publications include *Le Corbusier Before Le Corbusier* (Yale University Press, 2001); *Nicht Disneyland und andere Aufsätze* über *Modernität und Nostalgie* (Scheidegger & Spiess, 2004); and *Chandigarh 1956* (Scheidegger & Spies, 2010). He has been the curator of exhibitions such as *Le Corbusier: The Art of Architecture* and *Louis Kahn: The Power of Architecture*. His current research involves the impact of the East-West conflict on the history of architecture and urbanism as well as the cross-pollinations between architecture and the visual arts since 1940. A professor of Modern Art at the University of Zurich (1983–2005), he has lectured and taught widely in Europe and in the United States, including as Jean Labatut Visiting Professor at Princeton University (1997–98) and as Vincent Scully Visiting Professor at Yale University (2010–2014).

IMAGE CREDITS

The editors gratefully acknowledge the permissions granted to reproduce the copyrighted material in this publication. Every effort has been made to trace the ownership of all copyrighted material and to secure proper credits and permissions from the appropriate copyright holders. In the event of any omission or oversight, all necessary corrections will be made in future printings.

Unless otherwise noted, all images are courtesy of the author.

EDITORIAL STATEMENT

p. 4 — Courtesy of Edwynn Houk Gallery, New York; Photograph by Abelardo Morell

ESRA AKCAN

pp. 130–135 (3 images) — Courtesy of Collection Centre Canadien d'Architecture/Canadian Centre for Architecture, Montréal, John Hejduk fonds
p. 136 — Courtesy of Esra Akcan via IBA brochures
p. 140 — © Helene Binet

AMALE ANDRAOS

Courtesy of WORKac

p. 202 (above), 203 (below), 206, 207 & 209 (below)
p. 204 (above) — Courtesy of OMA / AMO; © Rem Koolhaas & OMA
p. 204 (below) — Courtesy of SFMOMA; © 2015 Estate of Gordon Matta-Clark / Artists Rights Society (ARS), New York

IWAN BAAN

All photographs are courtesy of Iwan Baan.

MARIO CARPO

p. 49 — Courtesy of Gallica – Bibliothèque Nationale de France; © Paris: Gauthier-Villars, 1922
p. 51 (above) — Courtesy of Collection Centre Canadien d'Architecture/Canadian Centre for Architecture, Montréal
p. 51 (below) & 52 — Courtesy of Michael Hansmeyer; Photograph by Demetris Shammas
p. 53 — Courtesy of Roland Snooks
p. 55 — Courtesy of Neri Oxman; Photograph by Yoran Reshef
p. 56 — Courtesy of Achim Menges; Photograph by Michael Haufmann

DAVID CHIPPERFIELD

pp. 16–17 (spread) — © Archiv Neue Nationalgalerie, Nationalgalerie, Staatliche Museen zu Berlin
p. 19 (above & below) — Courtesy of MoMA & Art Resources, NY; Artwork: © 2015 Artists Rights Society (ARS), New York & VG Bild-Kunst, Bonn. Digital image: © The Museum of Modern Art/Licensed by SCALA/Art Resource, NY

T. J. DEMOS

All images are courtesy of Marian Goodman Gallery and White Cube. © Julie Mehretu; photographs by Benjamin Westbody

KYLE DUGDALE

p. 110 — Courtesy of Beinecke Rare Book & Manuscript Library; © 2015 Artists Rights Society (ARS), New York / VG Bild-Kunst, Bonn
p. 112–113 — Bauhaus-Archiv Berlin via Ute Brüning, ed., *Das A und O des Bauhauses*, exhibition catalogue (Berlin: Bauhaus-Archiv, 1995), 64 Figure 47. nr. 84331/1–2
p. 115 — Courtesy of Linda Hall Library of Science, Engineering and Technology

EDWARD EIGEN

All images are courtesy of Edward Eigen with the exception of p. 34.
p. 34 — Courtesy of Yale Center for British Art, Paul Mellon Fund

MARCO FRASCARI

pp. 104–105 (spread) — Courtesy of FMR-Art'è
p. 106 (above) — Courtesy of Churches of Italy
p. 106 (below) — Courtesy of Montefeltro Vedute Rinascimentali

MARIA SHÉHÉRAZADE GIUDICI

All photographs are courtesy of Tommaso Franzolini, all drawings are courtesy of Maria Shéhérazade Giudici.

KARSTEN HARRIES

p. 6 — Courtesy of The Thomas Kinkade Company
p. 8 — Courtesy of Barbara Figal
p. 9 & 11 — Courtesy of U.S. Library of Congress Prints and Photographs Division
p. 12 — Courtesy of Winfried Brenne
p. 15 — Courtesy of The University of Virginia Digital Archives

SAM JACOB

p. 72 — Photograph by Edward Hsu
p. 73 — Courtesy of Foto Archivio Museo della Civiltà Romana, Roma
p. 74 — Courtesy of Aedes Ars
p. 75 (left & right) — Courtesy of Ivo Banac; Photograph by Željko Tutnjević
p. 76 — Photograph by Mim Davis
p. 78 (below) — Courtesy of HBO; Photograph by Paul Schiraldi

ANDREW KOVACS

p. 166, Figure 1
p. 166, Figure 2 — (above) Public domain image; (middle) Courtesy of Andrew Kovacs; (below) Courtesy of Editoriale Domus S.p.A. Rozzano, MI, Italy
p. 166, Figure 3 — Courtesy of Venturi, Scott Brown and Associates, Inc
p. 166, Figure 4 — (above left) Constant, Concert Hall for Electronic Music 19581961, © Fondation Constant c/o Pictoright 2015; (above right) Courtesy of Andrew Kovacs; (below left) Courtesy of Andrew Kovacs; (below right) Public domain image
p. 166, Figure 5 — (above) Courtesy of MIT Press and Fondation Le Corbusier; (below) Courtesy of Buchhandlung Walther König

Perspecta, The Yale Architectural Journal
is published in the United States of America
by the Yale School of Architecture and
distributed by the MIT Press.

Massachusetts Institute of Technology
Cambridge, MA 02142
http://mitpress.mit.edu

MIT Press books may be purchased at
special quantity discounts for business or
sales promotional use. For information,
please email special_sales@mitpress.mit.edu.

Printed and bound in Turkey.

ISBN: 978-0-262-52812-2
ISSN: 0079-0958

10 9 8 7 6 5 4 3 2 1

Perspecta 48
Amnesia

Editors
Aaron Dresben
Edward Hsu
Andrea Leung
Teo Quintana

Copy Editors
Cathryn Drake
Joan Strasbaugh

Graphic Design
Cactus LA
(Marina Mills Kitchen + Chris Svensson)

Printed and bound by
Offset Yapimevi, Istanbul

Perspecta Board
Peggy Deamer
Sheila Levrant de Bretteville
Keller Easterling
Gavin Macrae-Gibson
Cesar Pelli
Emmanuel Petit
Alan Plattus
Harold Roth
Robert A.M. Stern

Acknowledgements

This publication would not have been
possible without the generous support of
the following donors:

Marc F. Appleton, '72 M.Arch
Hans Baldauf, '81 BA, '88 M.Arch
Austin Church III, '60 BA Family Fund
Fred Koetter and Susie Kim
Elizabeth Lenahan
Cesar Pelli, '08 DFAH
Robert A.M. Stern, '65 M.Arch
Jeremy Scott Wood, '64 BA, '70 M.Arch
F. Anthony Zunino, '70 M.Arch

The editors thank the *Perspecta* board for
granting us the privilege of helming this issue
of the journal. We thank Robert A.M. Stern,
Keller Easterling, and the editorial teams
of previous issues of *Perspecta* whose advice
and wise council proved invaluable as we
navigated this process.

We thank our contributors for sharing
their work with us and giving so freely their
time. We are also grateful to the individuals
and institutions who permitted us to
reproduce works in their collections. Many
others helped in a myriad of ways to assemble
and edit our content across multiple media.
In particular, we thank Cathryn Drake and
Joan Strasbaugh, our copy editors, for their
unerring attention to detail.

Many others lent a hand in finding
images, securing permissions, and reviewing
edits. Among so many, we would especially
like to thank Ivo Banac, Brigid Boyle, Gary
Fox, Paola Frascari, Alex Maymind, Margel
Smit Nusbaumer, Max Shackleton, Thomas
Sutton, James Westcott, and Dan Wood.

At the Yale School of Architecture,
Richard DeFlumeri and John Jacobson kept
us on course with an ever-watchful eye.

At the MIT Press, Roger Conover,
Justin Kehoe, and Christine Bridget Savage
held fast and were both patient and accommo-
dating. Sandra Kohen Filizer at our printer,
Ofset Yapimevi, was instrumental in helping us
realize our design ambitions with enthusiasm
and alacrity.

Our deepest gratitude goes to our
graphic designers Marina Mills Kitchen and
Chris Svensson, both of whom outstripped
our highest expectations.

We thank Marvel Architects, Pelli
Clarke Pelli Architects, Robert A.M. Stern
Architects, and Steven Harris Architects for
providing us with comfortable quarters for
the duration.

We are indebted to our family and
friends for their unflagging support. And
finally, we thank all the others who we may
have forgotten.